Twentieth Century
Verse

Twentieth Century Verse

An Anthology

Chosen by

Ira Dilworth

Toronto
CLARKE, IRWIN & COMPANY LIMITED
1945

COPYRIGHT, CANADA, 1945
by CLARKE, IRWIN & COMPANY LIMITED

Reprinted,   April 1946

Mimeographing or reproducing
mechanically in any other way
passages from this book without the written permission of
the publishers is an infringement of the copyright law.

Printed in Canada

TO DUNCAN CAMPBELL SCOTT

'TIS true, the stuff I bring for sale
   Is not so brisk a brew as ale;
Out of a stem that scored the hand
I wrung it in a weary land.
But take it: if the smack is sour,
The better for the embittered hour;
It should do good to heart and head
When your soul is in my soul's stead;
And I will friend you, if I may,
In the dark and cloudy day.

   A. E. HOUSMAN, *A Shropshire Lad—LXII*

INTRODUCTION

I

PAUL ELMER MORE in the introduction to "A Century of Indian Epigrams"—an introduction cast in the form of a letter to his friend and fellow humanist, Irving Babbitt—wrote,

> We cannot to-day—it is better so—reproduce the literature of Greece; we should shudder at the Roman sternness; to call ourselves disciples of Buddha or followers of Brahma —as some unstable minds are prone to do— would be superstition and not spirituality: yet to each of these peoples we may turn for strength and consolation; nay, we must turn to them if we are to fortify our isolated life with the virtue and dignity of experience.

That is a profound and wise dictum, and one which our age needs badly to ponder; but it is true too that we may go to the poetry of our contemporaries or of those who have preceded us by a few years only and there find such fortification and enrichment of life as More speaks of. For the poet, to-day as yesterday, by virtue of his imaginative insight penetrates with sensitiveness and unaccountable wisdom the outer shows

INTRODUCTION

of the world and of life as it flows about him, and, by his shaping skill, sets down in memorable form what he has seen and thought and felt.

In 1940 there appeared a little collection of verses—all by living poets and all, by common consent, published anonymously. It had the arresting title—rich in connotation—"Fear no More". To one of its title pages the Poet Laureate, to whom it was dedicated, contributed this statement,

> In time of danger, the herd-mind has power; the individual mind, which alone creates the things of value, is neglected. By the herd-mind man resists his enemy; by the individual mind he conquers Death. Knowing this, the men who made this remarkable book bid you Fear No More.

The Editor of the volume in his brief introduction pointed out that "the importance of poetry is that it gives courage for contemplation, not that it signifies conclusions. . . . It offers no advice, no slogan,—it offers only the way of consciousness".

II

It is a platitude to say that in times such as ours the courage of a people and the spiritual

INTRODUCTION

resources which, in the final analysis, support that courage are tested often to the breaking point—and yet it is one of those truths which need to be repeated and may well give pause to those members of society who have a clear sense of responsibility. At such a time we must turn, and we do instinctively turn again and again, in upon those spiritual riches for sustenance and strength. We turn to the great creators—musicians, painters, sculptors, poets—hoping that somehow from the vision of life that was theirs we may find something that will comfort our sorrow, shed light through our bewilderment and give meaning to the apparently meaningless facts which surround us. We turn to those who, in Stephen Spender's fine phrase,

in their lives fought for life,
Who wore at their hearts the fire's centre.
Born of the sun they travelled a short while towards the sun
And left the vivid air signed with their honour.

Humbert Wolfe was conscious of this potency of verse when he said its chief impulse was "to smash one more fragment of shapelessness into shape, one piece more of folly and cruelty into partial sanity, one shard more of ugliness into

INTRODUCTION

limited beauty". And it was a part of the grief of Wilfred Owen, writing in the trenches, deploring "the undone years", the waste of youth, that

> by my glee might many men have laughed,
> And of my weeping something has been left,
> Which must die now. I mean the truth untold,
> The pity of war, the pity war distilled. . . .
> Then, when much blood had clogged their charriot-wheels,
> I would go up and wash them from sweet wells,
> Even with truths that lie too deep for taint.

III

The task of an anthologist is never an enviable one: it is always beset with danger and difficulty. Even when the passage of time and generations of criticism have set the work of a past age in some perspective the responsibility of selection is formidable. But when the anthologist undertakes to make a collection of the work of his contemporaries he embarks upon a sea so perilous that his friends may well look on with cynical pity and say, "Poor fellow! There, but for the grace of God and my own common sense go I!". For the most part he can have no other guide than his own judgement and taste. Time may prove both to have been faulty in an embarrassing number of instances.

INTRODUCTION

Every reader of an anthology is bound to experience disappointment and even to feel at times violent disagreement with the judgement that has governed the selection. His favourite poems are not here. Many which he considers much less valuable have been included. Now, there may be reasons for such omissions other than the limitations of the anthologist. Some poets, for good and sufficient reasons, do not wish their poems to be included in such collections. This is the explanation of the regrettable absence of selections from the work of Edith Sitwell, an extraordinarily interesting experimenter with diction and verse forms and a shrewd observer of life around her. In other cases poems may be so long that they cannot be quoted in their entirety and excerpts from them may be quite inadequate. This has been true in connection with the justly famous long narratives of the Poet Laureate. Mr. Masefield, with perfect justification, very much prefers not to permit the making of quotations from such works as "Dauber" and "The Everlasting Mercy". Consequently the reader may find himself impatient with an anthology which contains only examples of Masefield's shorter poems and does not represent the longer narrative, a form which the Poet Laureate has made so

INTRODUCTION

brilliantly his own special province and to which he has contributed a fresh beauty and strength.

IV

The present anthology has been prepared in an attempt to represent as fully as all the considerations and limitations will permit the verse which has been written in Great Britain, the United States and Canada during roughly the first forty years of this century. The magnitude of the task will be at once clear.

It is always difficult to set time limits for the creative spirit and, when they have been set, to justify them and to work consistently within them. The true creative artist knows neither the bounds of time nor space, and the historian or critic who would make definite divisions between movements and confine trends of thought and creative impulse within the limits of a definite space of time is running a grave danger. Some readers will find it difficult to know why the turn of the century should have been chosen as the further limit of this anthology. The choice was made arbitrarily for mere convenience sake: one had to begin somewhere. Other readers may object that, having established such a limit, the anthologist should have included such writers as Gerard Manley Hopkins, George Meredith and

INTRODUCTION

Archibald Lampman. The reasons are quite simple—whether or not they are satisfactory is another matter. The poetry of Hopkins, written almost wholly during the third and the first part of the fourth quarter of the last century, and therefore contemporary with the mature work of the great Victorians, has been fully represented here because it was not known to the reading public until it was published in 1918 by Robert Bridges. More than that, this verse reveals a vigorous and daring originality in the use of poetic form that makes it more contemporary in quality than the work of many poets living and writing to-day. George Meredith is in spirit very much a modern. "The Woods of Westermain", "Modern Love" and many of the brief lyrics which are represented here have much in common, both in form and content, with the most contemporary verse. The inclusion of Lampman who died just at the turn of the century is harder to justify. Perhaps one had better confess that in this case personal considerations weighed heavily—it was difficult to withstand the temptation to place Archibald Lampman side by side with the other poets of Canada among whom he towers and for whom his work has been and continues to be a powerful and vital inspiration.

INTRODUCTION
V

In this anthology the reader will find poetry as varied as the period in which it has been produced. There is the work of conscious, sometimes even self-conscious, experimenters, rebelling against artistic conventions that seemed to them to fetter the muse. There is poetry, democratic in theme and language. The poetry of the period immediately before the last war is represented—disillusioned, sometimes even cynical, increasingly pre-occupied with considerations of poetic technique, a pre-occupation which quickly produced its own formalism. There is poetry here of a realism so extreme that it sometimes becomes unreal and non-representative. There is poetry made out of the stark reality of the first world war, often bitter and angry, sometimes charged with a great and clear-eyed pity. There is poetry representing the great Celtic renaissance with its national enthusiasm, its fantasy and its sense of the beauty and dignity of simple character. There is the poetry of social revolt, dedicated, eagerly, almost at times fanatically, sincere. There is poetry that has no other justification (and needs none) than that it opens for the reader a way of escape into a world, different but not necessarily less true or real than the bewildering one in which he lives.

INTRODUCTION

The reader will find representative poems by great figures living and writing apart from movements and defying all generalised formulae in description of their achievement. Here is Thomas Hardy who, more than any other, perhaps, as novelist and poet, freed writers from conventions of form and subject matter, looking fearlessly beneath the surface of life and telling what he saw with challenging frankness and courage. Here are Masefield who went back to the amazing virility of Chaucer for his form, and has revealed men and women struggling in the grip of circumstance, entangled in stirring adventure, and Robert Bridges with his quiet dedication to beauty and wisdom. Here are Walter de la Mare, writing with superb sensitiveness to beauty, untroubled by any concern with political or social problems, taking the reader with complete naturalness and ease into lonely and remote areas of human character and experience, and William Butler Yeats who combined the rapturous, lyric abandon of the Celt with a deep mystical sense. Here is Kipling with his strong, manly feeling for life and people. Here is T. S. Eliot, a most searching critic of the life of his period, expressing his social criticism and his religious humanism in verse that is sometimes elusive but always impressive. Here is the noble beauty and dignity

INTRODUCTION

of thought and feeling of Duncan Campbell Scott, the virile awareness of E. J. Pratt, the young, penetrating vision of Earle Birney. Here is the polished lyric intensity of A. E. Housman, full of a deep wistful pity combined at times with reluctant and resentful stoicism, and here too the unaffected simple utterances of Robert Frost, the result of clear insight into the lives of plain people, tinged often with quiet, unobtrusive humour and almost always underlit by a rich but unpretentious philosophy.

VI

They have been remarkable, these first forty-odd years of our century—remarkable for many reasons but especially by virtue of the contradictions which they reveal. They have seen a vast advance in material and scientific achievement, an unparalleled development of resources, bringing within the reach of men of modest means an amazing increase in physical comfort and well-being, and this side by side with baffling problems of unemployment and poverty. They have heard on the one hand much said, and insistently, about human freedom and they have seen men submit to the "herd-mind" and regimentation as the result of the impact of publicity and ballyhoo, whether in the cause of commerce

INTRODUCTION

or politics. They have seen unparalleled humanitarian sentimentality side by side with the cruel ruthlessness of fanatical nationalism and racial hatred. They have heard the cult of world brotherhood preached, often with intense sincerity and zeal, and they have witnessed twice what Bridges in 1916 referred to as "the apostasy of a great people", and the world twice embarked upon war which has been little short of annihilative in its scope and violence.—A strange and remarkable period! And in nothing, perhaps, so remarkable as the evidence it has given (and nowhere more clearly than in its poetry) of the truth contained in Drinkwater's great lines,

> This is the wonder, always, everywhere—
> Not that vast mutability which is event,
> The pits and pinnacles of change,
> But man's desire and valiance that range
> All circumstance, and come to port unspent.
>
> Agents are these events, these ecstasies,
> And tribulations, to prove the purities
> Or poor oblivions that are our being. When
> Beauty and peace possess us, they are none
> But as they touch the beauty and peace of men,
> Nor, when our days are done,
> And the last utterance of doom must fall,
> Is the doom anything
> Memorable for its apparelling;
> The bearing of man facing it is all.

INTRODUCTION
VII

And so it may give us all courage to contemplate the poems contained in this anthology, bringing as they do evidence of the unquenchable spirit of mankind which, despite the convulsions which may rock the world, is still capable of producing work that is worthy of the long, "the calm and proud procession" of the achievement of the human race. For the poet, to-day as yesterday, will agree with Walt Whitman—

It avails not, time nor place—distance avails not,
I am with you, you men and women of a generation, or ever so many generations hence,
Just as you feel when you look on the river and sky, so I felt,
Just as any of you is one of a living crowd, I was one of a crowd,
Just as you are refresh'd by the gladness of the river and the bright flow, I was refresh'd,
Just as you stand and lean on the rail, yet hurry with the swift current, I stood yet was hurried,
Just as you look on the numberless masts of ships and the thick-stemm'd pipes of steamboats, I look'd . . .

Flow on, river! flow with the flood-tide, and ebb with the ebb-tide! . . .

Live, old life! play the part that looks back on the actor or actress!
Play the old role, the role that is great or small according as one makes it!

INTRODUCTION

Consider, you who peruse me, whether I may not in unknown ways be looking upon you;
Be firm, rail over the river, to support those who lean idly, yet haste with the hasting current. . . . .

You have waited, you always wait, you dumb beautiful ministers,
We receive you with free sense at last, and are insatiate henceforward,
Not you any more shall be able to foil us, or withhold yourselves from us,
We use you, and do not cast you aside—we plant you permanently within us,
We fathom you not—we love you—there is perfection in you also,
You furnish your parts toward eternity,
Great or small, you furnish your parts toward the soul.

Ira Dilworth

Christmas, 1944,
Vancouver, B.C.

ACKNOWLEDGEMENTS

THE publishers gratefully make the following acknowledgements to authors, their agents, executors or publishers, for the use of copyright poems:

To Mrs. H. D. Aldington (Hilda Doolittle), for the use of two poems *Evening* and *Cuckoo Song*; to Allen & Unwin Ltd., for *He is Jealous of the Heavens and Earth, He Wishes he Might Die and Follow Laura, He Understands the Great Cruelty of Death* and *Laura Waits for Him in Heaven* from *Petrarch*, and *An Old Woman's Lamentations* from *Villon*, by John Millington Synge; to Elise Aylen, for the use of two poems *Moon Spell* and *Wild Apple*; to Ernest Benn Ltd., for *She* from *The Saint*, and *The Lamb, The Green Parrot, Two Sparrows* and *Thrushes* from *Kensington Gardens*, by Humbert Wolfe, by permission of the executors; to Basil Blackwell & Mott, Ltd., for *The Farmer, A Dream in Early Spring* and *The New Ghost*, by Fredegond Shove; to Brandt & Brandt, for *Love is Not All* from *Fatal Interview*, *I Know I am But Summer* from *The Harp Weaver*, and *There Is No Peace on Earth Today* from *Conversation at Midnight*, published by Harper & Brothers and copyright 1931, 1922, and 1937 by Edna St. Vincent Millay, for *Prelude—The Slaver* and *John Brown's Body Lies A-Mouldering in the Grave* from *John Brown's Body*, copyright 1927, 1928 by Stephen Vincent Benet, for *next to of course god* and *Impression IV—the hours rise up* from *Collected Poems*,

ACKNOWLEDGEMENTS

published by Harcourt Brace & Company, copyright 1923, 1925, 1931, 1935, 1938 by E. E. Cummings; to Burns Oates & Washbourne Ltd., for *The House of Christmas*, by G. K. Chesterton; to Cambridge University Press, for *Pre-existence*, *To a Fat Lady Seen from the Train*, and *The Hills* from *Mountains and Molehills*, by Frances Cornford; to Jonathan Cape Ltd., for *Chamber Music V and XXXVI*, by James Joyce, for *The Kingfisher, Rich Days, Sweet Stay-at-Home, The Sleepers* and *In Spring Time* from *Collected Poems of William Henry Davies*, for extract from *The Flaming Terrapin*, by Roy Campbell, for *Fragment Thirty-Six*, by H. D. (Hilda Doolittle); to Chatto & Windus, for *The Cicadas* and *Song of Poplars*, by Aldous Huxley, by permission of the author, for *Strange Meeting, Dulce et Decorum Est, The Parable of the Old Men* and *Apologia pro Poemate Meo*, by Wilfred Owen, by kind permission of Mrs. Owen, for *Songs from Cypress*, by H. D. (Hilda Doolittle); to The Clarendon Press, for *I Heard a Linnet Courting, I Love All Beauteous Things, Spring Goeth All in White, A Passer-by* and *Nightingales* from *The Shorter Poems of Robert Bridges*; to Padraic Colum, for the use of five poems *An Old Woman of the Roads, What the Shuiler Said, The Furrow and the Hearth, The Plougher* and *She Moved through the Fair*; to Constable & Co. Ltd., for *Lucifer in Starlight, Dirge In Woods*, and *Woodland Peace*, by George Meredith, with permission of Charles Scribner's Sons; to Curtis Brown Ltd., for *Labour* and *Vintage* from *The Land*, and *Full Moon*

ACKNOWLEDGEMENTS

from *Orchard and Vineyard*, by Victoria Sackville-West; to J. M. Dent & Sons Ltd., for *The Donkey*, by G. K. Chesterton; to Lady Desborough, for *Into Battle*, by Julian Grenfell; to Doubleday, Doran & Co. Inc., for *the hen and the oriole* from *archy and mehitabel*, by Don Marquis; to Duckworth & Co. Ltd., for *South Country*, by Hilaire Belloc; to Faber & Faber Ltd., for *The Journey of the Magi, A Song for Simeon, The Hollow Men*, and two choruses from *The Rock*, by Thomas Stearns Eliot, for *Choosing a Mast* and *Tristan da Cunha*, by Roy Campbell, for *Watch any Day, It's No Use Raising a Shout, Consider This*, and *Doom is Dark*, from *Poems*, by W. H. Auden, for *A Flower for my Daughter* and *On the Beach at Fontana* from *Pomes Penyeach*, by James Joyce, for *The Scene of War—Fear* and *The Happy Warrior, September Fires*, and *Inbetweentimes*, by Herbert Read, for *I Think Continually, After They Have Tired, The Funeral* and *Who Live Under the Shadow of a War* from *Poems*, by Stephen Spender, for *All that's Past, Martha, Old Susan, Sam, The Listeners, Farewell, Nod, The Moth* and *Haunted*, by Walter de la Mare by permission of the author, for *The Grand Canyon of the Colorado* and *The Swan* from *Black Rock* by John Gould Fletcher; to F. S. Flint, for the use of three poems *Eau-Forte, Hats* and *London*; to Mrs. G. Freeman, for *Music Comes, It was the lovely Moon*, and *The Evening Sky*, by John Freeman, published by The Macmillan Co.; to Gollancz & Co., for *Snow*, by Humbert Wolfe, by permission of the executors; to Ralph Gustafson,

ACKNOWLEDGEMENTS

for the use of two poems *This Speaking were Enough* and *Dedication*; to *Hogarth Press*, for *You That Love England*, *I've Heard Them Lilting*, *Suppose That We Tomorrow or the Next Day* and *A Time to Dance*, by Cecil Day Lewis; to Henry Holt & Co. Inc., for *Chicago* from *Chicago Poems*, and *Cool Tombs* and *Loam* from *Cornhuskers*, by Carl Sandburg, for *The Sound of the Trees*, *Birches*, *Stopping by Woods on a Snowy Evening*, *The Pasture* and *Come In*, by Robert Frost; to Houghton Mifflin Co., for four choruses from *Abraham Lincoln*, by John Drinkwater, *Purple Grackles*, by Amy Lowell, *Immortal Autumn*, *Memorial Rain* and *1933*, by Archibald MacLeish; to Dorothy Livesay for the use of *Fantasia*; to Wilson MacDonald, for the use of *Exit*; to L. A. MacKay, for the use of three poems *Admonition for Spring*, *Non Nobis* and *Rend Your Heart and Not Your Garments;* to the Macmillan Co., New York, for *Strange Holiness*, *The Secret Heart* and *A Fire at Night* from *Collected Poems* of Robert P. Tristram Coffin, for *There Will be Stars*, *The Fountain*, *I Shall Not Care*, *Blue Squills* and *Winter Night Song* from *Collected Poems* of Sara Teasdale, for *General Booth Enters Heaven*, by Vachel Lindsay, for *Sea Fever*, *The Passing Strange* and *Sonnet XXIX*, by John Masefield; to Macmillan & Co. Ltd., for *Frolic*, *Babylon*, *Germinal* and *Promise* from A. E.'s *Collected Poems*, by permission of the author's representatives, for *The Ice Cart*, *Rupert Brooke II*, *Before Action*, *The Return* and *Lament* from Wilfrid Gibson's *Collected Poems 1905-1925*, by permission of the author,

ACKNOWLEDGEMENTS

for *The Last Chrysanthemum, The Darkling Thrush, Beyond the Last Lamp, When I Set Out For Lyonesse, Afterwards, The Oxen, In Time of 'The Breaking of Nations', Transformations, Life Laughs Onward* and *An Ancient to Ancients* from *Collected Poems of Thomas Hardy*, by permission of the Hardy Estate, for *Time You Old Gypsy Man, The Bells of Heaven, Stupidity Street* and lines from *The Song of Honour*, by Ralph Hodgson, by permission of the author, for *The Song of Wandering Aengus, The Wild Swans at Coole, Rose of the World, Down by the Salley Gardens, Aedh Wishes for the Cloths of Heaven, When You Are Old* and *The Fiddler of Dooney* from *Collected Poems of W. B. Yeats*, by permission of Mrs. Yeats, for *The Goat Paths, Deirdre, Hate* and *What Tomas Said In a Pub* from *Collected Poems of James Stephens*, by permission of the author; to The Macmillan Co. of Canada Ltd., for *Song, The Phoenix*, and selection from *Laodamia*, by Audrey Alexandra Brown, for *The Prize Cat, The Decision, Silences* and *Burial at Sea*, by E. J. Pratt; to McClelland & Stewart Ltd., for *The Great Lover, Dust, Heaven, The Dead* and *The Soldier*, by Rupert Brooke, for *Spring's Saraband, Low Tide on Grand Pre* and *A Northern Vigil*, by Bliss Carman, for *Pere Lalement, The Lamp of Poor Souls* and *Modern Endymion*, by Marjorie Pickthall, for *After Battle, The Forsaken, Spring in the Valley* and *A Song*, by Duncan Campbell Scott; to Methuen & Co. Ltd., for *Iliad* and *Journey's End*, by Humbert Wolfe, by permission of the executors; to Mrs. Alida Monro, for *Children of Love, The*

ACKNOWLEDGEMENTS

Nightingale Near the House, *Milk for the Cat*, and *There Are Some Men* from *Trees*, by Harold Monro, by permission of the Poetry Bookshop; to T. Sturge Moore (Michael Field's literary executor), for *Fifty Quatrains* and *A Kiss* from *Michael Field's Selected Poems* (Poetry Bookshop); to Thos. Nelson & Sons Ltd., for *Duncton Hill*, by Hilaire Belloc; to Captain Francis Newbolt, for *Drake's Drum*, *He Fell Among Thieves* and *Clifton Chapel* from *Poems New and Old*, by Sir Henry Newbolt, published by John Murray; to New York Herald Tribune, for *High Flight*, by John Gillespie Magee, with the kind permission of the author's parents; to Robert Nichols, for the use of *The Sprig of Lime*, published by William Collins Sons & Co. Ltd.; to Miss Ethel Oliver, for *In the Fields*, *Moorland Night* and *I Have Been Through the Gates*, by Charlotte Mew; to La Marchesa Origa, for *Faster*, *All Our Joy Is Enough* and *The Bridge*, by Geoffrey Scott; to Oxford University Press, for *God's Grandeur*, *Felix Randal*, *The Leaden Echo and the Golden Echo*, *Binsey Poplars* and *Spring*, by Gerard Manley Hopkins, for *Ode to Music* from *The Poetical Works of Robert Bridges*; to Pearn, Pollinger & Higham, Ltd., for *Humming Bird*, *Snake*, *Work* and *Bavarian Gentians*, by D. H. Lawrence, by permission of Mrs. Frieda Lawrence and Messrs. William Heinemann Ltd., for *Canto XIII*, *Ione Dead the Long Year*, *The Coming of War: Actaeon*, *The Return* and *Night Litany*, by Ezra Pound; to Random House, Inc., for *Suicide's Stone* and *Birds* from *Roan Stallion, Tamar*

ACKNOWLEDGEMENTS

and Other Poems, by Robinson Jeffers; to The Richards Press Ltd., for *Sehnsucht*, *The Mummer* and *The Cherry-Blossom Wand*, by Anna Wickham; to The Ryerson Press, for *The Wind Our Enemy*, *Woodyards In Rain* and *Sandstone*, by Anne Marriott, for *Prelude to Spring*, by Dorothy Livesay, for *David*, *Vancouver Lights* and *Hands*, by Earle Birney; for *A Summer Evening*, *A January Morning*, *Evening*, *Midnight* and *Late November*, by Archibald Lampman, for *Hath Hope Kept Vigil*, *The Solitary Woodsman* and *Tantramar Revisited*, by Charles G. D. Roberts, for *The Lonely Land*, *Ode on the Death of W. B. Yeats* and *Good Friday*, by A. J. M. Smith; to Siegfried Sassoon, for the use of seven poems *Grandeur of Ghosts*, *Base Details*, *The Heart's Journey (V)*, *The Heart's Journey (XXXIV)*, *The Glory of Women*, *Morning Glory* and *On Reading the War Diary of a Defunct Ambassador*; to Duncan Campbell Scott, for the use of two poems *Hymn for Those in the Air* and *Old Olives at Bordighera*; to Charles Scribner's Sons, for *All Lovely Things Will Have an Ending*, *Prelude XIV*, *Heaven You Say Will be a Field in April* and *Music I Heard With You*, by Conrad Aiken; to Secker & Warburg Ltd., for *Honey Harvest* and *The Buzzards*, by Martin Armstrong, for *The Old Ships*, *To a Poet a Thousand Years Hence*, *The Golden Journey to Samarkand* and *Yasmin*, by James Elroy Flecker; to The Society of Authors, for *Bredon Hill*, *Tell Me Not Here*, *As I Gird on for Fighting*, *Reveille*, *Loveliest of Trees*, *Oh See How Thick the Goldcup Flowers* and *Fancy's Knell*, by

ACKNOWLEDGEMENTS

A. E. Housman, by permission of The Society of Authors, as literary representatives of the Trustees of the Estate of the late A. E. Housman, and by permission of Jonathan Cape Ltd., publishers of *Collected Poems*, for *Hunger, For the Fallen* and *The Sirens*, by Laurence Binyon, by permission of Mrs. Binyon; to Mrs. Helen Thomas, for *The New House, If I Should Ever by Chance, Adlestrop* and *Out In the Dark*, by Edward Thomas, by permission of Messrs. Faber & Faber; to W. J. Turner, for the use of two poems *Romance* and *Ecstasy*; to A. P. Watt & Son, for *Star Talk* from *Over the Brazier*, and *Babylon*, by Robert Graves, for *Cities and Thrones and Powers, Harp Song of the Dane Women* from *Puck of Pook's Hill, Recessional* and *The Way Through the Woods*, by Rudyard Kipling, by permission of Mrs. Bambridge, for *The Barrel-Organ* and *The Highwayman* from *The Collected Poems of Alfred Noyes*, by permission of the author and Messrs. William Blackwood & Sons Ltd., for *The Song of Wandering Aengus, The Wild Swans at Coole, Rose of the World, Down by the Salley Gardens, Aedh Wishes for the Cloths of Heaven, When You Are Old* and *The Fiddler of Dooney* from *Collected Poems of W. B. Yeats*, by kind permission of Mrs. Yeats and Macmillan & Co. Ltd., for *Lepanto* and *The House of Christmas* from *The Collected Poems of G. K. Chesterton*, by permission of the executrix of the late Mr. Chesterton.

TABLE OF CONTENTS

	PAGE
'Æ' (George William Russell)	1
Conrad Aiken	6
Martin Armstrong	10
W. H. Auden	14
Elise Aylen	20
Hilaire Belloc	21
Stephen Vincent Benét	25
Laurence Binyon	39
Earle Birney	44
Robert Bridges	59
Rupert Brooke	67
Audrey Alexandra Brown	74
Roy Campbell	83
Bliss Carman	90
G. K. Chesterton	98
Robert P. Tristram Coffin	107
Padraic Colum	111
Frances Cornford	117
E. E. Cummings	119
William Henry Davies	121
Walter de la Mare	125
John Drinkwater	134
Thomas Stearns Eliot	141
Michael Field	151
James Elroy Flecker	152
John Gould Fletcher	156
F. S. Flint	161
John Freeman	166
Robert Frost	170
Wilfrid Gibson	175
Robert Graves	178
Julian Grenfell	181

CONTENTS

Ralph Gustafson	182
H. D. (Hilda Doolittle)	186
Thomas Hardy	194
Ralph Hodgson	205
Gerard Manley Hopkins	208
A. E. Housman	215
Aldous Huxley	222
Robinson Jeffers	226
James Joyce	228
Rudyard Kipling	230
Archibald Lampman	235
D. H. Lawrence	238
Cecil Day Lewis	245
Vachel Lindsay	250
Dorothy Livesay	252
Amy Lowell	258
Wilson MacDonald	263
L. A. MacKay	265
Archibald MacLeish	267
John Gillespie Magee	278
Don Marquis	279
Anne Marriott	280
John Masefield	287
George Meredith	292
Charlotte Mew	294
Edna St. Vincent Millay	297
Harold Munro	301
Sir Henry Newbolt	307
Robert Nichols	311
Alfred Noyes	314
Wilfred Owen	328
Marjorie Pickthall	333
Ezra Pound	338
E. J. Pratt	345
Herbert Read	352

CONTENTS

Sir Charles G. D. Roberts	355
Victoria Sackville-West	361
Carl Sandburg	364
Siegfried Sassoon	367
Duncan Campbell Scott	372
Geoffrey Scott	381
Fredegond Shove	384
A. J. M. Smith	387
Stephen Spender	391
James Stephens	395
John Millington Synge	399
Sara Teasdale	403
Edward Thomas	406
W. J. Turner	409
Anna Wickham	411
Humbert Wolfe	413
William Butler Yeats	421
Biographical Notes	
Index of Titles and First Lines	

Twentieth Century
Verse

'Æ' (GEORGE WILLIAM RUSSELL)
1867-1935

1 *Frolic*

THE children were shouting together
   And racing along the sands,
A glimmer of dancing shadows,
   A dovelike flutter of hands.

The stars were shouting in heaven,
   The sun was chasing the moon:
The game was the same as the children's,
   They danced to the self-same tune.

The whole of the world was merry,
   One joy from the vale to the height,
Where the blue woods of twilight encircled
   The lovely lawns of the light.

2 *Babylon*

THE blue dusk ran between the streets: my love
   was winged within my mind,
It left to-day and yesterday and thrice a thousand
   years behind.
To-day was past and dead for me, for from to-day my
   feet had run
Through thrice a thousand years to walk the ways of
   ancient Babylon.

'Æ' (GEORGE WILLIAM RUSSELL)

On temple top and palace roof the burnished gold
　　flung back the rays
Of a red sunset that was dead and lost beyond a
　　million days.
The tower of heaven turns darker blue, a starry
　　sparkle now begins;
The mystery and magnificence, the myriad beauty
　　and the sins
Come back to me. I walk beneath the shadowy
　　multitude of towers;
Within the gloom the fountain jets its pallid mist in
　　lily flowers.
The waters lull me and the scent of many gardens,
　　and I hear
Familiar voices, and the voice I love is whispering in
　　my ear.
Oh real as in dream all this; and then a hand on mine
　　is laid:
The wave of phantom time withdraws; and that
　　young Babylonian maid,
One drop of beauty left behind from all the flowing of
　　that tide,
Is looking with the self-same eyes, and here in Ireland
　　by my side.
Oh light our life in Babylon, but Babylon has taken
　　wings
While we are in the calm and proud procession of
　　eternal things.

'Æ' (GEORGE WILLIAM RUSSELL)
Germinal

CALL not thy wanderer home as yet
    Though it be late.
Now is his first assailing of
    The invisible gate.
Be still through that light knocking. The hour
    Is thronged with fate.

To that first tapping at the invisible door
    Fate answereth.
What shining image or voice, what sigh
    Or honied breath,
Comes forth, shall be the master of life
    Even to death.

Satyrs may follow after. Seraphs
    On crystal wing
May blaze. But the delicate first comer
    It shall be King.
They shall obey, even the mightiest,
    That gentle thing.

All the strong powers of Dante were bowed
    To a child's mild eyes,
That wrought within him that travail
    From depths up to skies,
Inferno, Purgatorio
    And Paradise.

'Æ' (GEORGE WILLIAM RUSSELL)

Amid the soul's grave councillors
    A petulant boy
Laughs under the laurels and purples, the elf
    Who snatched at his joy,
Ordering Caesar's legions to bring him
    The world for his toy.

In ancient shadows and twilights
    Where childhood had strayed,
The world's great sorrows were born
    And its heroes were made.
In the lost boyhood of Judas
    Christ was betrayed.

Let thy young wanderer dream on:
    Call him not home.
A door opens, a breath, a voice
    From the ancient room,
Speaks to him now. Be it dark or bright
    He is knit with his doom.

Promise

BE not so desolate
    Because thy dreams have flown
And the hall of the heart is empty
    And silent as stone,
As age left by children
    Sad and alone.

'Æ' (GEORGE WILLIAM RUSSELL)

Those delicate children,
Thy dreams, still endure:
All pure and lovely things
Wend to the Pure.
Sigh not: unto the fold
Their way was sure.

Thy gentlest dreams, thy frailest,
Even those that were
Born and lost in a heart-beat,
Shall meet thee there.
They are become immortal
In shining air.

The unattainable beauty
The thought of which was pain,
That flickered in eyes and on lips
And vanished again:
That fugitive beauty
Thou shalt attain.

The lights innumerable
That led thee on and on,
The Masque of Time ended,
Shall glow into one.
It shall be with thee for ever
Thy travel done.

CONRAD AIKEN

1889-

5 'All lovely things will have an ending'

ALL lovely things will have an ending,
All lovely things will fade and die,
And youth, that's now so bravely spending,
Will beg a penny by and by.

Fine ladies all are soon forgotten,
And goldenrod is dust when dead,
The sweetest flesh and flowers are rotten
And cobwebs tent the brightest head.

Come back, true love! Sweet youth, return!—
But time goes on, and will, unheeding,
Though hands will reach, and eyes will yearn,
And the wild days set true hearts bleeding.

Come back, true love! Sweet youth, remain!—
But goldenrod and daisies wither,
And over them blows autumn rain,
They pass, they pass, and know not whither.

6 Prelude XIV

--YOU went to the verge, you say, and came back safely?
Some have not been so fortunate,—some have fallen.
Children go lightly there, from crag to crag,
And coign to coign,—where even the goat is wary,—

CONRAD AIKEN

And make a sport of it. . . . They fling down pebbles,
Following, with eyes undizzied, the long curve,
The long slow outward curve, into the abyss,
As far as eye can follow; and they themselves
Turn back, unworried, to the here and now. . . .
But you have been there, too?—

         —I saw at length
The space-defying pine, that on the last
Outjutting rock has cramped its powerful roots.
There stood I too: under that tree I stood:
My hand against its resinous bark: my face
Turned out and downward to the fourfold kingdom.
The wind roared from all quarters. The waterfall
Came down, it seemed, from Heaven. The mighty
  sound
Of pouring elements,—earth, air, and water,—
The cry of eagles, chatter of falling stones,—
These were the frightful language of that place.
I understood it ill, but understood.—

—You understood it? Tell me, then, its meaning.
It was an all, a nothing, or a something?
Chaos, or divine love, or emptiness?
Water and earth and air and the sun's fire?
Or else, a question, simply?—

        —Water and fire were there,
And air and earth; there too was emptiness;
All, and nothing, and something too, and love.

CONRAD AIKEN

But these poor words, these squeaks of ours, in which
We strive to mimic, with strained throats and tongues,
The spawning and outrageous elements—
Alas, how paltry are they! For I saw—

—What did you see?

                              —I saw myself and God.
I saw the ruin in which godhead lives:
Shapeless and vast: the strewn wreck of the world:
Sadness unplumbed: misery without bound.
Wailing I heard, but also I heard joy.
Wreckage I saw, but also I saw flowers.
Hatred I saw, but also I saw love. . . .
And thus, I saw myself.

                              —And this alone?

—And this alone awaits you, when you dare
To that sheer verge where horror hangs, and tremble
Against the falling rock; and, looking down,
Search the dark kingdom. It is to self you come,—
And that is God. It is the seed of seeds:
Seed for disastrous and immortal worlds.

It is the answer that no question asked.

CONRAD AIKEN

7   *'Heaven, you say, will be a field in April'*

HEAVEN, you say, will be a field in April,
A friendly field, a long green wave of earth,
With one domed cloud above it. There you'll lie
In noon's delight, with bees to flash above you,
Drown amid buttercups that blaze in the wind,
Forgetting all save beauty. There you'll see
With sun-filled eyes your one great dome of cloud
Adding fantastic towers and spires of light,
Ascending, like a ghost, to melt in the blue.
Heaven enough, in truth, if you were there!
Could I be with you, I would choose your noon,
Drown amid buttercups, laugh with the intimate grass,
Dream there for ever. . . . But, being older, sadder,
Having not you, nor aught save thought of you,
It is not spring I'll choose, but fading summer;
Not noon I'll choose, but the charmed hour of dusk.
Poppies? A few! And a moon almost red.
But most I'll choose that subtler dusk that comes
Into the mind—into the heart, you say—
When, as we look bewildered at lovely things,
Striving to give their loveliness a name,
They are forgotten; and other things, remembered,
Flower in the heart with the fragrance we call grief.

8   *'Music I heard with you'*

MUSIC I heard with you was more than music,
And bread I broke with you was more than
    bread;
Now that I am without you, all is desolate;
All that was once so beautiful is dead.

CONRAD AIKEN

Your hands once touched this table and this silver,
And I have seen your fingers hold this glass.
These things do not remember you, beloved,
And yet your touch upon them will not pass.

For it was in my heart you moved among them,
And blessed them with your hands and with your eyes;
And in my heart they will remember always,—
They knew you once, O beautiful and wise.

MARTIN ARMSTRONG

1882-

Honey Harvest

LATE in March, when the days are growing longer
   And sight of early green
Tells of the coming spring and suns grow stronger,
Round the pale willow-catkins there are seen
   The year's first honey-bees
Stealing the nectar; and bee-masters know
This for the first sign of the honey-flow.

Then in the dark hillsides the Cherry-trees
Gleam white with loads of blossom where the gleams
Of piled snow lately hung, and richer streams
The honey. Now, if chilly April days
Delay the Apple-blossom, and the May's
First week come in with sudden summer weather,
The Apple and the Hawthorn bloom together,

MARTIN ARMSTRONG

And all day long the plundering hordes go round
And every overweighted blossom nods.
But from that gathered essence they compound
Honey more sweet than nectar of the gods.

Those blossoms fall ere June, warm June that brings
The small white Clover. Field by scented field,
Round farms like islands in the rolling weald,
It spreads thick-flowering or in wildness springs
Short-stemmed upon the naked downs, to yield
A richer store of honey than the Rose,
The Pink, the Honeysuckle. Thence there flows
Nectar of clearest amber, redolent
   Of every flowery scent
That the warm wind upgathers as he goes.

In mid-July be ready for the noise
Of million bees in old Lime-avenues,
As though hot noon had found a droning voice
To ease her soul. Here for those busy crews
Green leaves and pale-stemmed clusters of green
    flowers
Build heavily-perfumed, cool, green-twilight bowers
Whence, load by load, through the long summer days
   They fill their glassy cells
With dark green honey, clear as chrysoprase,
Which housewives shun; but the bee-master tells
This brand is more delicious than all else.

In August-time, if moors are near at hand,
Be wise and in the evening-twilight load

MARTIN ARMSTRONG

Your hives upon a cart, and take the road
By night; that, ere the early dawn shall spring
And all the hills turn rosy with the Ling,
   Each waking hive may stand
Established in its new-appointed land
Without harm taken, and the earliest flights
Set out at once to loot the heathery heights.

That vintage of the Heather yields so dense
And glutinous a syrup that it foils
Him who would spare the comb and drain from thence
   Its dark, full-flavoured spoils:
For he must squeeze to wreck the beautiful
Frail edifice. Not otherwise he sacks
Those many-chambered palaces of wax.

Then let a choice of every kind be made,
And, labelled, set upon your storehouse racks—
Of Hawthorn-honey that of almond smacks:
The luscious Lime-tree-honey, green as jade:
Pale Willow-honey, hived by the first rover:
   That delicate honey culled
From Apple-blossom, that of sunlight tastes:
And sunlight-coloured honey of the Clover.
   Then, when the late year wastes,
When night falls early and the noon is dulled
   And the last warm days are over,
Unlock the store and to your table bring
Essence of every blossom of the spring.
And if, when wind has never ceased to blow
All night, you wake to roofs and trees becalmed

MARTIN ARMSTRONG

In level wastes of snow,
Bring out the Lime-tree-honey, the embalmed
Soul of a lost July, or Heather-spiced
Brown-gleaming comb wherein sleeps crystallised
All the hot perfume of the heathery slope.
And, tasting and remembering, live in hope.

10 *The Buzzards*

WHEN evening came and the warm glow grew
    deeper
  And every tree that bordered the green meadows
  And in the yellow cornfields every reaper
And every corn-shock stood above their shadows
Flung eastward from their feet in longer measure,
Serenely far there swam in the sunny height
A buzzard and his mate who took their pleasure
Swirling and poising idly in golden light.

On great pied motionless moth-wings borne along,
  So effortless and so strong,
Cutting each other's paths, together they glided,
Then wheeled asunder till they soared divided
Two valleys' width (as though it were delight
To part like this, being sure they could unite
So swiftly in their empty, free dominion),
Curved headlong downward, towered up the sunny
    steep,
Then, with a sudden lift of the one great pinion,
Swung proudly to a curve, and from its height
Took half a mile of sunlight in one long sweep.

MARTIN ARMSTRONG

And we, so small on the swift immense hillside,
Stood tranced until our souls arose uplifted
  On those far-sweeping, wide,
Strong curves of flight—swayed up and hugely drifted,
Were washed, made strong and beautiful in the tide
Of sun-bathed air. But far beneath, beholden
Through shining deeps of air, the fields were golden
And rosy burned the heather where cornfields ended.

And still those buzzards wheeled, while light withdrew
Out of the vales and to surging slopes ascended,
Till the loftiest flaming summit died to blue.

W. H. AUDEN
1907-

11   *'It's no use raising a Shout'*

IT'S no use raising a shout.
  No, Honey, you can cut that right out.
I don't want any more hugs;
Make me some fresh tea, fetch me some rugs.
Here am I, here are you:
But what does it mean? What are we going to do?

A long time ago I told my mother
I was leaving home to find another:
I never answered her letter
But I never found a better.
Here am I, here are you:
But what does it mean? What are we going to do?

W. H. AUDEN

It wasn't always like this?
Perhaps it wasn't, but it is.
Put the car away; when life fails,
What's the good of going to Wales?
Here am I, here are you:
But what does it mean? What are we going to do?

In my spine there was a base;
And I knew the general's face:
But they've severed all the wires,
And I can't tell what the general desires.
Here am I, here are you:
But what does it mean? What are we going to do?

In my veins there is a wish,
And a memory of fish:
When I lie crying on the floor,
It says, 'You've often done this before.'
Here am I, here are you:
But what does it mean? What are we going to do?

A bird used to visit this shore:
It isn't going to come any more.
I've come a very long way to prove
No land, no water, and no love.
Here am I, here are you:
But what does it mean? What are we going to do?

W. H. AUDEN

'Watch any day'

WATCH any day his nonchalant pauses, see
His dextrous handling of a wrap as he
Steps after into cars, the beggar's envy.

'There is a free one', many say, but err.
He is not that returning conqueror,
Nor even the poles' circumnavigator.

But poised between shocking falls on razor-edge
Has taught himself this balancing subterfuge
Of the accosting profile, the erect carriage.

The song, the varied action of the blood
Would drown the warning from the iron wood
Would cancel the inertia of the buried:

Travelling by daylight on from house to house
The longest way to the intrinsic peace,
With love's fidelity and with love's weakness.

'Consider This and in Our Time'

CONSIDER this and in our time
As the hawk sees it or the helmeted airman:
The clouds rift suddenly—look there
At cigarette-end smouldering on a border
At the first garden party of the year.
Pass on, admire the view of the massif
Through plate-glass windows of the Sport Hotel;

W. H. AUDEN

Join there the insufficient units
Dangerous, easy, in furs, in uniform
And constellated at reserved tables
Supplied with feelings by an efficient band
Relayed elsewhere to farmers and their dogs
Sitting in kitchens in the stormy fens.

Long ago, supreme Antagonist,
More powerful than the great northern whale
Ancient and sorry at life's limiting defect,
In Cornwall, Mendip, or the Pennine moor,
Your comments on the highborn mining captains,
Found they no answer, made them wish to die
—Lie since in barrows out of harm.
You talk to your admirers every day
By silted harbours, derelict works,
In strangled orchards, and the silent comb
Where dogs have worried or a bird was shot.
Order the ill that they attack at once:
Visit the ports and, interrupting
The leisurely conversation in the bar
Within a stone's throw of the sunlit water,
Beckon your chosen out. Summon
Those handsome and diseased youngsters, those
    women
Your solitary agents in the country parishes;
And mobilize the powerful forces latent
In soils that make the farmer brutal
In the infected sinus, and the eyes of stoats.
Then, ready, start your rumour, soft

W. H. AUDEN

But horrifying in its capacity to disgust,
Which, spreading magnified, shall come to be
A polar peril, a prodigious alarm,
Scattering the people, as torn-up paper
Rags and utensils in a sudden gust,
Seized with immeasurable neurotic dread.

Financier, leaving your little room
Where the money is made but not spent,
You'll need your typist and your boy no more;
The game is up for you and for the others
Who, thinking, pace in slippers on the lawns
Of College Quad or Cathedral Close,
Who are born nurses, who live in shorts
Sleeping with people and playing fives.
Seekers after happiness, all who follow
The convolutions of your simple wish,
It is later than you think; nearer that day
Far other than that distant afternoon
Amid rustle of frocks and stamping feet
They gave the prizes to the ruined boys.
You cannot be away, then, no
Not though you pack to leave within an hour,
Escaping humming down arterial roads:
The date was yours; the prey to fugues,
Irregular breathing and alternate ascendancies
After some haunted migratory years
To disintegrate on an instant in the explosion of
    mania
Or lapse for ever into a classic fatigue.

W. H. AUDEN
'Doom is Dark'

DOOM is dark and deeper than any sea-dingle.
  Upon what man it fall
In spring, day-wishing flowers appearing,
Avalanche sliding, white snow from rock-face,
That he should leave his house,
No cloud-soft hand can hold him, restraint by women;
But ever that man goes
Through place-keepers, through forest trees,
A stranger to strangers over undried sea,
Houses for fishes, suffocating water,
Or lonely on fell as chat,
By pot-holed becks
A bird stone-haunting, an unquiet bird.

There head falls forward, fatigued at evening,
And dreams of home,
Waving from window, spread of welcome,
Kissing of wife under single sheet;
But waking sees
Bird-flocks nameless to him, through doorway voices
Of new men making another love.

Save him from hostile capture,
From sudden tiger's spring at corner;
Protect his house,
His anxious house where days are counted
From thunderbolt protect,
From gradual ruin spreading like a stain;
Converting number from vague to certain,
Bring joy, bring day of his returning,
Lucky with day approaching, with leaning dawn.

ELISE AYLEN

Moon Spell

THE moon has set fire
  To the icicles,
Their jets of crystal flame
Are flickering at the house-eaves.
Strangely that spirit ray
Fell, frozen to stillness,
And broke in pallid embers.
Frail hands stretch wanly
To the chill moon-kindling:
They come softly who gather
At this rime-pale hearth of night.
When a world is moon-spelled
Where shall we take comfort?
How come again to the sun-warmth,
When flame has dript and frozen
Round a naked heart?

Wild Apple

Uncertain still, new-mated birds
Give song unseen,
A little shyly still the fields
Wear their young green;

And, strange to their own beauty,
These wild buds unclose
Their lucent gleam of petal
Touched with dreamy rose.

ELISE AYLEN

Where all the naked moors
Spread bare of flower
This blush, strayed seedling hides
Its fragile dower.

The swarthy pines, like dark guards
Gathered round,
Hold the frail captive
In their secret ground,—

A maid, spring-veiled, who droops,
Wistful, austere,
Until her opened heart
With the full year

Shall know its hidden end
Of leaf and root,
And from the throe of beauty
Come to bitter fruit.

HILAIRE BELLOC

1870-

Duncton Hill

HE does not die that can bequeath
  Some influence to the land he knows,
Or dares, persistent, interweave
Love permanent with the wild hedgerows;
  He does not die, but still remains
  Substantiate with his darling plains.

HILAIRE BELLOC

The spring's superb adventure calls
His dust athwart the woods to flame;
His boundary river's secret falls
Perpetuate and repeat his name.
  He rides his loud October sky,
  He does not die. He does not die.

The beeches know the accustomed head
Which loved them, and a peopled air
Beneath their benediction spread
Comforts the silence everywhere;
  For native ghosts return and these
  Perfect the mystery in the trees.

So, therefore, though myself be crosst
The shuddering of that dreadful day
When friend and fire and home are lost,
And even children drawn away—
  The passer-by shall hear me still
  A boy that sings on Duncton Hill.

The South Country

WHEN I am living in the Midlands
    That are sodden and unkind,
I light my lamp in the evening:
  My work is left behind;
And the great hills of the South Country
  Come back into my mind.

HILAIRE BELLOC

The great hills of the South Country
  They stand along the sea;
And it's there walking in the high woods
  That I could wish to be,
And the men that were boys when I was a boy
  Walking along with me.

The men that live in North England
  I saw them for a day;
Their hearts are set upon the waste fells,
  Their skies are fast and grey;
From their castle-walls a man may see
  The mountains far away.

The men that live in West England
  They see the Severn strong,
A-rolling on rough water brown
  Light aspen leaves along.
They have the secret of the Rocks,
  And the oldest kind of song.

But the men that live in the South Country
  Are the kindest and most wise,
They get their laughter from the loud surf,
  And the faith in their happy eyes
Comes surely from our Sister the Spring
  When over the sea she flies;
The violets suddenly bloom at her feet,
  She blesses us with surprise.

HILAIRE BELLOC

I never get between the pines
    But I smell the Sussex air;
Nor I never come on a belt of sand
    But my home is there.
And along the sky the line of the Downs
    So noble and so bare.

A lost thing could I never find,
    Nor a broken thing mend:
And I fear I shall be all alone
    When I get towards the end.
Who will there be to comfort me
    Or who will be my friend?

I will gather and carefully make my friends
    Of the men of the Sussex Weald;
They watch the stars from silent folds,
    They stiffly plough the field.
By them and the God of the South Country
    My poor soul shall be healed.

If I ever become a rich man,
    Or if ever I grow to be old,
I will build a house with deep thatch
    To shelter me from the cold,
And there shall the Sussex songs be sung
    And the story of Sussex told.

I will hold my house in the high wood
    Within a walk of the sea,
And the men that were boys when I was a boy
    Shall sit and drink with me.

STEPHEN VINCENT BENÉT
1894-1943

19 *The Slaver*
(Prelude to 'John Brown's Body')

He closed the Bible carefully, putting it down
As if his fingers loved it.
      Then he turned.
'Mr. Mate.'
  'Yes, sir.'
      The captain's eyes held a shadow.
'I think, while this weather lasts,' he said, after a pause,
'We'd better get them on deck as much as we can.
They keep better that way. Besides,' he added, un-
  smiling,
'She's begun to stink already. You've noticed it?'

The mate nodded, a boyish nod of half-apology,
'And only a week out, too, sir.'
      'Yes,' said the skipper.
His eyes looked into themselves. 'Well. The trade,' he
  said,
'The trade's no damn perfume-shop.' He drummed
  with his fingers.
'Seems to be quiet tonight,' he murmured, at last.
'Oh yes sir, quiet enough.' The mate flushed. 'Not
What you'd call quiet at home but—quiet enough.'

'Um,' said the skipper. 'What about the big fellow?'

'Tarbarrel, sir? The man who says he's a king?
He was praying to something—it made the others
  restless.

STEPHEN VINCENT BENÉT

Mr. Olsen stopped it.'

'I don't like that,' said the skipper.

'It was only an idol, sir.'

'Oh.'

'A stone or something.'

'Oh.'

'But he's a bad one, sir—a regular sullen one—
He—eyes in the dark—like a cat's—enough to give you—'
The mate was young. He shivered. 'The creeps,' he said.

'We've had that kind,' said the skipper. His mouth was hard,
Then it relaxed. 'Damn cheating Arabs!' he said,
'I told them I'd take no more of their pennyweight kings,
Worth pounds to look at, and then when you get them aboard
Go crazy so they have to be knocked on the head
Or else just eat up their hearts and die in a week
Taking up room for nothing.'

The mate hardly heard him, thinking of something else.
'I'm afraid we'll lose some more of the women,' he said.
'Well, they're a scratch lot,' said the skipper. 'Any sickness?'

STEPHEN VINCENT BENÉT

'Just the usual, sir.'
                    'But nothing like plague or—'
                                                'No sir.'

'The Lord is merciful,' said the skipper.
His voice was wholly sincere—an old ship's bell
Hung in the steeple of a meeting-house
With all New England and the sea's noise in it.
'Well, you'd better take another look-see, Mr. Mate.'
The mate felt his lips go dry. 'Aye aye, sir,' he said,
Wetting his lips with his tongue. As he left the cabin
He heard the Bible being opened again.

Lantern in hand, he went down to the hold.
Each time he went he had a trick of trying
To shut the pores of his body against the stench
By force of will, by thinking of salt and flowers,
But it was always useless.

                          He kept thinking:
When I get home, when I get a bath and clean food,
When I've gone swimming out beyond the Point
In that cold green, so cold it must be pure
Beyond the purity of a dissolved star,
When I get my shore-clothes on, and one of those shirts
Out of the linen-closet that smells of lavender,
Will my skin smell black even then, will my skin smell black?

27

STEPHEN VINCENT BENÉT

The lantern shook in his hand.

                        This was black, here;
This was black to see and feel and smell and taste,
The blackness of black, with one weak lamp to light it
As ineffectually as a firefly in Hell,
And, being so, should be silent.

                                But the hold
Was never silent.

                  There was always that breathing.
Always that thick breathing, always those shivering cries.

A few of the slaves
Knew English—at least the English for water and Jesus.
'I'm dying.' 'Sick.' 'My name Caesar.'

                               Those who knew
These things, said these things now when they saw the lantern
Mechanically, as tamed beasts answer the whipcrack.
Their voices beat at the light like heavy moths.
But most made merely liquid or guttural sounds
Meaningless to the mate, but horribly like
The sounds of palateless men or animals trying
To talk through a human throat.

                          The mate was used
To the confusion of limbs and bodies by now.
At first it had made him think of the perturbed
Blind coil of blacksnakes thawing on a rock
In the bleak sun of Spring, or Judgment Day

STEPHEN VINCENT BENÉT

Just after the first sounding of the trump
When all earth seethes and crumbles with the slow
Vast, mouldy resurrection of the dead.
But he had passed such fancies.
                          He must see
As much as he could. He couldn't see very much.
They were too tightly packed but—no plague yet,
And all the chains were fast. Then he saw something.
The woman was asleep but her baby was dead.
He wondered whether to take it from her now.
No, it would only rouse the others. Tomorrow.
He turned away with a shiver.
                      His glance fell
On the man who said he had been a king, the man
Called Tarbarrel, the image of black stone
Whose eyes were savage gods.
                            The huge suave muscles
Rippled like stretching cats as he changed posture,
Magnificence in chains that yet was ease.
The smoulder in those eyes. The steady hate.

The mate made himself stare till the eyes dropped.
Then he turned back to the companionway.
His forehead was hot and sweaty. He wiped it off,
But then the rough cloth of his sleeve smelt black.

The captain shut the Bible as he came in.
'Well, Mister Mate?'
               'All quiet, sir.'
                          The captain

Looked at him sharply. 'Sit down,' he said in a bark.
The mate's knees gave as he sat. 'It's—hot down there,'
He said, a little weakly, wanting to wipe
His face again, but knowing he'd smell that blackness
Again, if he did.
        'Takes you that way, sometimes,'
Said the captain, not unkindly, 'I remember
Back in the twenties.'
        Something hot and strong
Bit the mate's throat. He coughed.
        'There,' said the captain,
Putting the cup down. 'You'll feel better now.
You're young for this trade, Mister, and that's a fact.'

The mate coughed and didn't answer, much too glad
To see the captain change back to himself
From something made of steam, to want to talk.
But, after a while, he heard the captain talking,
Half to himself.
        'It's a fact, that,' he was saying.
'They've even made a song of me—ever heard it?'
The mate shook his head, quickly. 'Oh yes you have.
You know how it goes.' He cleared his throat and hummed:

> *'Captain Ball was a Yankee slaver,*
> *Blow, blow, blow the man down!*
> *He traded in niggers and loved his Saviour,*
> *Give me some time to blow the man down.'*

30

STEPHEN VINCENT BENÉT

The droning chanty filled the narrow cabin
An instant with grey Massachusetts sea,
Wave of the North, wave of the melted ice,
The hard salt-sparkles on the harder rock,
The stony islands.
>   Then it died away.

'Well,' said the captain, 'if that's how it strikes them—
They mean it bad but I don't take it bad.
I get my sailing-orders from the Lord.'
He touched the Bible. 'And it's down there, Mister,
Down there in black and white—the sons of Ham—
Bondservants—sweat of their brows.' His voice trailed off
Into texts. 'I tell you, Mister,' he said fiercely,
'The pay's good pay, but it's the Lord's work, too.
We're spreading the Lord's seed—spreading his seed—'

His hand made the outflung motion of a sower
And the mate, staring, seemed to hear the slight
Patter of fallen seeds on fertile ground,
Black, shining seeds, robbed from a black king's storehouse,
Falling and falling on American earth
With light, inexorable patter and fall,
To strike, lie silent, quicken.
>   Till the Spring
Came with its weeping rains, and the ground bore
A blade, a shadow-sapling, a tree of shadow,
A black-leaved tree whose trunk and roots were shadow,

STEPHEN VINCENT BENÉT

A tree shaped like a yoke, growing and growing
Until it blotted all the seamen's stars.

Horses of anger trampling, horses of anger,
Trampling behind the sky in ominous cadence,
Beat of the heavy hooves like metal on metal,
Trampling something down....
                        Was it they, was it they?
Or was it cold wind in the leaves of the shadow-tree
That made such grievous music?

>Oh Lordy Je-sus,
>Won't you come and find me?
>They put me in jail, Lord,
>Way down in the jail.
>Won't you send me a pro-phet,
>Just one of your prophets
>Like Moses and Aaron,
>To get me some bail?

>I'm feeling poorly,
>Yes, mighty poorly,
>I ain't got no strength, Lord,
>I'm all trampled down.
>So send me an angel,
>Just any old angel,
>To give me a robe, Lord,
>And give me a crown.

STEPHEN VINCENT BENÉT

>Oh Lordy Je-sus,
>It's a long time comin',
>It's a long time co-o-min',
>That Jubilee time.
>We'll wait and we'll pray, Lord,
>We'll wait and we'll pray, Lord,
>But it's a long time, Lord,
>Yes, it's a long time.

The dark sobbing ebbed away.
The captain was still talking. 'Yes,' he said,
'And yet we treat 'em well enough. There's no one
From Salem to the Guinea Coast can say
They lose as few as I do.' He stopped.
                                      'Well, Mister?'
The mate arose. 'Good night sir and—'
                                              'Good night.'

The mate went up on deck. The breeze was fresh.
There were the stars, steady. He shook himself
Like a dog coming out of water and felt better.
Six weeks, with luck, and they'd be back in port
And he could draw his pay and see his girl.
Meanwhile, it wasn't his watch, so he could sleep.
The captain still below, reading that Bible. . . .
Forget it—and the noises, still half-heard—
He'd have to go below to sleep, this time,
But after, if the weather held like this,
He'd have them sling a hammock up on deck.
You couldn't smell the black so much on deck
And so you didn't dream it when you slept.

STEPHEN VINCENT BENÉT

20 *John Brown's body lies a-mouldering*
       (Finale from 'John Brown's Body')

JOHN BROWN'S body lies a-mouldering in the grave.
Spread over it the bloodstained flag of his song,
For the sun to bleach, the wind and the birds to tear,
The snow to cover over with a pure fleece
And the New England cloud to work upon
With the grey absolution of its slow, most lilac-
    smelling rain,
Until there is nothing there
That ever knew a master or a slave
Or, brooding on the symbol of a wrong,
Threw down the irons in the field of peace.
John Brown is dead, he will not come again,
A stray ghost-walker with a ghostly gun.
Let the strong metal rust
In the enclosing dust,
And the consuming coal
That was the furious soul
And still like iron groans,
Anointed with the earth,
Grow colder than the stones
While the white roots of grass and little weeds
Suck the last hollow wildfire from the singing bones.

Bury the South together with this man,
Bury the bygone South.
Bury the minstrel with the honey-mouth,
Bury the broadsword virtues of the clan,

STEPHEN VINCENT BENÉT

Bury the unmachined, the planters' pride,
The courtesy and the bitter arrogance,
The pistol-hearted horsemen who could ride
Like jolly centaurs under the hot stars.
Bury the whip, bury the branding-bars,
Bury the unjust thing
That some tamed into mercy, being wise,
But could not starve the tiger from its eyes
Or make it feed where beasts of mercy feed.
Bury the fiddle-music and the dance,
The sick magnolias of the false romance
And all the chivalry that went to seed
Before its ripening.

And with these things, bury the purple dream
Of the America we have not been,
The tropic empire seeking the warm sea,
The last foray of aristocracy
Based not on dollars or initiative
Or any blood for what that blood was worth
But on a certain code, a manner of birth,
A certain manner of knowing how to live,
The pastoral rebellion of the earth
Against machines, against the Age of Steam,
The Hamiltonian extremes against the Franklin mean,
The genius of the land
Against the metal hand,
The great, slave-driven bark,
Full-oared upon the dark,
With gilded figurehead,

STEPHEN VINCENT BENÉT

With fetters for the crew
And spices for the few,
The passion that is dead,
The pomp we never knew,
Bury this, too.

Bury this destiny unmanifest,
This system broken underneath the test,
Beside John Brown and though he knows his enemy
    is there
He is too full of sleep at last to care.

He was a stone, this man who lies so still,
A stone flung from a sling against a wall,
A sacrificial instrument of kill,
A cold prayer hardened to a musket-ball:
And yet, he knew the uses of a hill,
And he must have his justice, after all.

He was a lover of certain pastoral things,
He had the shepherd's gift.
When he walked at peace, when he drank from the
    watersprings,
His eyes would lift

To see God, robed in a glory, but sometimes, too,
Merely the sky,
Untroubled by wrath or angels, vacant and blue,
Vacant and high.

STEPHEN VINCENT BENÉT

He knew not only doom but the shape of the land,
Reaping and sowing.
He could take a lump of any earth in his hand
And feel the growing.

He was a farmer, he didn't think much of towns,
The wheels, the vastness.
He liked the wide fields, the yellows, the lonely browns,
The black ewe's fastness.

Out of his body grows revolving steel,
Out of his body grows the spinning wheel
Made up of wheels, the new, mechanic birth,
No longer bound by toil
To the unsparing soil
Or the old furrow-line,
The great, metallic beast
Expanding West and East,
His heart a spinning coil,
His juices burning oil,
His body serpentine.
Out of John Brown's strong sinews the tall skyscrapers grow,
Out of his heart the chanting buildings rise,
Rivet and girder, motor and dynamo,
Pillar of smoke by day and fire by night,
The steel-faced cities reaching at the skies,
The whole enormous and rotating cage
Hung with hard jewels of electric light,
Smoky with sorrow, black with splendor, dyed

STEPHEN VINCENT BENÉT

Whiter than damask for a crystal bride
With metal suns, the engine-handed Age,
The genie we have raised to rule the earth,
Obsequious to our will
But servant-master still,
The tireless serf already half a god—

Touch the familiar sod
Once, then gaze at the air
And see the portent there,
With eyes for once washed clear
Of worship and of fear:
There is its hunger, there its living thirst,
There is the beating of the tremendous heart
You cannot read for omens.
      Stand apart
From the loud crowd and look upon the flame
Alone and steadfast, without praise or blame.
This is the monster and the sleeping queen
And both have roots struck deep in your own mind;
This is reality that you have seen,
This is reality that made you blind.

So, when the crowd gives tongue
And prophets, old or young,
Bawl out their strange despair
Or fall in worship there,
Let them applaud the image or condemn,
But keep your distance and your soul from them.
And, if the heart within your breast must burst
Like a cracked crucible and pour its steel

STEPHEN VINCENT BENÉT

White-hot before the white heat of the wheel,
Strive to recast once more
That attar of the ore
In the strong mold of pain
Till it is whole again,
And while the prophets shudder or adore
Before the flame, hoping it will give ear,
If you at last must have a word to say,
Say neither, in their way,
'It is a deadly magic and accursed,'
Nor, 'It is blest,' but only, 'It is here.'

LAURENCE BINYON
1869-

Hunger

I COME among the peoples like a shadow;
I sit down by each man's side.

None sees me, but they look on one another,
And know that I am there.

My silence is like the silence of the tide
That buries the playground of children;

Like the deepening of frost in the slow night,
When birds are dead in the morning.

Armies trample, invade, destroy,
With guns roaring from earth and air.

LAURENCE BINYON

I am more terrible than armies,
I am more feared than the cannon.

Kings and chancellors give commands;
I give no command to any;

But I am listened to more than kings
And more than passionate orators.

I unswear words, and undo deeds.
Naked things know me.

I am first and last to be felt of the living.
I am Hunger.

For the Fallen
1914

WITH proud thanksgiving, a mother for her children,
England mourns for her dead across the sea.
Flesh of her flesh they were, spirit of her spirit,
Fallen in the cause of the free.

Solemn the drums thrill: Death august and royal
Sings sorrow up into immortal spheres;
There is music in the midst of desolation
And a glory that shines upon our tears.

They went with songs to the battle, they were young,
Straight of limb, true of eye, steady and aglow.
They were staunch to the end against odds uncounted,
They fell with their faces to the foe.

LAURENCE BINYON

They shall grow not old, as we that are left grow old:
Age shall not weary them, nor the years condemn.
At the going down of the sun and in the morning
We will remember them.

They mingle not with their laughing comrades again;
They sit no more at familiar tables of home;
They have no lot in our labour of the day-time:
They sleep beyond England's foam.

But where our desires are and our hopes profound,
Felt as a well-spring that is hidden from sight,
To the innermost heart of their own land they are
    known
As the stars are known to the Night;

As the stars that shall be bright when we are dust
Moving in marches upon the heavenly plain,
As the stars that are starry in the time of our darkness,
To the end, to the end, they remain.

23 *The Sirens*

WHITHER is she gone, wing'd by the evening
    airs,
Yon sail that draws the last of light afar,
On the sea-verge alone, despising other cares
Than her own errand and her guiding star?
She leaves the safe land, leaves the roofs, and the long
    roads
Travelling the hills to end for each at his own hearth.
She leaves the silence under slowly-darkening elms,

LAURENCE BINYON

The friendly human voices, smell of dew and dust,
And generations of men asleep in the old earth.
Between two solitudes she glides and fades,
And round us falls the darkness she invades.

Waters empty and outcast, O barren waters!
What have your wastes to do
With the earth-treader, the earth-tiller; this frail
Body of man; the sower, whom the green shoot
    gladdens;
Hewer of trees; the builder, who houses him from the
    bleak winds,
And whom awaits at last long peace beneath the grass
In soil his fathers knew?
What shall he hope for from your careless desolation,
Lion-indolence, or cold roar of your risen wrath?
What sows he in your furrows, or what fruit gathers
But hazard, loss, and his own hard courage? . . .
Yon sail goes like a spirit seeking you.

I heard a trumpet from beyond the moon,
Piercing ice-blue gulfs of air,
Cry down the secret waters of the world,
Under the far sea-streams, to summon there
The foundered ships, the splendid ships, the lost ships.
In their ribb'd ruin and age-long sleep they heard,
Where each had found her shadowy burial-bed,
Clutched in blind reef, shoal-choked or shingle-bound;
Heard from betraying isles and capes of dread
In corners of all oceans, where the light
Gropes faltering over their split merchandize:

LAURENCE BINYON

And shapes at last were stirred
On glimmerless abysses' oozy floors
Known to the dark fins only and drowned eyes;—
Sunk out of memory, they that glided forth
Bound from cold rivers to the tropic shores,
Or questing up the white gloom of the North;
Or shattered in the glory of old wars,
The laden ships, the gallant ships, the lost ships!

I saw them clouding up over the verge,
Ghosts that arose out of an unknown grave,
Strange to the buoyant seas that young they rode
    upon
And strange to the idle glitter of the wave.
Magically rebuilded, rigged and manned,
They stole in their slow beauty toward the land.
Mariners, O mariners!
I heard a voice cry: Home, come home!
Here is the rain-fresh earth, leaf-changing seasons;
    here
Spring the flowers; and here, older than memory, peace
Tastes on the air sweet as honey in the honey-comb.
Smells not the hearth-smoke better than spices of
    India?
Are not children's kisses dearer than ivory and pearls?
And sleep in the hill kinder than nameless water
And the cold, wandering foam?

Dear are the names of home, I heard a far voice
    answer,

LAURENCE BINYON

Pleasant the tilled valley, the flocks and farms; and sweet
The hum in cities of men, and words of our own kin.
But we have tasted wild fruit, listened to strange music;
And all shores of the earth are but as doors of an inn;
We knocked at the doors, and slept; to arise at dawn and go.
We spilt blood for gold, trafficked in costly cargoes,
But knew in the end it was not these we sailed to win;
Only a wider sea; room for the winds to blow,
And a world to wander in.

EARLE BINYON
1904-

David

I

DAVID and I that summer cut trails on the Survey,
All week in the valley for wages, in air that was steeped
In the wail of mosquitoes, but over the sunalive weekends
We climbed, to get from the ruck of the camp, the surly

EARLE BIRNEY

Poker, the wrangling, the snoring under the fetid
Tents, and because we had joy in our lengthening coltish
Muscles, and mountains for David were made to see over,
Stairs from the valleys and steps to the sun's retreats.

II
Our first was Mount Gleam. We hiked in the long afternoon
To a curling lake and lost the lure of the faceted
Cone in the swell of its sprawling shoulders. Past
The inlet we grilled our bacon, the strips festooned

On a poplar prong, in the hurrying slant of the sunset.
Then the two of us rolled in the blanket while round us the cold
Pines thrust at the stars. The dawn was a floating
Of mists till we reached to the slopes above timber, and won

To snow like fire in the sunlight. The peak was upthrust
Like a fist in a frozen ocean of rock that swirled
Into valleys the moon could be rolled in. Remotely unfurling
Eastward the alien prairie glittered. Down through the dusty

EARLE BIRNEY

Skree on the west we descended, and David showed me
How to use the give of shale for giant incredible
Strides. I remember, before the larches' edge,
That I jumped a long green surf of juniper flowing

Away from the wind, and landed in gentian and saxifrage
Spilled on the moss. Then the darkening firs
And the sudden whirring of water that knifed down a fern-hidden
Cliff and splashed unseen into mist in the shadows.

III

One Sunday on Rampart's arête a rainsquall caught us,
And passed, and we clung by our blueing fingers and bootnails
An endless hour in the sun, not daring to move
Till the ice had steamed from the slate. And David taught me

How time on a knife-edge can pass with the guessing of fragments
Remembered from poets, the naming of strata beside one,
And matching of stories from schooldays. . . . We crawled astride
The peak to feast on the marching ranges flagged

EARLE BIRNEY

By the fading shreds of the shattered stormcloud.
    Lingering
There it was David who spied to the south, remote,
And unmapped, a sunlit spire on Sawback, an overhang
Crooked like a talon. David named it the Finger.

That day we chanced on the skull and the splayed white ribs
Of a mountain goat underneath a cliff, caught tight
On a rock. Around were the silken feathers of kites.
And that was the first I knew that a goat could slip.

IV

And then Inglismaldie. Now I remember only
The long ascent of the lonely valley, the live
Pine spirally scarred by lightning, the slicing pipe
Of invisible pika, and great prints, by the lowest

Snow, of a grizzly. There it was too that David
Taught me to read the scroll of coral in limestone
And the beetle-seal in the shale of ghostly trilobites,
Letters delivered to man from the Cambrian waves.

V

On Sundance we tried from the col and the going was hard.
The air howled from our feet to the smudged rocks
And the papery lake below. At an outthrust we balked
Till David clung with his left to a dint in the scarp,

EARLE BIRNEY

Lobbed the iceaxe over the rocky lip,
Slipped from his holds and hung by the quivering pick,
Twisted his long legs up into space and kicked
To the crest. Then, grinning, he reached with his freckled wrist

And drew me up after. We set a new time for that climb.
That day returning we found a robin gyrating
In grass, wing-broken. I caught it to tame but David
Took and killed it, and said, 'Could you teach it to fly?'

VI

In August, the second attempt, we ascended The Fortress.
By the Forks of the Spray we caught five trout and fried them
Over a balsam fire. The woods were alive
With the vaulting of mule-deer and drenched with clouds all the morning,

Till we burst at noon to the flashing and floating round
Of the peaks. Coming down we picked in our hats the bright
And sunhot raspberries, eating them under a mighty
Spruce, while a marten moving like quicksilver scouted us.

EARLE BIRNEY
VII

But always we talked of the Finger on Sawback, unknown
And hooked, till the first afternoon in September we slogged
Through the musky woods, past a swamp that quivered with frog-song,
And camped by a bottle-green lake. But under the cold

Breath of the glacier sleep would not come, the moonlight
Etching the Finger. We rose and trod past the feathery
Larch, while the stars went out, and the quiet heather
Flushed, and the skyline pulsed with the surging bloom

Of incredible dawn in the Rockies. David spotted
Bighorns across the moraine and sent them leaping
With yodels the ramparts redoubled and rolled to the peaks,
And the peaks to the sun. The ice in the morning thaw

Was a gurgling world of crystal and cold blue chasms,
And seracs that shone like frozen salt-green waves.
At the base of the Finger we tried once and failed. Then David
Edged to the west and discovered the chimney; the last

Hundred feet we fought the rock and shouldered and
    kneed
Our way for an hour and made it. Unroping we
    formed
A cairn on the rotting tip. Then I turned to look
    north
At the glistening wedge of giant Assiniboine, heedless

Of handhold. And one foot gave. I swayed and
    shouted.
David turned sharp and reached out his arm and
    steadied me
Turning again with a grin and his lips ready
To jest. But the strain crumbled his foothold. Without

A gasp he was gone. I froze to the sound of grating
Edge-nails and fingers, the slither of stones, the lone
Second of silence, the nightmare thud. Then only
The wind and the muted beat of unknowing cascades.

VIII
Somehow I worked down the fifty impossible feet
To the ledge, calling and getting no answer but echoes
Released in the cirque, and trying not to reflect
What an answer would mean. He lay still, with his
    lean

Young face upturned and strangely unmarred, but his
    legs
Splayed beneath him, beside the final drop,

EARLE BIRNEY

Six hundred feet sheer to the ice. My throat stopped
When I reached him, for he was alive. He opened his
    grey

Straight eyes and brokenly murmured, 'over . . . over.'
And I, feeling beneath him a cruel fang
Of the ledge thrust in his back, but not understanding,
Mumbled stupidly, 'Best not to move,' and spoke

Of his pain. But he said, 'I can't move . . . If only
    I felt
Some pain.' Then my shame stung the tears to my
    eyes
As I crouched, and I cursed myself, but he cried
Louder, 'No, Bobbie! Don't ever blame yourself.

I didn't test my foothold.' He shut the lids
Of his eyes to the stare of the sky, while I moistened
    his lips
From our water flask and tearing my shirt into strips
I swabbed the shredded hands. But the blood slid

From his side and stained the stone and the thirsting
    lichens,
And yet I dared not lift him up from the gore
Of the rock. Then he whispered, 'Bob, I want to go
    over!'
This time I knew what he meant and I grasped for a
    lie

EARLE BIRNEY

And said, 'I'll be back here by midnight with ropes
And men from the camp and we'll cradle you out.'
    But I knew
That the day and the night must pass and the cold
    dews
Of another morning before such men unknowing

The ways of mountains could win to the chimney's
    top.
And then, how long? And he knew . . . and the hell
    of hours
After that, if he lived till we came, roping him out.
But I curled beside him and whispered, 'The bleeding
    will stop.

You can last.' He said only, 'Perhaps . . . For what?
    A wheelchair,
Bob?' His eyes brightening with fever upbraided me.
I could not look at him more and said, 'Then I'll stay
With you.' But he did not speak, for the clouding
    fever.

I lay dazed and stared at the long valley,
The glistening hair of a creek on the rug stretched
By the firs, while the sun leaned round and flooded
    the ledge,
The moss, and David still as a broken doll.

I hunched to my knees to leave, but he called and
    his voice
Now was sharpened with fear. 'For Christ's sake
    push me over!

EARLE BIRNEY

If I could move . . . or die. . . .' The sweat ran from
    his forehead,
But only his head moved. A kite was buoying

Blackly its wings over the wrinkled ice.
The purr of a waterfall rose and sank with the wind.
Above us climbed the last joint of the Finger
Beckoning bleakly the wide indifferent sky.

Even then in the sun it grew cold lying there. . . .
    And I knew
He had tested his holds. It was I who had not. . . .
    I looked
At the blood on the ledge, and the far valley. I looked
At last in his eyes. He breathed, 'I'd do it for you,
    Bob.'

IX

I will not remember how nor why I could twist
Up the wind-devilled peak, and down through the
    chimney's empty
Horror, and over the traverse alone. I remember
Only the pounding fear I would stumble on It

When I came to the grave-cold maw of the berg-
    schrund . . . reeling
Over the sun-cankered snowbridge, shying the caves
In the névé . . . the fear, and the need to make sure
    It was there
On the ice, the running and falling and running,
    leaping

EARLE BIRNEY

Of gaping green-throated crevasses, alone and pursued
By the Finger's lengthening shadow. At last through the fanged
And blinding seracs I slid to the milky wrangling
Falls at the glacier's snout, through the rocks piled huge

On the humped moraine, and into the spectral larches,
Alone. By the glooming lake I sank and chilled
My mouth but I could not rest and stumbled still
To the valley, losing my way in the ragged marsh.

I was glad of the mire that covered the stains, on my ripped
Boots, of his blood, but panic was on me, the reek
Of the bog, the purple glimmer of toadstools obscene
In the twilight. I staggered clear to a firewaste, tripped

And fell with a shriek on my shoulder. It somehow eased
My heart to know I was hurt, but I did not faint
And I could not stop while over me hung the range
Of the Sawback. In blackness I searched for the trail by the creek

And found it.... My feet squelched a slug and horror
Rose again in my nostrils. I hurled myself
Down the path. In the woods behind some animal yelped.
Then I saw the glimmer of tents and babbled my story.

EARLE BIRNEY

I said that he fell straight to the ice where they found him,
And none but the sun and incurious clouds have lingered
Around the marks of that day on the ledge of the Finger,
That day, the last of my youth, on the last of our mountains.

25   *Vancouver Lights*

ABOUT me the night, moonless, wimples the mountains,
wraps ocean, land, air, and mounting
sucks at the stars. The city, away and below,
webs the sable peninsula. Streaming, the golden
strands leap the sea-jet, by bridge and by buoy,
vault the shears of the inlet, climb the woods
toward me, falter and halt. Across to the firefly
haze of a ship on the gulf's erased horizon
roll the lambent spokes of a restless lighthouse.

Now through the feckless years we have come to the time
when to look on this quilt of lamps is a troubling delight.
Welling from Europe's bog, through Africa flowing
and Asia, drowning the lonely lumes on the oceans,
tiding up over Halifax, and now to this winking
outpost, comes flooding the primal ink.

EARLE BIRNEY

On this mountain's brutish forehead, with terror of space
I stir, of the changeless night and the stark ranges
of nothing, pulsing down from beyond and between
the fragile planets. We are a spark beleaguered
by darkness; this twinkle we make in a corner of emptiness,
how shall we utter our fear lest the black Experimentress
never in the range of her microscope find it? Our Phoebus
himself is a bubble that dries on Her slide, while the Nubian
wears for an evening's whim a necklace of nebulae.

Yet we must speak, we the unique glowworms.
Out of the waters and rocks of our little world
we cunningly conjured these flames, hooped these sparks
for our will. From blankness and cold we fashioned stars
to our size, rulered with manplot the velvet chaos
and signalled Aldebaran. This we must say,
whoever may be to hear us, if the murk devour,
and none weave again in gossamer:

        These rays were ours,
we made and unmade them. Not the shudder of continents
doused us, the moon's passion, nor crash of comets.

EARLE BIRNEY

In the fathomless heat of our dwarfdom, our dream's
    combustion,
we contrived the power, the blast that snuffed us.
No one slew Prometheus. Himself he chained
and consumed his own bright liver. O stranger,
Plutonian, descendant, or beast in the stretching
    night—
there was light.

26   *Hands*

IN the amber morning by the inlet's high shore
  My canoe drifts and the slim trees come bending
Arching the palms of their still green hands
Juggling the shimmer of ripples.
                        Too bewildering
Even in the dead days of peace was this manumission,
The leaves' illogical loveliness. Now am I frustrate,
Alien. Here is the battle steeped in silence,
The fallen have use and fragrantly nourish the quick.
My species would wither, away from the radio's bark-
    ings,
The headline beating its chimpanzee breast, the
    nimble
Young digits at levers and triggers. Lithe are these
    balsam
Fingers, gaunt as a Jew's in Poland, but green,
Green, not of us, our colours are black and red.
Cold and unskilled is the cedar, his webbed claws
Drooping over the water shall focus no bombsight

57

EARLE BIRNEY

Nor suture the bayoneted bowel, his jade tips
Alert but to sea-dew and air and the soundless touch
Of the light winked by the wind from the breathing ocean,
Inept to clutch the parachute cord, the uniformed
Throat, the mud by the Thames in ebbing agony.
These alders cupping their womanish palms, pulsing
To the startled light when the long unpredictable swell
Reaches from the grey heart of the far Pacific,
Are not of my flesh. Their hands speak for Brutus,
And signal sedition to the poet interned and the lover
Suppressed; they render nought unto Caesar.

                             My fingers
Must close on the paddle. Back to the safe dead
Wood of the docks, the whining poles of the city,
And to hands the extension of tools, of the militant typewriter,
The self-filling patriot pen, back to the paws
Clasping warmly over the bomber contract,
Applauding the succulent orators, back to the wrinkled
Index weaving the virtuous sock, pointing the witch hunt,
While the splayed fist thrusts at the heart of hereafter.
We are gloved with steel, and a magnet is set us in Europe.
We are not of these woods, we are not of these woods,
Our roots are in autumn, and store for no spring.

ROBERT BRIDGES
1844-1930

27 *'I heard a Linnet courting'*

I HEARD a linnet courting
  His lady in the spring:
His mates were idly sporting,
  Nor stayed to hear him sing
    His song of love.—
I fear my speech distorting
    His tender love.

The phrases of his pleading
  Were full of young delight;
And she that gave him heeding
  Interpreted aright
    His gay, sweet notes,—
So sadly marred in the reading,—
    His tender notes.

And when he ceased, the hearer
  Awaited the refrain,
Till swiftly perching nearer
  He sang his song again,
    His pretty song:—
Would that my verse spake clearer
    His tender song!

Ye happy, airy creatures!
  That in the merry spring
Think not of what misfeatures
  Or cares the year may bring;
    But unto love
Resign your simple natures,
    To tender love.

ROBERT BRIDGES

28 *'I love all Beauteous Things'*

I LOVE all beauteous things,
  I seek and adore them;
God hath no better praise,
And man in his hasty days
  Is honoured for them.

I too will something make
  And joy in the making;
Altho' tomorrow it seem
Like the empty words of a dream
  Remembered on waking.

29 *'Spring goeth all in White'*

SPRING goeth all in white,
  Crowned with milk-white may:
In fleecy flocks of light
O'er heaven the white clouds stray:

White butterflies in the air;
White daisies prank the ground:
The cherry and hoary pear
Scatter their snow around.

30 *A Passer-by*

WHITHER, O splendid ship, thy white sails crowding,
  Leaning across the bosom of the urgent West,
That fearest nor sea rising, nor sky clouding,

ROBERT BRIDGES

Whither away, fair rover, and what thy quest?
  Ah! soon, when Winter has all our vales opprest,
When skies are cold and misty, and hail is hurling,
  Wilt thou glide on the blue Pacific, or rest
In a summer haven asleep, thy white sails furling.

I there before thee, in the country that well thou knowest,
  Already arrived am inhaling the odorous air:
I watch thee enter unerringly where thou goest,
  And anchor queen of the strange shipping there,
  Thy sails for awnings spread, thy masts bare;
Nor is aught from the foaming reef to the snow-capp'd, grandest
  Peak, that is over the feathery palms more fair
Than thou, so upright, so stately and still thou standest.

And yet, O splendid ship, unhail'd and nameless,
  I know not if, aiming a fancy, I rightly divine
That thou hast a purpose joyful, a courage blameless,
  Thy port assured in a happier land than mine.
  But for all I have given thee, beauty enough is thine,
As thou, aslant with trim tackle and shrouding,
  From the proud nostril curve of a prow's line
In the offing scatterest foam, thy white sails crowding.

ROBERT BRIDGES
Nightingales

BEAUTIFUL must be the mountains whence ye come,
And bright in the fruitful valleys the streams, wherefrom
    Ye learn your song:
Where are those starry woods? O might I wander there,
Among the flowers, which in that heavenly air
    Bloom the year long!

Nay, barren are those mountains and spent the streams:
Our song is the voice of desire, that haunts our dreams,
    A throe of the heart,
Whose pining visions dim, forbidden hopes profound,
No dying cadence nor long sigh can sound,
    For all our art.

Alone, aloud in the raptured ear of men
We pour our dark nocturnal secret; and then,
    As night is withdrawn
From these sweet-springing meads and bursting boughs of May,
Dream, while the innumerable choir of day
    Welcome the dawn.

ROBERT BRIDGES
From 'Ode to Music'
V

1

LOVE to Love calleth,
Love unto Love replieth;
From the ends of the earth, drawn by invisible bands,
Over the dawning and darkening lands
    Love cometh to Love,
    To the pangs of desire;
To the heart by courage and might
Escaped from hell,
From the torment of raging fire,
From the sighs of the drowning main,
From shipwreck of fear and pain,
From the terror of night.

2

All mankind by love shall be banded
To combat Evil, the many-handed:
For the spirit of man on beauty feedeth,
The airy fancy he heedeth,
He regardeth Truth in the heavenly height,
In changeful pavilions of loveliness dight,
The sovran sun that knows not the night;
He loveth the beauty of earth,
And the sweet birds' mirth;
And out of his heart there falleth

ROBERT BRIDGES

A melody-making river
Of passion, that runneth ever
To the ends of the earth and crieth,
That yearneth and calleth;
And Love from the heart of man
To the heart of man replieth:
    On the wings of desire
    Love cometh to Love.

VII
Dirge

Man born of desire
Cometh out of the night,
A wandering spark of fire,
A lonely world of eternal thought
Echoing in chance and forgot.

I

He seeth the sun,
He calleth the stars by name,
He saluteth the flowers.—
Wonders of land and sea,
The mountain towers
Of ice and air
He seeth, and calleth them fair:
  Then he hideth his face;—
Whence he came to pass away
Where all is forgot,
Unmade—lost for aye
With the things that are not.

ROBERT BRIDGES

2

He striveth to know,
To unravel the Mind
That veileth in horror:
He wills to adore.
In wisdom he walketh
And loveth his kind;
His labouring breath
Would keep evermore:
   Then he hideth his face;—
Whence he came to pass away
Where all is forgot,
Unmade—lost for aye
With the things that are not.

3

He dreameth of beauty,
He seeks to create
Fairer and fairer
To vanquish his Fate;
No hindrance he—
No curse will brook,
He maketh a law
No ill shall be:
Then he hideth his face;—
Whence he came to pass away
Where all is forgot,
Unmade—lost for aye
With the things that are not.

* * *

ROBERT BRIDGES

Rejoice, ye dead, where'er your spirits dwell,
Rejoice that yet on earth your fame is bright,
And that your names, remember'd day and
  night,
Live on the lips of those who love you well.
  'Tis ye that conquer'd have the powers of
    Hell
Each with the special grace of your delight;
Ye are the world's creators, and by might
Alone of Heavenly love ye did excel.
  Now ye are starry names
  Behind the sun ye climb
    To light the glooms of Time
    With deathless flames.

* * *

Open for me the gates of delight,
The gates of the garden of man's desire;
Where spirits touch'd by heavenly fire
  Have planted the trees of life.—
Their branches in beauty are spread,
  Their fruit divine
To the nations is given for bread,
  And crush'd into wine.

RUPERT BROOKE
1887-1915

33 *The Great Lover*

I HAVE been so great a lover: filled my days
  So proudly with the splendour of Love's praise,
The pain, the calm, and the astonishment,
Desire illimitable, and still content,
And all dear names men use, to cheat despair,
For the perplexed and viewless streams that bear
Our hearts at random down the dark of life.
Now, ere the unthinking silence on that strife
Steals down, I would cheat drowsy Death so far,
My night shall be remembered for a star
That outshone all the suns of all men's days.
Shall I not crown them with immortal praise
Whom I have loved, who have given me, dared with
    me
High secrets, and in darkness knelt to see
The inenarrable godhead of delight?
Love is a flame:—we have beaconed the world's night.
A city:—and we have built it, these and I.
An emperor:—we have taught the world to die.
So, for their sakes I loved, ere I go hence,
And the high cause of Love's magnificence,
And to keep loyalties young, I'll write those names
Golden for ever, eagles, crying flames,
And set them as a banner, that men may know,
To dare the generations, burn, and blow
Out on the wind of Time, shining and streaming. . . .

These I have loved:
          White plates and cups, clean-gleaming,
Ringed with blue lines; and feathery, faery dust;

RUPERT BROOKE

Wet roofs, beneath the lamplight; the strong crust
Of friendly bread; and many-tasting food;
Rainbows; and the blue bitter smoke of wood;
And radiant raindrops couching in cool flowers;
And flowers themselves, that sway through sunny hours,
Dreaming of moths that drink them under the moon;
Then, the cool kindliness of sheets, that soon
Smooth away trouble; and the rough male kiss
Of blankets; grainy wood; live hair that is
Shining and free; blue-massing clouds; the keen
Unpassioned beauty of a great machine;
The benison of hot water; furs to touch;
The good smell of old clothes; and other such—
The comfortable smell of friendly fingers,
Hair's fragrance, and the musty reek that lingers
About dead leaves and last year's ferns. . . .
                                          Dear names,
And thousand other throng to me! Royal flames;
Sweet water's dimpling laugh from tap or spring;
Holes in the ground; and voices that do sing;
Voices in laughter, too; and body's pain,
Soon turned to peace; and the deep-panting train;
Firm sands; the little dulling edge of foam
That browns and dwindles as the wave goes home;
And washen stones, gay for an hour; the cold
Graveness of iron; moist black earthen mould;
Sleep; and high places; footprints in the dew;
And oaks; and brown horse-chestnuts, glossy-new;
And new-peeled sticks; and shining pools on grass;—
All these have been my loves. And these shall pass,

RUPERT BROOKE

Whatever passes not, in the great hour,
Nor all my passion, all my prayers, have power
To hold them with me through the gate of Death.
They'll play deserter, turn with the traitor breath,
Break the high bond we made, and sell Love's trust
And sacramental covenant to the dust.
—Oh, never a doubt but, somewhere, I shall wake,
And give what's left of love again; and make
New friends, now strangers. . . .
                     But the best I've known,
Stays here, and changes, breaks, grows old, is blown
About the winds of the world, and fades from brains
Of living men, and dies.
                  Nothing remains.

O dear my loves, O faithless, once again
This one last gift I give: that after men
Shall know, and later lovers, far-removed,
Praise you, "All these were lovely"; say, "He loved."

Dust

WHEN the white flame in us is gone,
    And we that lost the world's delight
Stiffen in darkness, left alone
    To crumble in our separate night;

When your swift hair is quiet in death,
    And through the lips corruption thrust
Has stilled the labour of my breath—
    When we are dust, when we are dust!—

RUPERT BROOKE

Not dead, not undesirous yet,
   Still sentient, still unsatisfied,
We'll ride the air, and shine, and flit,
   Around the places where we died,

And dance as dust before the sun,
   And light of foot, and unconfined,
Hurry from road to road, and run
   About the errands of the wind.

And every mote, on earth or air,
   Will speed and gleam, down later days,
And like a secret pilgrim fare
   By eager and invisible ways,

Nor ever rest, nor ever lie,
   Till, beyond thinking, out of view,
One mote of all the dust that's I
   Shall meet one atom that was you.

Then in some garden hushed from wind,
   Warm in a sunset's afterglow,
The lovers in the flowers will find
   A sweet and strange unquiet grow

Upon the peace; and, past desiring,
   So high a beauty in the air,
And such a light, and such a quiring,
   And such a radiant ecstasy there,

RUPERT BROOKE

They'll not know if it's fire, or dew,
 Or out of earth, or in the height,
Singing, or flame, or scent, or hue,
 Or two that pass, in light, to light,

Out of the garden, higher, higher. . . .
 But in that instant they shall learn
The shattering ecstasy of our fire,
 And the weak passionless hearts will burn

And faint in that amazing glow,
 Until the darkness close above;
And they will know—poor fools, they'll know!—
 One moment, what it is to love.

Heaven

FISH (fly-replete, in depth of June,
 Dawdling away their wat'ry noon)
Ponder deep wisdom, dark or clear,
Each secret fishy hope or fear.
Fish say, they have their Stream and Pond;
But is there anything Beyond?
This life cannot be All, they swear,
For how unpleasant, if it were!
One may not doubt that, somehow, Good
Shall come of Water and of Mud;
And, sure, the reverent eye must see
A Purpose in Liquidity.
We darkly know, by Faith we cry,
The future is not Wholly Dry.

RUPERT BROOKE

Mud unto mud!—Death eddies near—
Not here the appointed End, not here!
But somewhere, beyond Space and Time,
Is wetter water, slimier slime!
And there (they trust) there swimmeth One
Who swam ere rivers were begun,
Immense, of fishy form and mind,
Squamous, omnipotent, and kind;
And under that Almighty Fin,
The littlest fish may enter in.
Oh! never fly conceals a hook,
Fish say, in the Eternal Brook,
But more than mundane weeds are there,
And mud, celestially fair;
Fat caterpillars drift around,
And Paradisal grubs are found;
Unfading moths, immortal flies,
And the worm that never dies.
And in that Heaven of all their wish,
There shall be no more land, say fish.

The Dead

THESE hearts were woven of human joys and cares,
    Washed marvellously with sorrow, swift to mirth.
The years had given them kindness. Dawn was theirs,
    And sunset, and the colours of the earth.
These had seen movement, and heard music; known
    Slumber and waking; loved; gone proudly friended;

RUPERT BROOKE

Felt the quick stir of wonder; sat alone;
  Touched flowers and furs and cheeks. All this is ended.

There are waters blown by changing winds to laughter
And lit by the rich skies, all day. And after,
  Frost, with a gesture, stays the waves that dance
And wandering loveliness. He leaves a white
  Unbroken glory, a gathered radiance,
A width, a shining peace, under the night.

37   *The Soldier*

IF I should die, think only this of me:
  That there's some corner of a foreign field
That is for ever England. There shall be
  In that rich earth a richer dust concealed;
A dust whom England bore, shaped, made aware,
  Gave, once, her flowers to love, her ways to roam,
A body of England's, breathing English air,
  Washed by the rivers, blest by suns of home.

And think, this heart, all evil shed away,
  A pulse in the eternal mind, no less
    Gives somewhere back the thoughts by England given;
Her sights and sounds; dreams happy as her day;
  And laughter, learnt of friends; and gentleness,
    In hearts at peace, under an English heaven.

AUDREY ALEXANDRA BROWN
1904-

Song

WHAT will be left when my life is over?
    What will be left when I shut, some spring,
My ears on the drone of the bees in clover,
    My eyes on the flash of the swallow's wing?

What will be left of the seagull's crying,
    The wraith-white mist on the harbour spread,
The bright leaves blown, and the spindrift's flying,
    When I am laid away with the dead?

These will remain for the hearts that love them:
    Many and many, though I am gone,
Will spare a thought for the skies above them,
    Burnt in the rose-red fires of dawn.

April's breath in the alders sighing,
    The fruited ash with its eardrops red,
The silver weft from the hedgetops flying,
    All will endure when I am dead.

And I think, when the long train mourning passes—
    When they shall lay me away to rest
Under a roof of the tasselled grasses,
    Hands laid lightly across my breast—

I shall be blithe for the bloom new-moulded,
    I shall be fain for the lark in May,
Though the eyes be shut and the hands be folded
    In the long, long rest at the end of day!

AUDREY ALEXANDRA BROWN
The Phoenix

THE Phoenix said to me
  (That wild and lovely bird in the ash tree
Which never in its double-score of springs
Bloomed with such dark wood-opal glimmerings
As dropped from the purple fall of his shut wings)—

Calmly, incuriously,
The Phoenix said to me,
'After so many a year do I return:
As always, I behold the trampled seed
And I behold again the roofs that burn
And I behold again the men that bleed.

'Is it so for ever?' Quietly while I gazed,
He stooped his head to the gold fruit I raised:
'Again, and again, and again,
Shall the shouting massed armies pack the plain,
Slaying and being slain?
Poor men, you toss away your warm live breath
As if there were no death:
Believe me, goodly though you stand and brave—
Strong jaws has the grave.'

I answered with a proud and passionate word:
'O brightest creature ever seen or heard,
O loveliest bird, still you are but a bird!
Born and re-born, albeit eternally,
You see, not understanding what you see.
It is because death *is*, and sets a bound

AUDREY ALEXANDRA BROWN

To our life's little round—
It is because we have a flesh too frail
To long outwear the gale—
It is because our thought and our desire
Burn us away like fire—
We dare cut narrower yet our narrow span:
And to die steadfastly
In a good cause for conscience' sake, shall be,
And is, the glory and the crown of man.'

Very clear and bold
That sardonic topaz eye
Ringed with transparent gold!
He rose, and standing high
Settled those plumes that on the dazzled sight
Glowed like a tropic night.

He said, 'Blue as a gentian is your sky;
The small fields lie
Russet and olive and emerald-hued between
Hedges of quicker green.
—So much for any gathering hand to take!
Do you do wisely for whatever sake
To cast away a world as rich in bliss,
Beauty and mirth as this?'

I answered: 'We do well to lightly hold
Even this fair earth, which being prized too high
Would fail us sorely in our growing old.
Though it delight the eye,
If we should feed our hearts upon it, slowly

AUDREY ALEXANDRA BROWN

We should dwindle, spirit, flesh and bone—
For man, that cannot live by bread alone,
Lives not by beauty wholly.'

Pruning the prismy feathers of his breast,
Replied the bird: 'I never had a nest,
Nor ever had a son,
Nor shall have one:
But see, the star-flowered strawberry plants run wild
Along the hedge, and look, a two-years' child
Chuckles and fills his hands with coral fruit.
—Tell true or else be mute!
Do they do well, whatever good they seek,
Who change the dimpled cheek,
The close arms, the warm breath
Of child or love, for the embrace of death?'

At first I had no voice—
Remembering one who made that bitterest choice
And made it smiling. Afterwards I said:
'O Phoenix, these our dead
Knew as we know that all the best in life—
Lover and child and wife,
Being once possessed cannot be lost to death:
This is our faith—
That they are part of us as we of them—
Flowers of one stem.

'But if it were not so—
Too well we know
That even man's tenderest tie of love is less

Than that divine duress
Which rather than suffer him to live in shame
Drives him upon the steel, the flame.

'We are as you, O Phoenix! dying in fire
To rise with glory from our little dust:
We trust, we are bold to trust
That in itself the existence of desire
Argues desire's fulfilment: that to climb
Presumes the crest achieved in God's good time:
And that to dare to die, for such as we,
Is evidence enough of immortality!'

40 *From 'Laodamia'*

'AT dawn they launched the ships; and all went well.
　The slender galleys dipped with masts asway
　Until their wroughten figureheads drank spray:
Lightly they rode the seaward-moving swell;
　Lightly the harbour took the glistening oar,
And as a dream they passed from sight and sound of shore.

'The wide sea held them, and their eager prows
　Cleft a cool ocean, violet-smooth and deep;
　The tides were netted in a trancèd sleep
Fragrant of cinnamon and almond boughs:
　Soft air that filled the sail and stirred the tree
Was all that waked or breathed in that enchanted sea.

AUDREY ALEXANDRA BROWN

'All day they moved before a tranquil breeze:
   On many a green mysterious isle they came,
   Blossomed with brazen orchis wild as flame
And strangely set with brooding secret trees:
   Clear lay the small lagoon; they entered not,
But trimmed their sails anew, and fled the haunted spot.

'Night-long they floated in a silver stream
   Shed by the moon athwart the rippled night:
   The sails were silver in that silver light—
The oarsmen rowed as in a silver dream.
   In a still trance untouched of grief or joy
Upon the summer's end they came at last to Troy.

'Mighty is Troy. Those makers builded well
   Who raised its proud pale splendour at command,
   Fronting the white rocks and the whiter sand,
Immaculate, unassailed, invincible—
   Scorning the level menace of the sea
With towers and temples shaped for immortality.

'Scarcely the sea-breeze stirred the palms a-row;
   Fair in the sun the ivory turrets gleamed;
   In its unwatchfulness the city seemed
As it disdained the presence of the foe—
   As the wild tumult, the alarm of war
Might beat upon its gates, unheard, forever more.

'Thus from the sea they looked upon their goal.
   So long they had pursued their quest, the deep

AUDREY ALEXANDRA BROWN

Had lulled them with the poppy-flowers of sleep
And laid a heavy peace upon their soul:
　As men awaking from a dream they turned,
And near and high the glory of the city burned.

'No warder kept the wall; no trumpet rang.
　. . . So near they were, a leap and one might stand
　Safe on the silken spread of empty sand
That waited for the eager foot that sprang.
　None stirred: again they caught, with failing breath,
The hollow-spoken words that prophesied of death.

'Death—not in battle, half its anguish past,
　But as the heifer at the altar dies,
　Uncomprehending terror in the eyes
That glaze so slowly and are dumb at last,
　Shuttered with night. . . . . "Who leads you to the shore
Shall see these happy fields of blossomed vine no more."

'Remembering, hesitation took them then,
　And spread from man to man about the ship:
　They say Achilles wore a paler lip,
And Ajax look'd aside: for these were men
　Who loved mad battle; yet they held their breath
Before they leapt clear-eyed upon their certain death.

'An ugly silence round the vessels crept . . .
　Then turned Protesilaus where he stood,
　And crying—"Follow to avenge my blood!"

AUDREY ALEXANDRA BROWN

Clad in his armour as he was he leapt
  To the white sand—and on that sand fell dead,
Pierced with a hundred wounds that stained its white-
      ness red.

'Nor passed he unavenged; but as he fell
  There rose a great and furious-throated cry
  From all that fleet whose ships had watched him
      die:
Their decks were empty, and the shoreward swell
  Flashed with a springing horde that from the sea
Leapt up to snatch the fruits of glittering victory.

'Lo, they have wrapped him rich in cloth of pride
  And woven purple: they have made his grave
  In hearing of the ceaseless narrow wave
Which brims the place of battle where he died—
  And they have lettered deep in shining stone
The legend of his death to ages yet unknown.

'Moreover, children's lips shall learn his name
  With their first language: and the youth of Greece
  In happier years of ripe unshadowed peace
Shall bring their laurels to adorn his fame,
  Dreaming of him who turned with steadfast breath
From a most glorious life to a more glorious death.'

He paused. Behind her by the silent loom
  She heard her maidens weeping: but the smart
  Of some great ache that could not be her heart
Beat, beat and fluttered in the listening room—

81

AUDREY ALEXANDRA BROWN

And she was still, lest any had divined
That strangely, in that hour, her tearless eyes were
    blind.

Ah, but her heart could see! . . . A little space
    She stirred not; and her damsels hushed their grief
    To look upon her, lovely past belief,
The great eyes burning in her crystal face
    Where all that year of soul-sick hopes and fears
Closed now in agony beyond relief of tears.

And still she spoke not, and her lips were cold
    With bitter air from off the Stygian deep. . . . .
    At last she moved, as waking from a sleep,
Gave the pale messenger his wonted gold,
    Gently, but yet as one who did not hear
The stammering gratitude that died upon her ear.

And she unloosed the clinging hands, whose care
    Laid timid hold, with weeping, on her dress;
    With eyes that saw not, yet with gentleness,
She put her maidens from her. Wan and fair,
    Glimmering from light to shade, from shade to light,
Up the long hall she moved, and passed beyond their
    sight.

ROY CAMPBELL
1902-

41 *Choosing a Mast*

THIS mast, new-shaved, through whom I rive
    the ropes,
Says she was once an oread of the slopes,
Graceful and tall upon the rocky highlands,
A slender tree, as vertical as noon,
And her low voice was lovely as the silence
Through which a fountain whistles to the moon,
Who now of the white spray must take the veil
And, for her songs, the thunder of the sail.

I chose her for her fragrance, when the spring
With sweetest resins swelled her fourteenth ring
And with live amber welded her young thews:
I chose her for the glory of the Muse,
Smoother of forms, that her hard-knotted grain,
Grazed by the chisel, shaven by the plane,
Might from the steel as cool a burnish take
As from the bladed moon a windless lake.

I chose her for her eagerness of flight
Where she stood tiptoe on the rocky height
Lifted by her own perfume to the sun,
While through her rustling plumes with eager sound
Her eagle spirit, with the gale at one,
Spreading wide pinions, would have spurned the
    ground
And her own sleeping shadow, had they not
With thymy fragrance charmed her to the spot.

ROY CAMPBELL

Lover of song, I chose this mountain pine
Not only for the straightness of her spine
But for her songs: for these she loved to sing
Through a long noon's repose of wave and wing—
The fluvial swirling of her scented hair
Sole rill of song in all that windless air
And her slim form the naiad of the stream
Afloat upon the languor of its theme;

And for the soldier's fare on which she fed—
Her wine the azure, and the snow her bread;
And for her stormy watches on the height—
For only out of solitude or strife
Are born the sons of valour and delight;
And lastly for her rich exulting life
That with the wind stopped not its singing breath
But carolled on, the louder for its death.

Under a pine, when summer days were deep,
We loved the most to lie in love or sleep:
And when in long hexameters the west
Rolled his grey surge, the forest for his lyre,
It was the pines that sang us to our rest
Loud in the wind and fragrant in the fire,
With legioned voices swelling all night long,
From Pelion to Provence, their storm of song.

It was the pines that fanned us in the heat,
The pines that cheered us in the time of sleet,
For which sweet gifts I set one dryad free—
No longer to the wind a rooted foe,

ROY CAMPBELL

This nymph shall wander where she longs to be
And with the blue north wind arise and go,
A silver huntress with the moon to run
And fly through rainbows with the rising sun;

And when to pasture in the glittering shoals
The guardian mistral drives his thundering foals,
And when like Tartar horsemen racing free
We ride the snorting fillies of the sea,
My pine shall be the archer of the gale
While on the bending willow curves the sail
From whose great bow the long keel shooting home
Shall fly, the feathered arrow of the foam.

42 *Tristan da Cunha*

SNORE in the foam; the night is vast and blind;
The blanket of the mist around your shoulders,
Sleep your old sleep of rock, snore in the wind,
Snore in the spray! The storm your slumber lulls,
His wings are folded on your nest of boulders
As on their eggs the grey wings of your gulls.

No more as when, ten thousand years ago,
You hissed a giant cinder from the ocean—
Around your rocks you furl the shawling snow,
Half sunk in your own darkness, vast and grim,
And round you on the deep with surly motion
Pivot your league-long shadow as you swim.

ROY CAMPBELL

Why should you haunt me thus but that I know
My surly heart is in your own displayed,
Round whom such wastes in endless circuit flow,
Whose hours in such a gloomy compass run—
A dial with its league-long arm of shade
Slowly revolving to the moon and sun.

My heart has sunk, like your grey fissured crags,
By its own strength o'ertoppled and betrayed:
I too have burned the wind with fiery flags,
Who now am but a roost for empty words—
An island of the sea whose only trade
Is in the voyages of its wandering birds.

Did you not, when your strength became your pyre,
Deposed and tumbled from your flaming tower,
Awake in gloom from whence you sank in fire
To find Antaeus-like, more vastly grown,
A throne in your own darkness, and a power
Sheathed in the very coldness of your stone?

Your strength is that you have no hope or fear,
You march before the world without a crown:
The nations call you back, you do not hear:
The cities of the earth grow grey behind you,
You will be there when their great flames go down
And still the morning in the van will find you.

You march before the continents: you scout
In front of all the earth: alone you scale
The masthead of the world, a lorn look-out,

ROY CAMPBELL

Waving the snowy flutter of your spray
And gazing back in infinite farewell
To suns that sink, and shores that fade away.

From your grey tower what long regrets you fling
To where, along the low horizon burning,
The great swan-breasted seraphs soar and sing,
And suns go down, and trailing splendours dwindle,
And sails on lonely errands unreturning,
Glow with a gold no sunrise can rekindle.

Turn to the Night, these flames are not for you
Whose steeple for the thunder swings its bells:
Grey Memnon, to the tempest only true,
Turn to the night, turn to the shadowing foam,
And let your voice, the saddest of farewells,
With sullen curfew toll the grey wings home.

The wind, your mournful syren, haunts the gloom;
The rocks, spray-coloured, are your signal-guns
Whose stony nitre, puffed with flying spume,
Rolls forth in grim salute your broadside hollow,
Over the gorgeous burials of suns,
To sound the tocsin of the storms to follow.

Plunge forward like a ship to battle hurled;
Slip the long cables of the failing light,
The level rays that moor you to the world:
Sheathed in your armour of eternal frost,
Plunge forward, in the thunder of the fight
To lose yourself as I would fain be lost.

ROY CAMPBELL

Exiled like you, and severed from my race
By the cold ocean of my own disdain,
Do I not freeze in such a wintry space,
Do I not travel through a storm as vast
And rise at times, victorious from the main,
To fly the sunrise at my shattered mast?

Your path is but a desert where you reap
Only the bitter knowledge of your soul;
You fish with nets of seaweed in the deep
As fruitlessly as I with nets of rhyme,—
Yet forth you stride: yourself the way, the goal,
The surges are your strides, your path is time.

Hurled by what aim to what tremendous range!
A missile from the great sling of the past
Your passage leaves its track of death and change
And ruin on the world: you fly beyond,
Leaping the current of the ages vast
As lightly as a pebble skims a pond.

The years are undulations in your flight
Whose awful motion we can only guess:
Too swift for sense, too terrible for sight,
We only know how fast behind you darken
Our days like lonely beacons of distress:
We know that you stride on and will not harken.

Now in the eastern sky the fairest planet
Pierces the dying wave with dangled spear,
And in the whirring hollows of your granite

ROY CAMPBELL

That vaster Sea, to which you are a shell,
Sighs with a ghostly rumour like the drear
Moan of the nightwind in a hollow cell.

We shall not meet again: over the wave
Our ways divide, and yours is straight and endless—
But mine is short and crooked to the grave:
Yet what of these dark crowds, amid whose flow
I battle like a rock, aloof and friendless—
Are not their generations, vague and endless,
The waves, the strides, the feet on which I go?

43 *From 'The Flaming Terrapin'*

FOR when the winds have ceased their ghostly speech
And the long waves roll moaning from the beach,
The Flaming Terrapin that towed the Ark
Rears up his hump of thunder on the dark,
And like a mountain, seamed with rocky scars,
Tufted with forests, barnacled with stars,
Crinkles white rings, as from its ancient sleep
Into a foam of life he wakes the Deep.
His was the crest that from the angry sky
Tore down the hail: he made the boulders fly
Like balls of paper, splintered icebergs, hurled
Lassoes of dismal smoke around the world,
And like a bunch of crisp and crackling straws,
Coughed the sharp lightning from his craggy jaws.
His was the eye that blinked beyond the hill
After the fury of the flood was done,

ROY CAMPBELL

And breaching from the bottom, cold and still,
Leviathan reared up to greet the Sun.
Perched on the stars around him in the air,
White angels rinsed the moonlight from their hair
And the drowned trees into new flowers unfurled
As it sank dreaming down upon the world.
As he rolled by, all evil things grew dim.
The Devil, who had scoffed, now slunk from him
And sat in Hell, dejected and alone,
Rasping starved teeth against an old dry bone.

BLISS CARMAN
1861-1929

Spring's Saraband

OVER the hills of April
With soft winds hand in hand,
Impassionate and dreamy-eyed,
Spring leads her saraband.
Her garments float and gather
And swirl along the plain,
Her headgear is the golden sun,
Her cloak the silver rain.

With colour and with music,
With perfumes and with pomp,
By meadowland and upland,
Through pasture, wood, and swamp,

BLISS CARMAN

With promise and enchantment
Leading her mystic mime,
She comes to lure the world anew
With joys as old as time.

The bluebird in the orchard
Is lyrical for her,
The blackbird with his meadow pipe
Sets all the wood astir,
The hooded white spring-beauties
Are curtsying in the breeze,
The blue hepaticas are out
Under the chestnut trees.

The maple-buds make glamour,
Viburnum waves its bloom,
The daffodils and tulips
Are risen from the tomb.
The lances of Narcissus
Have pierced the wintry mould;
The commonplace seems paradise
Through veils of greening gold.

Quick lifts the marshy chorus
To transport, trill on trill;
There's not a rod of stony ground
Unanswering on the hill.
The brooks and little rivers
Dance down their wild ravines,
And children in the city squares
Keep time, to tambourines.

BLISS CARMAN

O heart, hear thou the summons,
Put every grief away,
When all the motley masques of earth
Are glad upon a day.
Alack that any mortal
Should less than gladness bring
Into the choral joy that sounds
The saraband of spring!

Low Tide on Grand Pré

THE sun goes down, and over all
   These barren reaches by the tide
Such unelusive glories fall,
   I almost dream they yet will bide
   Until the coming of the tide.

And yet I know that not for us,
   By any ecstasy of dream,
He lingers to keep luminous
   A little while the grievous stream,
   Which frets, uncomforted of dream—

A grievous stream, that to and fro
   Athrough the fields of Acadie
Goes wandering, as if to know
   Why one belovèd face should be
   So long from home and Acadie.

BLISS CARMAN

Was it a year or lives ago
  We took the grasses in our hands,
And caught the summer flying low
  Over the waving meadow lands,
  And held it there between our hands?

The while the river at our feet—
  A drowsy inland meadow stream—
At set of sun the after-heat
  Made running gold, and in the gleam
  We freed our birch upon the stream.

There down along the elms at dusk
  We lifted dripping blade to drift,
Through twilight scented fine like musk,
  Where night and gloom awhile uplift,
  Nor sunder soul and soul adrift.

And that we took into our hands
  Spirit of life or subtler thing—
Breathed on us there, and loosed the bands
  Of death, and taught us, whispering,
  The secret of some wonder-thing.

Then all your face grew light, and seemed
  To hold the shadow of the sun;
The evening faltered, and I deemed
  The time was ripe, and years had done
  Their wheeling underneath the sun.

BLISS CARMAN

So all desire and all regret,
  And fear and memory, were naught;
One to remember or forget
  The keen delight our hands had caught;
  Morrow and yesterday were naught.

The night has fallen, and the tide ...
  Now and again comes drifting home,
Across these aching barrens wide,
  A sigh like driven wind or foam:
  In grief the flood is bursting home.

A Northern Vigil

HERE by the gray north sea,
  In the wintry heart of the wild,
Comes the old dream of thee,
  Guendolen, mistress and child.

The heart of the forest grieves
  In the drift against my door;
A voice is under the eaves,
  A footfall on the floor.

Threshold, mirror and hall,
  Vacant and strangely aware,
Wait for their soul's recall
  With the dumb expectant air.

Here where the smouldering west
  Burns down into the sea,
I take no heed of rest
  And keep the watch for thee.

BLISS CARMAN

I sit by the fire and hear
  The restless wind go by,
On the long dirge and drear,
  Under the low bleak sky.

When day puts out to sea
  And night makes in for land,
There is no lock for thee,
  Each door awaits thy hand!

When night goes over the hill
  And dawn comes down the dale,
It's O for the wild sweet will
  That shall no more prevail!

When the zenith moon is round,
  And snow-wraiths gather and run,
And there is set no bound
  To love beneath the sun,

O wayward will, come near
  The old mad wilful way,
The soft mouth at my ear
  With words too sweet to say!

Come, for the night is cold,
  The ghostly moonlight fills
Hollow and rift and fold
  Of the eerie Ardise hills!

BLISS CARMAN

The windows of my room
    Are dark with bitter frost,
The stillness aches with doom
    Of something loved and lost.

Outside, the great blue star
    Burns in the ghostland pale,
Where giant Algebar
    Holds on the endless trail.

Come, for the years are long,
    And silence keeps the door,
Where shapes with the shadows throng
    The firelit chamber floor.

Come, for thy kiss was warm,
    With the red embers' glare
Across thy folding arm
    And dark tumultuous hair!

And though thy coming rouse
    The sleep-cry of no bird,
The keepers of the house
    Shall tremble at thy word.

Come, for the soul is free!
    In all the vast dreamland
There is no lock for thee,
    Each door awaits thy hand.

BLISS CARMAN

Ah, not in dreams at all,
  Fleering, perishing, dim,
But thy old self, supple and tall,
  Mistress and child of whim!

The proud imperious guise,
  Impetuous and serene,
The sad mysterious eyes,
  And dignity of mien!

Yea, wilt thou not return,
  When the late hill-winds veer,
And the bright hill-flowers burn
  With the reviving year?

When April comes, and the sea
  Sparkles as if it smiled,
Will they restore to me
  My dark Love, empress and child?

The curtains seem to part;
  A sound is on the stair,
As if at the last . . . I start;
  Only the wind is there.

Lo, now far on the hills
  The crimson fumes uncurled,
Where the cauldron mantles and spills
  Another dawn on the world!

G. K. CHESTERTON

1874-1936

47   *Lepanto*

WHITE founts falling in the courts of the sun,
And the Soldan of Byzantium is smiling as they run;
There is laughter like the fountains in that face of all men feared,
It stirs the forest darkness, the darkness of his beard,
It curls the blood-red crescent, the crescent of his lips,
For the inmost sea of all the earth is shaken with his ships.
They have dared the white republics up the capes of Italy,
They have dashed the Adriatic round the Lion of the Sea,
And the Pope has cast his arms abroad for agony and loss,
And called the kings of Christendom for swords about the Cross.
The cold queen of England is looking in the glass;
The shadow of the Valois is yawning at the Mass;
From evening isles fantastical rings faint the Spanish gun,
And the Lord upon the Golden Horn is laughing in the sun.

Dim drums throbbing, in the hills half heard,
Where only on a nameless throne a crownless prince has stirred,
Where, risen from a doubtful seat and half-attainted stall,

G. K. CHESTERTON

The last knight of Europe takes weapons from the wall,
The last and lingering troubadour to whom the bird has sung,
That once went singing southward when all the world was young,
In that enormous silence, tiny and unafraid,
Comes up along a winding road the noise of the Crusade.
Strong gongs groaning as the guns boom far,
Don John of Austria is going to the war,
Stiff flags straining in the night-blasts cold,
In the gloom black-purple, in the glint old-gold,
Torchlight crimson on the copper kettle-drums,
Then the tuckets, then the trumpets, then the cannon, and he comes,
Don John laughing in the brave beard curled,
Spurning of his stirrups like the thrones of all the world,
Holding his head up for a flag of all the free.
Love-light of Spain—hurrah!
Death-light of Africa!
Don John of Austria
Is riding to the sea.
Mahound is in his paradise above the evening star,
(*Don John of Austria is going to the war.*)
He moves a mighty turban on the timeless houri's knees,
His turban that is woven of the sunset and the seas.
He shakes the peacock gardens as he rises from his ease,

G. K. CHESTERTON

And he strides among the tree-tops and is taller than
    the trees,
And his voice through all the garden is a thunder sent
    to bring
Black Azrael and Ariel and Ammon on the wing,
Giants and the Genii,
Multiplex of wing and eye,
Whose strong obedience broke the sky
When Solomon was king.

They rush in red and purple from the red clouds of
    the morn
From temples where the yellow gods shut up their
    eyes in scorn;
They rise in green robes roaring from the green hells
    of the sea
Where fallen skies and evil hues and eyeless creatures
    be;
On them the sea-valves cluster and the grey sea-
    forests curl,
Splashed with a splendid sickness, the sickness of
    the pearl;
They swell in sapphire smoke out of the blue cracks
    of the ground,—
They gather and they wonder and give worship to
    Mahound.
And he saith, "Break up the mountains where the
    hermit-folk can hide,
And sift the red and silver sands lest bone of saint
    abide

G. K. CHESTERTON

And chase the Giaours flying night and day, not
    giving rest,
For that which was our trouble comes again out of
    the west.
We have set the seal of Solomon on all things under
    sun,
Of knowledge and of sorrow and endurance of things
    done,
But a noise is in the mountains, in the mountains,
    and I know
The voice that shook our palaces—four hundred years
    ago:
It is he that saith not 'Kismet'; it is he that knows not
    Fate;
It is Richard, it is Raymond, it is Godfrey in the gate!
It is he whose loss is laughter when he counts the
    wager worth;
Put down your feet upon him that our peace be on
    the earth."
For he heard drums groaning and he heard guns jar,
(Don John of Austria is going to the war.)
Sudden and still—hurrah!
Bolt from Iberia!
Don John of Austria
Is gone by Alcalar.

St. Michael's on his Mountain in the sea-roads of the
    north
(Don John of Austria is girt and going forth.)
Where the grey seas glitter and the sharp tides shift
And the sea-folk labour and the red sails lift.

101

G. K. CHESTERTON

He shakes his lance of iron and he claps his wings of stone;
The noise is gone through Normandy; the noise is gone alone;
The North is full of tangled things and texts and aching eyes
And dead is all the innocence of anger and surprise,
And Christian killeth Christian in a narrow dusty room,
And Christian dreadeth Christ that hath a newer face of doom,
And Christian hateth Mary that God kissed in Galilee,
But Don John of Austria is riding to the sea,
Don John calling through the blast and the eclipse
Crying with the trumpet, with the trumpet of his lips,
Trumpet that sayeth ha!
Domino gloria!
Don John of Austria
Is shouting to the ships.

King Philip's in his closet with the Fleece about his neck,
(*Don John of Austria is armed upon the deck.*)
The walls are hung with velvet that is black and soft as sin,
And little dwarfs creep out of it and little dwarfs creep in.
He holds a crystal phial that has colours like the moon,
He touches, and it tingles, and he trembles very soon,
And his face is as a fungus of a leprous white and grey
Like plants in the high houses that are shuttered from the day,

G. K. CHESTERTON

And death is in the phial, and the end of noble work;
But Don John of Austria has fired upon the Turk.
Don John's hunting, and his hounds have bayed—
Booms away past Italy the rumour of his raid.
Gun upon gun, ha! ha!
Gun upon gun, hurrah!
Don John of Austria
Has loosed the cannonade.

The Pope was in his chapel before day or battle broke,
(*Don John of Austria is hidden in the smoke.*)
The hidden room in man's house where God sits all the year,
The secret window whence the world looks small and very dear.
He sees as in a mirror on the monstrous twilight sea
The crescent of his cruel ships whose name is mystery;
They fling great shadows foe-wards, making Cross and Castle dark,
They veil the plumèd lions on the galleys of St. Mark;
And above the ships are palaces of brown, black-bearded chiefs,
And below the ships are prisons, where with multitudinous griefs,
Christian captives sick and sunless, all a labouring race, repines
Like a race in sunken cities, like a nation in the mines.
They are lost like slaves that swat, and in the skies of morning hung
The stairways of the tallest gods when tyranny was young.

G. K. CHESTERTON

They are countless, voiceless, hopeless as those fallen or fleeing on
Before the high King's horses in the granite of Babylon.
And many a one grows witless in his quiet room in hell
Where a yellow face looks inward through the lattice of his cell,
And he finds his God forgotten, and he seeks no more a sign—
(*But Don John of Austria has burst the battle-line!*)
Don John pounding from the slaughter-painted poop,
Purpling all the ocean like a bloody pirate's sloop,
Scarlet running over on the silvers and the golds,
Breaking of the hatches up and bursting of the holds,
Thronging of the thousands up that labour under sea
White for bliss and blind for sun and stunned for liberty.
Vivat Hispania!
Domino gloria!
Don John of Austria
Has set his people free!

Cervantes on his galley sets the sword back in the sheath,
(*Don John of Austria rides homeward with a wreath.*)
And he sees across a weary land a straggling road in Spain,
Up which a lean and foolish knight forever rides in vain,

G. K. CHESTERTON

And he smiles, but not as Sultans smile, and settles
    back the blade . . .
(*But Don John of Austria rides home from the
    Crusade.*)

The House of Christmas

THERE fared a mother driven forth
    Out of an inn to roam;
In the place where she was homeless
    All men are at home.
The crazy stable close at hand,
With shaking timber and shifting sand,
Grew a stronger thing to abide and stand
    Than the square stones of Rome.

For men are homesick in their homes,
    And strangers under the sun,
And they lay their heads in a foreign land
    Whenever the day is done.
Here we have battle and blazing eyes
And chance and honour and high surprise;
But our homes are under miraculous skies
    Where the yule tale was begun.

A child in a foul stable,
    Where the beasts feed and foam;
Only where He was homeless
    Are you and I at home;
We have hands that fashion and heads that know,

G. K. CHESTERTON

But our hearts we lost—how long ago!—
In a place no chart nor ship can show
　Under the sky's dome.

The world is wild as an old wives' tale,
　And strange the plain things are,
The earth is enough and the air is enough
　For our wonder and our war;
But our rest is as far as the fire-drake swings,
And our peace is put in impossible things
Where clashed and thundered unthinkable wings
　Round an incredible star.

To an open house in the evening
　Home shall men come,
To an older place than Eden
　And a taller town than Rome;
To the end of the way of the wandering star,
To the things that cannot be and that are,
To the place where God was homeless
　And all men are at home.

The Donkey

WHEN fishes flew and forests walked
　And figs grew upon thorn,
Some moment when the moon was blood
　Then surely I was born;

G. K. CHESTERTON

With monstrous head and sickening cry
  And ears like errant wings,
The devil's walking parody
  On all four-footed things.

The tattered outlaw of the earth,
  Of ancient crooked will;
Starve, scourge, deride me: I am dumb,
  I keep my secret still.

Fools! For I also had my hour;
  One far fierce hour and sweet:
There was a shout about my ears,
  And palms before my feet.

ROBERT P. TRISTRAM COFFIN
1892-

Strange Holiness

THERE is strange holiness around
  Our common days on common ground.

I have heard it in the birds
Whose voices reach above all words,

Going upward, bars on bars,
Until they sound as high as stars.

I have seen it in the snake,
A flowing jewel in the brake.

ROBERT P. TRISTRAM COFFIN

It has sparkled in my eyes
In luminous breath of fireflies.

I have come upon its track
Where trilliums curled their petals back.

I have seen it flash in under
The towers of the midnight thunder.

Once, I met it face to face
In a fox pressed by the chase.

He came down the road on feet,
Quiet and fragile, light as heat.

He had a fish still wet and bright
In his slender jaws held tight.

His ears were conscious, whetted darts,
His eyes had small flames in their hearts.

The preciousness of life and breath
Glowed through him as he outran death.

Strangeness and secrecy and pride
Ran rippling down his golden hide.

His beauty was not meant for me,
With my dull eyes, so close to see.

Unconscious of me, rapt, alone,
He came, and then stopped still as stone.

ROBERT P. TRISTRAM COFFIN

His eyes went out as in a gust,
His beauty crumbled into dust.

There was but a ruin there,
A hunted creature, stripped and bare.

Then he faded at one stroke
Like a dingy, melting smoke.

But there his fish lay like a key
To the bright, lost mystery.

51 *The Secret Heart*

ACROSS the years he could recall
His father one way best of all.

In the stillest hour of night
The boy awakened to a light.

Half in dreams, he saw his sire
With his great hands full of fire.

The man had struck a match to see
If his son slept peacefully.

He held his palms each side the spark
His love had kindled in the dark.

His two hands were curved apart
In the semblance of a heart.

ROBERT P. TRISTRAM COFFIN

He wore, it seemed to his small son,
A bare heart on his hidden one,

A heart that gave out such a glow
No son awake could bear to know.

It showed a look upon a face
Too tender for the day to trace.

One instant, it lit all about,
And then the secret heart went out.

But it shone long enough for one
To know that hands held up the sun.

A Fire at Night

A MAN should kindle once a year
A fire after dark and peer
Across his little world of light
Into the faces of the night.

On such a night of sparks and gust
He reads the Apocalypse of dust,
　Knows, without his brain to guide him,
　The emptiness and fear inside him,
The loneliness and bitter plight
Of a creature fed on light
　Which must burn out. He hears the tread
　Of vast feet above his head
Where the future and the dark
Lean above his dying spark.

ROBERT P. TRISTRAM COFFIN

And as he tends the sudden shoots
Of fire, he can feel the roots
   That grow from him and reach out far
   Till their tendrils clutch a star.
He feels the safety of the sky
Curved about him cold and high,
   He comprehends eternal life
   Keen before him, like a knife
Between him and the silence going
Beyond the reach of any knowing.

It is good to stand with flame
By the gulf that has no name.

PADRAIC COLUM
1881-

53   *An Old Woman of the Roads*

O, to have a little house!
   To own the hearth and stool and all!
The heaped-up sods upon the fire,
The pile of turf against the wall!

To have a clock with weights and chains
And pendulum swinging up and down!
A dresser filled with shining delph,
Speckled and white and blue and brown!

I could be busy all the day
Clearing and sweeping hearth and floor,
And fixing on their shelf again
My white and blue and speckled store!

PADRAIC COLUM

I could be quiet there at night
Beside the fire and by myself,
Sure of a bed and loath to leave
The ticking clock and the shining delph!

Och! but I'm weary of mist and dark,
And roads where there's never a house nor bush,
And tired I am of bog and road,
And the crying wind and the lonesome hush!

And I am praying to God on high,
And I am praying Him night and day,
For a little house—a house of my own—
Out of the wind's and the rain's way.

54 *What the Shuiler Said as she Lay by the Fire in the Farmer's House*

I'M glad to lie on a sack of leaves
By a wasted fire and take my ease,
For the wind would strip me bare as a tree—
The wind would blow old age upon me.
And I'm dazed with the wind, the rain, and the cold.
 If I had only the good red gold
To buy me the comfort of a roof,
And under the thatch the brown of the smoke!
 I'd lie up in my painted room
Until my hired girl would come;
And when the sun had warmed my walls
I'd rise up in my silks and shawls,
And break my fast before the fire.

PADRAIC COLUM

And I'd watch them that had to sweat
And shiver for shelter and what they ate:
The farmer digging in the fields;
The beggars going from gate to gate;
The horses striving with their loads,
And all the sights upon the roads.

I'd live my lone without clan or care,
And none about me to crave a share.
The young have mocking, impudent ways,
And I'd never let them a-nigh my place.
And a child has often a pitiful face.
  I'd give the rambling fiddler rest,
And for me he would play his best.
And he'd have something to tell of me
From the Moat of Granard down to the sea!
And, though I'd keep distant, I'd let in
Old women who would card and spin
And clash with me, and I'd hear it said,
  'Mór who used to carry her head
As if she was a lady bred—
Has little enough in her house, they say—
And such-a-one's child I saw on the way
Scaring crows from a crop, and glad to get,
In a warmer house, the bit to eat.
O! none are safe, and none secure,
And it's well for some whose bit is sure!'

  I'd never grudge them the weight of their lands
If I had only the good red gold
To huggle between my breast and hands!

PADRAIC COLUM

The Furrow and the Hearth (I)

STRIDE the hill, sower,
Up to the sky-ridge,
Flinging the seed,
Scattering, exultant!
Mouthing great rhythms
To the long sea beats
On the wide shore, behind
The ridge of the hillside.

Below in the darkness—
The slumber of mothers—
The cradles at rest—
The fire-seed sleeping
Deep in white ashes!

Give to darkness and sleep,
O sower, O seer!
Give me to the Earth.
With the seed I would enter.
O! the growth thro' the silence
From strength to new strength;
Then the strong bursting forth
Against primal forces,
To laugh in the sunshine,
To gladden the world!

PADRAIC COLUM

The Plougher

SUNSET and silence! A man: around him earth savage, earth broken;
Beside him two horses—a plough!
Earth savage, earth broken, the brutes, the dawn man there in the sunset,
And the Plough that is twin to the Sword, that is founder of cities!

'Brute-tamer, plough-maker, earth-breaker! Canst hear? There are ages between us.
Is it praying you are as you stand there alone in the sunset?

'Surely our sky-born gods can be naught to you, earth child and earth master?
Surely your thoughts are of Pan, or of Wotan, or Dana?

'Yet, why give thought to the gods? Has Pan led your brutes where they stumble?
Has Dana numbed pain of the child-bed, or Wotan put hands to your plough?

'What matter your foolish reply? O man, standing lone and bowed earthward,
Your task is a day near its close. Give thanks to the night-giving God.'

. . . .

Slowly the darkness falls, the broken lands blend with the savage;
The brute-tamer stands by the brutes, a head's breadth only above them.

A head's breadth? Ay, but therein is hell's depth, and the height up to heaven,
And the thrones of the gods and their halls, their chariots, purples, and splendours.

57 *She Moved through the Fair*

MY young love said to me, 'My brothers won't mind,
And my parents won't slight you for your lack of kind.'
Then she stepped away from me, and this she did say,
'It will not be long, love, till our wedding day.'

She stepped away from me and she moved through the fair,
And fondly I watched her go here and go there,
Then she went her way homeward with one star awake,
As the swan in the evening moves over the lake.

The people were saying no two were e'er wed
But one had a sorrow that never was said,
And I smiled as she passed with her goods and her gear,
And that was the last that I saw of my dear.

PADRAIC COLUM

I dreamt it last night that my young love came in,
So softly she entered, her feet made no din;
She came close beside me, and this she did say,
'It will not be long, love, till our wedding day.'

FRANCES CORNFORD
1883-
Pre-Existence

I LAID me down upon the shore
  And dreamed a little space;
I heard the great waves break and roar;
  The sun was on my face.

My idle hands and fingers brown
  Played with the pebbles grey;
The waves came up, the waves went down,
  Most thundering and gay.

The pebbles they were smooth and round
  And warm upon my hands,
Like little people I had found
  Sitting among the sands.

The grains of sand so shining-small
  Soft through my fingers ran;
The sun shone down upon it all,
  And so my dream began:

How all of this had been before;
　　How ages far away
I lay on some forgotten shore
　　As here I lie today.

The waves came shining up the sands,
　　As here today they shine;
And in my pre-Pelasgian hands
　　The sand was warm and fine.

I have forgotten whence I came,
　　Or what my home might be,
Or by what strange and savage name
　　I called that thundering sea.

I only know the sun shone down
　　As still it shines today,
And in my fingers long and brown
　　The little pebbles lay.

59 *To a Fat Lady seen from the Train*

O WHY do you walk through the fields in gloves,
　　Missing so much and so much?
O fat white woman whom nobody loves,
Why do you walk through the fields in gloves,
When the grass is soft as the breast of doves
　　And shivering-sweet to the touch?
O why do you walk through the fields in gloves,
　　Missing so much and so much?

FRANCES CORNFORD

60 *The Hills*

OUT of the complicated house come I
  To walk beneath the sky.
Here mud and stones and turf, here everything
Is mutely comforting.
Now hung upon the twigs and thorns appear
A host of lovely raindrops cold and clear.
And on the bank
Or deep in brambly hedges dank
The small birds nip about and say:
"Brothers, the Spring is not so far away!"
The hills like mother-giantesses old
Lie in the cold,
And with a complete patience, let
The cows come cropping on their bosoms wet,
And even tolerate that such as I
Should wander by
With paltry leathern heel which cannot harm
Their bodies calm;
And, with a heart they cannot know, to bless
The enormous power of their peacefulness.

E. E. CUMMINGS
1894-

61 *next to of course god*

'next to of course god america i
love you land of the pilgrims' and so forth oh
say can you see by the dawn's early my
country 'tis of centuries come and go

119

E. E. CUMMINGS

and are no more what of it we should worry
in every language even deafanddumb
thy sons acclaim your glorious name by gorry
by jingo by gee by gosh by gum
why talk of beauty what could be more beautiful than those heroic happy dead
who rushed like lions to the roaring slaughter
they did not stop to think they died instead
then shall the voices of liberty be mute?'

He spoke. And drank rapidly a glass of water.

62 *Impression—IV*

the hours rise up putting off stars and it is
dawn
into the street of the sky light walks scattering poems

on earth a candle is
extinguished   the city
wakes
with a song upon her
mouth having death in her eyes

and it is dawn
the world
goes forth to murder dreams . . . .

i see in the street where strong
men are digging bread
and i see the brutal faces of
people contented hideous hopeless cruel happy

E. E. CUMMINGS

and it is day,

in the mirror
i see a frail
man
dreaming
dreams
dreams in the mirror
and it
is dusk   on earth

a candle is lighted
and it is dark.
the people are in their houses
the frail man is in his bed
the city

sleeps with death upon her mouth having a song in
    her eyes
the hours descend
putting on stars . . . .

in the street of the sky night walks scattering poems

WILLIAM HENRY DAVIES
1871-

The Kingfisher

IT was the Rainbow gave thee birth,
  And left thee all her lovely hues;
And, as her mother's name was Tears,
  So runs it in thy blood to choose
For haunts the lonely pools, and keep
In company with trees that weep.

WILLIAM HENRY DAVIES

Go you and, with such glorious hues,
   Live with proud peacocks in green parks;
On lawns as smooth as shining glass,
   Let every feather show its marks;
Get thee on boughs and clap thy wings
Before the windows of proud kings.

Nay, lovely Bird, thou art not vain;
   Thou hast no proud, ambitious mind;
I also love a quiet place
   That's green, away from all mankind;
A lonely pool, and let a tree
Sigh with her bosom over me.

64 *Rich Days*

WELCOME to you, rich Autumn days,
   Ere comes the cold, leaf-picking wind;
When golden stooks are seen in fields,
   All standing arm-in-arm entwined;
And gallons of sweet cider seen
On trees in apples red and green;

With mellow pears that cheat our teeth,
   Which melt that tongues may suck them in;
With cherries red, and blue-black plums
   Now sweet and soft from stone to skin;
And woodnuts rich, to make us go
Into the loveliest lanes we know.

WILLIAM HENRY DAVIES
'Sweet Stay-at-Home'

SWEET Stay-at-Home, sweet Well-content,
Thou knowest of no strange continent;
Thou hast not felt thy bosom keep
A gentle motion with the deep;
Thou hast not sailed in Indian seas,
Where scent comes forth in every breeze;
Thou hast not seen the rich grape grow
For miles, as far as eyes can go;
Thou hast not seen a summer's night
When maids could sew by a worm's light;
Nor the North Sea in spring send out
Bright hues that like birds flit about
In solid cages of white ice—
Sweet Stay-at-Home, sweet Love-one-place.
Thou hast not seen black fingers pick
White cotton where the bloom is thick,
Nor heard black throats in harmony;
Nor hast thou sat on stones that lie
Flat on the earth, that once did rise
To hide proud kings from common eyes;
Thou hast not seen plains full of bloom
Where green things had such little room
They pleased the eye like fairer flowers—
Sweet Stay-at-Home, all these long hours.
Sweet Well-content, sweet Love-one-place,
Sweet, simple maid, bless thy dear face;
For thou hast made more homely stuff
Nurture thy gentle self enough;
I love thee for a heart that's kind—
Not for the knowledge in thy mind.

WILLIAM HENRY DAVIES
The Sleepers

As I walked down the waterside
  This silent morning, wet and dark;
Before the cocks in farmyards crowed,
  Before the dogs began to bark;
Before the hour of five was struck
By old Westminster's mighty clock:

As I walked down the waterside
  This morning, in the damp cold air,
I saw a hundred women and men
  Huddled in rags and sleeping there:
These people have no work, thought I,
And long before their time they die.

That moment, on the waterside,
  A lighted car came at a bound;
I looked inside, and saw a score
  Of pale and weary men that frowned;
Each man sat in a huddled heap,
Carried to work while fast asleep.

Ten cars rushed down the waterside,
  Like lighted coffins in the dark;
With twenty dead men in each car,
  That must be brought alive by work:
These people work too hard, thought I,
And long before their time they die.

WILLIAM HENRY DAVIES

In Spring-Time

THERE'S many a pool that holds a cloud
   Deep down for miles, to float along;
There's many a hedge that's white with may,
   To bring the backward birds to song;
There's many a country lane that smells
   Of beanfields, through the night and day;
Then why should I be here this hour,
   In Spring-time, when the month is May?

There's nothing else but stone I see,
   With but this ribbon of a sky;
And not a garden big enough
   To share it with a butterfly.
Why do I walk these dull dark streets,
   In gloom and silence, all day long—
In Springtime, when the blackbird's day
   Is four and twenty hours of song?

WALTER DE LA MARE
1873-
All that's Past

VERY old are the woods;
   And the buds that break
Out of the brier's boughs,
   When March winds wake,
So old with their beauty are—

WALTER DE LA MARE

    Oh, no man knows
Through what wild centuries
    Roves back the rose.

Very old are the brooks;
    And the rills that rise
Where snow sleeps cold beneath
    The azure skies
Sing such a history
    Of come and gone,
Their every drop is as wise
    As Solomon.

Very old are we men;
    Our dreams are tales
Told in dim Eden
    By Eve's nightingales;
We wake and whisper awhile,
    But, the day gone by,
Silence and sleep like fields
    Of amaranth lie.

Martha

'ONCE ... once upon a time ...'
    Over and over again,
Martha would tell us her stories
    In the hazel glen.

WALTER DE LA MARE

Hers were those clear grey eyes
    You watch, and the story seems
Told by their beautifulness
    Tranquil as dreams.

She would sit with her two slim hands
    Clasped round her bended knees;
While we on our elbows lolled,
    And stared at ease.

Her voice, her narrow chin,
    Her grave small lovely head,
Seemed half the meaning
    Of the words she said.

'Once . . . once upon a time . . .'
    Like a dream you dream in the night,
Fairies and gnomes stole out
    In the leaf-green light.

And her beauty far away
    Would fade, as her voice ran on,
Till hazel and summer sun
    And all were gone—

All fordone and forgot;
    And like clouds in the height of the sky,
Our hearts stood still in the hush
    Of an age gone by.

WALTER DE LA MARE

70 *Old Susan*

WHEN Susan's work was done she would sit,
With one fat guttering candle lit,
And window opened wide to win
The sweet night air to enter in;
There, with a thumb to keep her place,
She would read, with stern and wrinkled face,
Her mild eyes gliding very slow
Across the letters to and fro,
While wagged the guttering candle flame
In the wind that through the window came.
And sometimes in the silence she
Would mumble a sentence audibly,
Or shake her head as if to say,
'You silly souls, to act this way!'
And never a sound from night I would hear,
Unless some far-off cock crowed clear;
Or her old shuffling thumb should turn
Another page; and rapt and stern,
Through her great glasses bent on me,
She would glance into reality;
And shake her round old silvery head,
With—'You!—I thought you was in bed!'—
Only to tilt her book again,
And rooted in Romance remain.

71 *Sam*

WHEN Sam goes back in memory,
    It is to where the sea
Breaks on the shingle, emerald-green,
    In white foam, endlessly;
He says—with small brown eye on mine—

WALTER DE LA MARE

'I used to keep awake,
And lean from my window in the moon,
  Watching those billows break;
And half a million tiny hands,
  And eyes, like sparks of frost,
Would dance and come tumbling into the moon,
  On every breaker tossed.
And all across from star to star,
  I've seen the watery sea,
With not a single ship in sight,
  Just ocean there, and me;
And heard my father snore. And once,
  As sure as I'm alive,
Out of those wallowing, moon-flecked waves
  I saw a mermaid dive;
Head and shoulders above the wave,
  Plain as I now see you,
Combing her hair, now back, now front,
  Her two eyes peeping through;
Calling me, "Sam!"—quietlike—"Sam!" . . .
  But me . . . I never went,
Making believe I kind of thought
  'Twas some one else she meant . . .
Wonderful lovely there she sat,
  Singing the night away,
All in the solitudinous sea
  Of that there lonely bay.

'P'raps,' and he'd smooth his hairless mouth,
  'P'raps, if 'twere now, my son,
P'raps, if I heard a voice say, "Sam!" . . .
  Morning would find me gone.'

WALTER DE LA MARE

The Listeners

'Is there anybody there?' said the Traveller,
  Knocking on the moonlit door;
And his horse in the silence champed the grasses
  Of the forest's ferny floor:
And a bird flew up out of the turret,
  Above the Traveller's head:
And he smote upon the door again a second time;
  'Is there anybody there?' he said.
But no one descended to the Traveller;
  No head from the leaf-fringed sill
Leaned over and looked into his grey eyes,
  Where he stood perplexed and still.
But only a host of phantom listeners
  That dwelt in the lone house then
Stood listening in the quiet of the moonlight
  To that voice from the world of men:
Stood thronging the faint moonbeams on the dark stair,
  That goes down to the empty hall,
Hearkening in an air stirred and shaken
  By the lonely Traveller's call.
And he felt in his heart their strangeness,
  Their stillness answering his cry,
While his horse moved, cropping the dark turf,
  'Neath the starred and leafy sky;
For he suddenly smote on the door, even
  Louder, and lifted his head:—
'Tell them I came, and no one answered,
  That I kept my word,' he said.

WALTER DE LA MARE

Never the least stir made the listeners,
  Though every word he spake
Fell echoing through the shadowiness of the still house
  From the one man left awake:
Ay, they heard his foot upon the stirrup,
  And the sound of iron on stone,
And how the silence surged softly backward,
  When the plunging hoofs were gone.

73 — Farewell

WHEN I lie where shades of darkness
    Shall no more assail mine eyes,
Nor the rain make lamentation
    When the wind sighs;
How will fare the world whose wonder
Was the very proof of me?
Memory fades, must the remembered
    Perishing be?

Oh, when this my dust surrenders
Hand, foot, lip, to dust again,
May these loved and loving faces
    Please other men!
May the rusting harvest hedgerow
Still the Traveller's Joy entwine,
And as happy children gather
    Posies once mine.

Look thy last on all things lovely
Every hour. Let no night

WALTER DE LA MARE

Seal thy sense in deathly slumber
 Till to delight
Thou have paid thy utmost blessing;
Since that all things thou wouldst praise
Beauty took from those who loved them
 In other days.

Nod

SOFTLY along the road of evening,
 In a twilight dim with rose,
Wrinkled with age, and drenched with dew,
 Old Nod, the shepherd, goes.

His drowsy flock streams on before him,
 Their fleeces charged with gold,
To where the sun's last beam leans low
 On Nod the shepherd's fold.

The hedge is quick and green with briar,
 From their sand the conies creep;
And all the birds that fly in heaven
 Flock singing home to sleep.

His lambs outnumber a noon's roses,
 Yet, when night's shadows fall,
His blind old sheep-dog, Slumber-soon,
 Misses not one of all.

His are the quiet steeps of dreamland,
 The waters of no-more-pain,
His ram's bell rings 'neath an arch of stars,
 'Rest, rest, and rest again.'

WALTER DE LA MARE
The Moth

ISLED in the midnight air,
  Musked with the dark's faint bloom,
Out into glooming and secret haunts
    The flame cries, 'Come!'

Lovely in dye and fan,
A-tremble in shimmering grace,
A moth from her winter swoon
    Uplifts her face:

Stares from her glamorous eyes;
Wafts her on plumes like mist;
In ecstasy swirls and sways
    To her strange tryst.

Haunted

THE rabbit in his burrow keeps
  No guarded watch, in peace he sleeps;
The wolf that howls in challenging night
Cowers to her lair at morning light;
The simplest bird entwines a nest
Where she may lean her lovely breast,
Couched in the silence of the bough.
But thou, O man, what rest hast thou?

Thy emptiest solitude can bring
Only a subtler questioning
In thy divided heart. Thy bed
Recalls at dawn what midnight said.

WALTER DE LA MARE

Seek how thou wilt to feign content,
Thy flaming ardour is quickly spent;
Soon thy last company is gone,
And leaves thee—with thyself—alone.

Pomp and great friends may hem thee round,
A thousand busy tasks be found;
Earth's thronging beauties may beguile
Thy longing lovesick heart awhile;
And pride, like clouds of sunset, spread
A changing glory round thy head;
But fade will all; and thou must come,
Hating thy journey, homeless, home.

Rave how thou wilt; unmoved, remote,
That inward presence slumbers not,
Frets out each secret from thy breast,
Gives thee no rally, pause, nor rest,
Scans close thy very thoughts, lest they
Should sap his patient power away,
Answers thy wrath with peace, thy cry
With tenderest taciturnity.

JOHN DRINKWATER
1882-1937

77 *Choruses from 'Abraham Lincoln'*

I

Two Chroniclers (speaking together): Kinsmen, you
      shall behold
   Our stage, in mimic action, mould
   A man's character.

JOHN DRINKWATER

This is the wonder, always, everywhere—
Not that vast mutability which is event,
The pits and pinnacles of change,
But man's desire and valiance that range
All circumstance, and come to port unspent.

Agents are these events, these ecstasies,
And tribulations, to prove the purities
Or poor oblivions that are our being. When
Beauty and peace possess us, they are none
But as they touch the beauty and peace of men,
Nor, when our days are done,
And the last utterance of doom must fall,
Is the doom anything
Memorable for its apparelling;
The bearing of man facing it is all.

So, kinsmen, we present
This for no loud event
That is but fugitive,
But that you may behold
Our mimic action mould
The spirit of man immortally to live.

First Chronicler: Once when a peril touched the days
Of freedom in our English ways,
And none renowned in government
Was equal found,
Came to the steadfast heart of one,
Who watched in lonely Huntingdon,
A summons, and he went,
And tyranny was bound,
And Cromwell was the lord of his event.

JOHN DRINKWATER

Second Chronicler: And in that land where voyaging
  The pilgrim Mayflower came to rest,
  Among the chosen, counselling,
  Once, when bewilderment possessed
  A people, none there was might draw
  To fold the wandering thoughts of men,
  And make as one the names again
  Of liberty and law.
  And then, from fifty fameless years
  In quiet Illinois was sent
  A word that still the Atlantic hears,
  And Lincoln was the lord of his event.

The two speaking together: So the uncounted spirit wakes
  To the birth
  Of uncounted circumstance,
  And time in a generation makes
  Portents majestic a little story of earth
  To be remembered by chance
  At a fireside.
  But the ardours that they bear,
  The proud and invincible motions of character—
  These—these abide.

II

The two Chroniclers: Lonely is the man who understands.
  Lonely is vision that leads a man away
  From the pasture-lands,
  From the furrows of corn and the brown loads of hay,

JOHN DRINKWATER

To the mountain-side,
To the high places where contemplation brings
All his adventurings
Among the sowers and the tillers in the wide
Valleys to one fused experience,
That shall control
The courses of his soul,
And give his hand
Courage and continence.

First Chronicler: Shall a man understand,
He shall know bitterness because his kind,
Being perplexed of mind,
Hold issues even that are nothing mated.
And he shall give
Counsel out of his wisdom that none shall hear;
And steadfast in vain persuasion must he live,
And unabated
Shall his temptation be.

Second Chronicler: Coveting the little, the instant gain,
The brief security,
And easy-tongued renown,
Many will mock the vision that his brain
Builds to a far, unmeasured monument,
And many bid his resolutions down
To the wages of content.

First Chronicler: A year goes by.

JOHN DRINKWATER

The two together: Here contemplate
  A heart, undaunted to possess
  Itself among the glooms of fate,
  In vision and in loneliness.

III

The two Chroniclers: You who have gone gathering
    Cornflowers and meadowsweet,
  Heard the hazels glancing down
    On September eves,
  Seen the homeward rooks on wing
    Over fields of golden wheat,
  And the silver cups that crown
    Water-lily leaves;

  You who know the tenderness
    Of old men at eve-tide,
  Coming from the hedgerows,
    Coming from the plough,
  And the wandering caress
    Of winds upon the woodside,
  When the crying yaffle goes
    Underneath the bough;

First Chronicler: You who mark the flowing
    Of sap upon the May-time,
  And the waters welling
    From the watershed,
  You who count the growing
    Of harvest and hay-time,
  Knowing these the telling
    Of your daily bread;

JOHN DRINKWATER

Second Chronicler: You who cherish courtesy
    With your fellows at your gate,
And about your hearthstone sit
    Under love's decrees,
You who know that death will be
    Speaking with you soon or late,

The two together: Kinsmen, what is mother-wit
    But the light of these?

Knowing these, what is there more
    For learning in your little years?
Are not these all gospels bright
    Shining on your day?
How then shall your hearts be sore
    With envy and her brood of fears,
How forget the words of light
    From the mountain way? . . .

Blessed are the merciful. . . .
    Does not every threshold seek
Meadows and the flight of birds
    For compassion still?
Blessed are the merciful. . . .
    Are we pilgrims yet to speak
Out of Olivet the words
    Of knowledge and good-will?

First Chronicler: Two years of darkness, and this man
            but grows
    Greater in resolution, more constant in compassion.

JOHN DRINKWATER

He goes
The way of dominion in pitiful, high-hearted
    fashion.

IV

The two Chroniclers: A wind blows in the night,
    And the pride of the rose is gone,
    It laboured, and was delight,
    And rains fell, and shone
    Suns of the summer days,
    And dews washed the bud,
    And thanksgiving and praise
    Was the rose in our blood.

And out of the night it came,
A wind, and the rose fell,
Shattered its heart of flame,
And how shall June tell
The glory that went with May,
How shall the full year keep
The beauty that ere its day
Was blasted into sleep?

Roses. Oh, heart of man:
Courage, that in the prime
Looked on truth, and began
Conspiracies with time
To flower upon the pain
Of dark and envious earth. . . .
A wind blows, and the brain
Is the dust that was its birth.

JOHN DRINKWATER

What shall the witness cry,
He who has seen alone
With imagination's eye
The darkness overthrown?
Hark: from the long eclipse
The wise words come—
A wind blows, and the lips
Of prophecy are dumb.

THOMAS STEARNS ELIOT
1888-

78 *Journey of the Magi*

'A COLD coming we had of it,
Just the worst time of the year
For a journey, and such a long journey:
The ways deep and the weather sharp,
The very dead of winter.'
And the camels galled, sore-footed, refractory,
Lying down in the melting snow.
There were times we regretted
The summer palaces on slopes, the terraces,
And the silken girls bringing sherbet.
Then the camel men cursing and grumbling
And running away, and wanting their liquor and
    women,
And the night-fires going out, and the lack of shelters,
And the cities hostile and the towns unfriendly

THOMAS STEARNS ELIOT

And the villages dirty and charging high prices:
A hard time we had of it.
At the end we preferred to travel all night,
Sleeping in snatches,
With the voices singing in our ears, saying
That this was all folly.

Then at dawn we came down to a temperate valley,
Wet, below the snow line, smelling of vegetation;
With a running stream and a water-mill beating the
    darkness,
And three trees on the low sky,
And an old white horse galloped away in the meadow.
Then we came to a tavern with vine-leaves over the
    lintel,
Six hands at an open door dicing for pieces of silver,
And feet kicking the empty wine-skins.
But there was no information, and so we continued
And arrived at evening, not a moment too soon
Finding the place; it was (you may say) satisfactory.

All this was a long time ago, I remember,
And I would do it again, but set down
This set down
This: were we led all that way for
Birth or Death? There was a Birth, certainly,
We had evidence and no doubt. I had seen birth and
    death,
But had thought they were different; this Birth was
Hard and bitter agony for us, like Death, our death.
We returned to our places, these Kingdoms,

THOMAS STEARNS ELIOT

But no longer at ease here, in the old dispensation,
With an alien people clutching their gods.
I should be glad of another death.

A Song for Simeon

LORD, the Roman hyacinths are blooming in bowls and
The winter sun creeps by the snow hills;
The stubborn season has made stand.
My life is light, waiting for the death wind,
Like a feather on the back of my hand.
Dust in sunlight and memory in corners
Wait for the wind that chills towards the dead land.

Grant us thy peace.
I have walked many years in this city,
Kept faith and fast, provided for the poor,
Have given and taken honour and ease.
There went never any rejected from my door.
Who shall remember my house, where shall live my
    children's children
When the time of sorrow is come?
They will take to the goat's path, and the fox's home,
Fleeing from the foreign faces and the foreign swords.

Before the time of cords and scourges and lamentation
Grant us thy peace.
Before the stations of the mountain of desolation,
Before the certain hour of maternal sorrow,
Now at this birth season of decease,

THOMAS STEARNS ELIOT

Let the Infant, the still unspeaking and unspoken
    Word,
Grant Israel's consolation
To one who has eighty years and no to-morrow.

According to thy word.
They shall praise Thee and suffer in every generation
With glory and derision,
Light upon light, mounting the saints' stair.
Not for me the martyrdom, the ecstasy of thought
    and prayer,
Not for me the ultimate vision.
Grant me thy peace.
(And a sword shall pierce thy heart,
Thine also.)
I am tired with my own life and the lives of those
    after me,
I am dying in my own death and the deaths of those
    after me.
Let thy servant depart,
Having seen thy salvation.

80   *The Hollow Men*

(A penny for the Old Guy)

I

WE are the hollow men
    We are the stuffed men
Leaning together
Headpiece filled with straw. Alas!
Our dried voices, when

THOMAS STEARNS ELIOT

We whisper together
Are quiet and meaningless
As wind in dry grass
Or rats' feet over broken glass
In our dry cellar

Shape without form, shade without colour,
Paralysed force, gesture without motion;

Those who have crossed
With direct eyes, to death's other Kingdom
Remember us—if at all—not as lost
Violent souls, but only
As the hollow men
The stuffed men.

II

Eyes I dare not meet in dreams
In death's dream kingdom
These do not appear:
There, the eyes are
Sunlight on a broken column
There, is a tree swinging
And voices are
In the wind's singing
More distant and more solemn
Than a fading star.

Let me be no nearer
In death's dream kingdom
Let me also wear

THOMAS STEARNS ELIOT

Such deliberate disguises
Rat's coat, crowskin, crossed staves
In a field
Behaving as the wind behaves
No nearer—

Not that final meeting
In the twilight kingdom

III

This is the dead land
This is cactus land
Here the stone images
Are raised, here they receive
The supplication of a dead man's hand
Under the twinkle of a fading star.

Is it like this
In death's other kingdom
Waking alone
At the hour when we are
Trembling with tenderness
Lips that would kiss
Form prayers to broken stone.

IV

The eyes are not here
There are no eyes here
In this valley of dying stars
In this hollow valley
This broken jaw of our lost kingdoms

THOMAS STEARNS ELIOT

In this last of meeting places
We grope together
And avoid speech
Gathered on this beach of the tumid river

Sightless, unless
The eyes reappear
As the perpetual star
Multifoliate rose
Of death's twilight kingdom
The hope only
Of empty men.

V

Here we go round the prickly pear
Prickly pear prickly pear
Here we go round the prickly pear
At five o'clock in the morning.

Between the idea
And the reality
Between the motion
And the act
Falls the Shadow
        For Thine is the Kingdom

Between the conception
And the creation
Between the emotion
And the response
Falls the Shadow
        Life is very long

THOMAS STEARNS ELIOT

Between the desire
And the spasm
Between the potency
And the existence
Between the essence
And the descent
Falls the Shadow
          For Thine is the Kingdom

For Thine is
Life is
For Thine is the

This is the way the world ends
This is the way the world ends
This is the way the world ends
Not with a bang but a whimper.

81   *Two Choruses from 'The Rock'*

I

THE Eagle soars in the summit of Heaven,
   The Hunter with his dogs pursues his circuit.
O perpetual revolution of configured stars,
O perpetual recurrence of determined seasons,
O world of spring and autumn, birth and dying!
The endless cycle of idea and action,
Endless invention, endless experiment,
Brings knowledge of motion, but not of stillness;

THOMAS STEARNS ELIOT

Knowledge of speech, but not of silence;
Knowledge of words, and ignorance of the Word.
All our knowledge brings us nearer to our ignorance,
All our ignorance brings us nearer to death,
But nearness to death no nearer to God.
Where is the life we have lost in living?
Where is the wisdom we have lost in knowledge?
Where is the knowledge we have lost in information?
The cycles of Heaven in twenty centuries
Bring us farther from God and nearer to the Dust.

II

O Light Invisible, we praise Thee!
Too bright for mortal vision.
O Greater Light, we praise Thee for the less;
The eastern light our spires touch at morning,
The light that slants upon our western doors at evening,
The twilight over stagnant pools at bat-flight,
Moon light and star light, owl and moth light,
Glow-worm glow-light on a grass-blade.
O Light Invisible, we worship Thee!

We thank Thee for the lights that we have kindled,
The light of altar and of sanctuary,
Small lights of those who meditate at midnight
And lights directed through the coloured panes of windows
And light reflected from the polished stone,
The gilded carven wood, the coloured fresco.

THOMAS STEARNS ELIOT

Our gaze is submarine, our eyes look upward
And see the light that fractures through unquiet water.
We see the light but see not whence it comes.
O Light Invisible, we glorify Thee!
In our rhythm of earthly life we tire of light. We are
    glad when the day ends, when the play ends;
    and ecstasy is too much pain.
We are children quickly tired: children who are up in
    the night and fall asleep as the rocket is fired;
    and the day is long for work or play.
We tire of distraction or concentration, we sleep and
    are glad to sleep,
Controlled by the rhythm of blood and the day and
    the night and the seasons.
And we must extinguish the candle, put out the light
    and relight it;
For ever must quench, for ever relight the flame.
Therefore we thank Thee for our little light, that is
    dappled with shadow.
We thank Thee who hast moved us to building, to
    finding, to forming at the ends of our fingers
    and beams of our eyes.
And when we have built an altar to the Invisible
    Light, we may set thereon the little lights for
    which our bodily vision is made.
And we thank Thee that darkness reminds us of light.
O Light Invisible, we give Thee thanks for Thy great
    glory!

MICHAEL FIELD
Katherine Bradley 1846-1914
Edith Cooper 1862-1913

82   *Fifty Quatrains*

'TWAS fifty quatrains: and from unknown strands
   The woman came who sang them on the floor.
I saw her, I was leaning by the door,
—Saw her strange raiment and her lovely hands;
And saw . . . but *that* I think she sang—the bands
Of low-voiced women on a happy shore:
Incomparable was the haze, and bore
The many blossoms of soft orchard lands.
'Twas fifty quatrains, for I caught the measure;
And all the royal house was full of kings,
Who listened and beheld her and were dumb;
Nor dared to seize the marvellous rich pleasure,
Too fearful even to ask in whisperings,
The ramparts being closed, whence she had come.

A Kiss

83   *David's Reconciliation with Absalom*

THE fury of a creature when it drips
   Wet-fanged, and thirsty with the desert dust,
The clench in battle on a sword that must
Ravish the foe, the pang of finger tips—
Joy of a captain in recovered ships,
Joy, verity of a long-buried lust
Delightsome to the flesh, is in the thrust
Toward Absalom of the king's tarried lips.

MICHAEL FIELD

And, lo, beneath that awful benison,
A thief's face glittered, sniffing at the gems
Of the bent crown as they were cassia-stems;
While the young ears heard but the rolling on
Of chariots, and a tumult, broke amain
By rumour of an agèd monarch slain.

JAMES ELROY FLECKER
1884-1915

84 *The Old Ships*

I HAVE seen old ships sail like swans asleep
Beyond the village which men still call Tyre,
With leaden age o'ercargoed, dipping deep
For Famagusta and the hidden sun
That rings black Cyprus with a lake of fire;
And all those ships were certainly so old
Who knows how oft with squat and noisy gun,
Questing brown slaves or Syrian oranges,
The pirate Genoese
Hell-raked them till they rolled
Blood, water, fruit and corpses up the hold.
But now through friendly seas they softly run,
Painted the mid-sea blue or shore-sea green,
Still patterned with the vine and grapes in gold.

But I have seen,
Pointing her shapely shadows from the dawn
And image tumbled on a rose-swept bay,
A drowsy ship of some yet older day;

JAMES ELROY FLECKER

And, wonder's breath indrawn,
Thought I—who knows—who knows—but in
    that same
(Fished up beyond Ææa, patched up new
—Stern painted brighter blue—)
That talkative, bald-headed seaman came
(Twelve patient comrades sweating at the oar)
From Troy's doom-crimson shore,
And with great lies about his wooden horse
Set the crew laughing, and forgot his course.

It was so old a ship—who knows, who knows?
—And yet so beautiful, I watched in vain
To see the mast burst open with a rose,
And the whole deck put on its leaves again.

To a Poet a Thousand Years Hence

I WHO am dead a thousand years,
    And wrote this sweet archaic song,
Send you my words for messengers
    The way I shall not pass along.

I care not if you bridge the seas,
    Or ride secure the cruel sky,
Or build consummate palaces
    Of metal or of masonry.

But have you wine and music still,
    And statues and a bright-eyed love,
And foolish thoughts of good and ill,
    And prayers to them who sit above?

JAMES ELROY FLECKER

How shall we conquer? Like a wind
   That falls at eve our fancies blow,
And old Maeonides the blind
   Said it three thousand years ago.

O friend unseen, unborn, unknown,
   Student of our sweet English tongue,
Read out my words at night, alone:
   I was a poet, I was young.

Since I can never see your face,
   And never shake you by the hand,
I send my soul through time and space
   To greet you. You will understand.

The Golden Journey to Samarkand
Prologue

WE who with songs beguile your pilgrimage
   And swear that Beauty lives though lilies die,
We poets of the proud old lineage
   Who sing to find your hearts, we know not why,—

What shall we tell you? Tales, marvellous tales
   Of ships and stars and isles where good men rest,
Where nevermore the rose of sunset pales,
   And winds and shadows fall toward the West:

And there the world's first huge white-bearded kings,
   In dim glades sleeping, murmur in their sleep,
And closer round their breasts the ivy clings,
   Cutting its pathway slow and red and deep.

JAMES ELROY FLECKER

II

And how beguile you? Death has no repose
  Warmer and deeper than that Orient sand
Which hides the beauty and bright faith of those
  Who made the Golden Journey to Samarkand.

And now they wait and whiten peaceably,
  Those conquerors, those poets, those so fair:
They know time comes, not only you and I,
  But the whole world shall whiten, here or there;

When those long caravans that cross the plain
  With dauntless feet and sound of silver bells
Put forth no more for glory or for gain,
  Take no more solace from the palm-girt wells,

When the great markets by the sea shut fast
  All that calm Sunday that goes on and on;
When even lovers find their peace at last,
  And Earth is but a star, that once had shone.

87   *Yasmin*

A Ghazel

HOW splendid in the morning glows the lily: with what grace he throws
His supplication to the rose: do roses nod the head, Yasmin?

But when the silver dove descends I find the little flower of friends
Whose very name that sweetly ends I say when I have said Yasmin.

JAMES ELROY FLECKER

The morning light is clear and cold: I dare not in that light behold
A whiter light, a deeper gold, a glory too far shed, Yasmin.

But when the deep red eye of day is level with the lone highway,
And some to Meccah turn to pray, and I toward thy bed, Yasmin;

Or when the wind beneath the moon is drifting like a soul aswoon,
And harping planets talk love's tune with milky wings outspread, Yasmin,

Shower down thy love, O burning bright! For one night or the other night
Will come the Gardener in white, and gathered flowers are dead, Yasmin.

JOHN GOULD FLETCHER
1886-

88 *The Grand Canyon of the Colorado*

I

I HAVE seen that which is mysterious,
Aloof, divided, silent;
Something not of this earth.

JOHN GOULD FLETCHER

Suddenly the endless dark green piney uplands
Stopped.
Yellow, red, grey-green, purple-black chasms fell swiftly below each other.

On the other side,
Strong-built, arose
Towers whose durable terraces were hammered from red sandstone,
Purple granite, and gold.

Beyond
A golden wall,
Aloof, inscrutable.

It was hidden
Behind layers of white silence.
No voice might reach it;
It was not of this earth.

II

When the free thunder-spirit
Had built and carved these terraced walls,
Completing his task of ages,
He wrote upon them
In dark invisible words,
'It is finished.'

Silent and windless,
The forever completed
Is never broken but by clouds.
Sometimes dark eagles slow-sailing
Rise out of it, like spirits,
Wheeling away.

JOHN GOULD FLETCHER

Now in the steady glare,
Some will moves darkly,
Driving the clouds, piling them,
Shaping masses of shadow
That move slowly forward
Over the array of towers.

Yet still behind them,
Unscarred, unaltered,
The work stands finished,
Without a cry of protest, for protest is uncompletion,
Moulded and fashioned for ever in durable ageless
    stone,
And on every surface is written
In strong invisible words:
'It is finished.'

III

Should I by chance deserve some last reward from
    earth,—
The rewards of earth are usually unwholesome;—
One single thing I would ask for,
Burn my body here.

Kindle the pyre
Upon this jutting point:
Dry aromatic juniper,
Lean flame, blue smoke,
Ashes and dust.

JOHN GOULD FLETCHER

The winds would drift the ash
Outwards across the canyon,
To the rose-purple rim of the desert
Beyond the red-barred towers.

The rabbits in the morning
Would come and snuff at the embers,
While the chasm, rekindling,
Would build up its silent poem of colour to the sun.

IV

Shadows of clouds
March across the canyon,
Shadows of blue hands passing
Over a curtain of flame.

Clutching, staggering, upstriking,
Darting in blue-black fury,
To where the pinnacles, green and orange,
Await.

The winds are battling and striving to break them;
Thin lightnings spit and flicker;
The peaks seem a dance of scarlet demons
Flitting amid the shadows.

Grey rain-curtains wave afar off;
Wisps of vapour curl and vanish:
The sun throws soft shafts of golden light
Over rose-buttressed palisades.

JOHN GOULD FLETCHER

Now the clouds are a lazy procession:
Blue balloons bobbing solemnly
Over black-dappled walls:

Where rise sharp-fretted, golden-roofed cathedrals
Exultantly, and split the sky with light.

89   *The Swan*

UNDER a wall of bronze
Where beeches dip and trail
Thin branches in the water,
With red-tipped head and wings,
A beaked ship under sail,
There glides a great black swan.

Under the autumn trees
He goes. The branches quiver,
Dance in the wraith-like water,
Which ripples beneath the sedge
With the slackening furrow that glides
In his wake when he is gone:
The beeches bow dark heads.

Into the windless dusk,
Where in mist great towers stand
Guarding a lonely strand
That is bodiless and dim,
He speeds with easy stride;
And I would go beside,
Till the low brown hills divide
At last, for me and him.

F. S. FLINT

1885-

90   *Eau-Forte*

ON black bare trees a stale cream moon
   Hangs dead, and sours the unborn buds.

Two gaunt old hacks, knees bent, heads low,
Tug, tired and spent, an old horse tram.

Damp smoke, rank mist fill the dark square;
And round the bend six bullocks come.

A hobbling, dirt-grimed drover guides
Their clattering feet—
        their clattering feet!
            to the slaughterhouse.

91   *Hats*

THE hollow sound of your hard felt hat
   As you clap it on your head
Is echoed over two thousand miles of trenches
By a thousand thousand guns;
And thousands of thousands of men have been killed,
And still more thousands of thousands have bled
And been maimed and have drowned
Because of that sound.

Towns battered and shattered,
Villages blasted to dust and mud,
Forests and woods stripped bare,
Rivers and streams befouled,

161

F. S. FLINT

The earth between and beyond the lines
Ravaged and sown with steel
And churned with blood
And astink with decaying men,
Nations starving, women and children murdered,
Genius destroyed, minds deformed and twisted,
And waste, waste, waste
Of the earth's fruits, of the earth's riches,—
All in obedience to your voice;
And the sound of your hat
Is in the same gamut of void and thoughtless
And evil sounds.

O estimable man,
Keeper of the season ticket,
Walker on the pavement,
Follower of the leader writer,
Guardian of the life policy,
Insured against all harm—
Fire, burglary, servants' accidents—
Warden and ward of the church,
Wallflower of the suburbs,
Primrose of respectability,
As you go home beneath your hard felt hat
The tradesmen do you homage.
Happily, the trees do not know you.

You have scoffed at the poet,
Because you are a practical man:
And does not your house bear you out?
Have poets such houses?

F. S. FLINT

It has a garden in front with a plot of grass,
And in the middle of that a flower-bed,
With a rose-tree in its midst, and other rose-trees
Against the walls, and a privet hedge,
And stocks and delphiniums, flowers in season!
The path is irregularly paved for quaintness;
There is a rustic porch, and a street door
With a polished brass letter-box and knocker,
And stained glass panels, showing a bird and flowers,
And an electric-bell push.
But you have a key, and you let yourself in
To the quiet red-tiled hall, where the doormat
Says "Welcome," and the stand receives your umbrella
And your coat and your hard felt hat.
A drawing-room, a dining-room (because
All your fellows have them), and a kitchen
All clean and neat; and because the kitchen is comfortable
You have your tea there with your wife and child—
Only one child, for are you not practical?
On the upper floor are a bathroom and three bedrooms.
Let your furniture stand undisturbed,
I will not describe it: a hundred shops in London
Show off the like in their windows. As for your books
They are as haphazard and as futile as your pictures.
But here is your comfort and you are comfortable;
And on summer evenings and Saturday afternoons
You wander out into the garden at the back,
Which is fenced off on three sides from similar gardens,
And you potter around with garden tools and are happy.

F. S. FLINT

O insured against all harm,
Waiter on the pension at sixty,
Domestic vegetable, cultivated flower,
You have laughed at the poet, the unpractical dreamer:
You have seen life as bookkeeping and accountancy;
Your arithmetic has pleased you, your compound interest
Your business, more than the earth and the heavens;
And if your brother suffered, you took no heed,
Or read a liberal newspaper, and salved your conscience.
Ant, ant, oblivious of the water being boiled in the cauldron!

But when the time came for your chastisement,
For the punishment of your apathy, your will-less ignorance,
When the atmospheric pressure was just equivalent
To the weight of the seventy-six centimetre column of mercury,
And the water had exactly reached the hundredth degree of centigrade,
You felt, though you feared it, that the time had come,
That you had something called a collective honour, some patriotism;
And those others too felt the same honourable sentiment,
And you called for the slaughter that sanctifies honour,
And the boiling water was poured on us all. Ants! Ants!

F. S. FLINT

Friend and brother, you have not been killed;
Chance still allows you to wear your bowler hat,
The helmet of the warrior in its degeneracy,
The symbol of gracelessness and of the hate of beauty,
The signature of your sameness and innocuousness.
Take off your hat; let your hair grow; open your eyes;
Look at your neighbour; his suffering is your hurt.
Become dangerous; let the metaphysical beast
Whose breath poisons us all fear your understanding,
And recoil from our bodies, his prey, and fall back
    before you,
And shiver and quake and thirst and starve and die.

92 *London*

LONDON, my beautiful,
it is not the sunset
nor the pale green sky
shimmering through the curtain
of the silver birch,
nor the quietness;
it is not the hopping
of birds
upon the lawn,
nor the darkness
stealing over all things
that moves me.

But as the moon creeps slowly
over the tree-tops
among the stars,
I think of her

F. S. FLINT

and the glow her passing
sheds on men.

London, my beautiful,
I will climb
into the branches
to the moonlit tree-tops,
that my blood may be cooled
by the wind.

JOHN FREEMAN
1880-1929

93 *'Music Comes'*

MUSIC comes
Sweetly from the trembling string
When wizard fingers sweep
Dreamily, half asleep;
When through remembering reeds
Ancient airs and murmurs creep,
Oboe oboe following,
Flute answering clear high flute,
Voices, voices—falling mute,
And the jarring drums.

At night I heard
First a waking bird
Out of the quiet darkness sing. . . .
Music comes

JOHN FREEMAN

Strangely to the brain asleep!
And I heard
Soft, wizard fingers sweep
Music from the trembling string,
And through remembering reeds
Ancient airs and murmurs creep;
Oboe oboe following,
Flute calling clear high flute,
Voices faint, falling mute,
And low jarring drums;
Then all those airs
Sweetly jangled—newly strange,
Rich with change . . .
Was it the wind in the reeds?
Did the wind range
Over the trembling string;
Into flute and oboe pouring
Solemn music; sinking, soaring
Low to high,
Up and down the sky?
Was it the wind jarring
Drowsy far-off drums?

Strangely to the brain asleep
Music comes.

94   *'It was the lovely Moon'*

IT was the lovely moon—she lifted
 Slowly her white brow among
Bronze cloud-waves that ebbed and drifted
Faintly, faintlier afar.

JOHN FREEMAN

Calm she looked, yet pale with wonder,
Sweet in unwonted thoughtfulness,
Watching the earth that dwindled under
Faintly, faintlier afar.
It was the lovely moon that lovelike
Hovered over the wandering, tired
Earth, her bosom gray and dovelike,
Hovering beautiful as a dove. . . .
The lovely moon:—her soft light falling
Lightly on roof and poplar and pine—
Tree to tree whispering and calling,
Wonderful in the silvery shine
Of the round, lovely, thoughtful moon.

The Evening Sky

ROSE-bosom'd and rose-limb'd
With eyes of dazzling bright
Shakes Venus mid the twined boughs of the night;
Rose-limb'd, soft-stepping
From low bough to bough
Shaking the wide-hung starry fruitage—dimmed
Its bloom of snow
By that sole planetary glow.

Venus, avers the astronomer,
Not thus idly dancing goes
Flushing the eternal orchard with wild rose.
She through ether burns
Outpacing planetary earth,

JOHN FREEMAN

And ere two years triumphantly returns,
And again wave-like swelling flows,
And again her flashing apparition comes and goes.
This we have not seen,
No heavenly courses set,
No flight unpausing through a void serene:
But when eve clears,
Arises Venus as she first uprose
Stepping the shaken boughs among,
And in her bosom glows
The warm light hidden in sunny snows.

She shakes the clustered stars
Lightly, as she goes
Amid the unseen branches of the night,
Rose-limb'd, rose-bosom'd bright.
She leaps: they shake and pale; she glows
And who but knows
How the rejoiced heart aches
When Venus all his starry vision shakes;

When through his mind
Tossing with random airs of an unearthly wind,
Rose-bosom'd, rose-limb'd,
The mistress of his starry vision arises,
And the boughs glittering sway
And the stars pale away,
And the enlarging heaven glows
As Venus light-foot mid the twined branches goes?

ROBERT FROST
1875-

The Sound of the Trees

I WONDER about the trees.
Why do we wish to bear
Forever the noise of these
More than another noise
So close to our dwelling-place?
We suffer them by the day
Till we lose all measure of pace,
And fixity in our joys,
And acquire a listening air.
They are that that talks of going
But never gets away;
And that talks no less for knowing,
As it grows wiser and older,
That now it means to stay.
My feet tug at the floor
And my head sways to my shoulder
Sometimes when I watch trees sway,
From the window or the door.
I shall set forth for somewhere,
I shall make the reckless choice
Some day when they are in voice
And tossing so as to scare
The white clouds over them on.
I shall have less to say,
But I shall be gone.

ROBERT FROST
Birches

WHEN I see birches bend to left and right
    Across the line of straighter darker trees,
I like to think some boy's been swinging them.
But swinging doesn't bend them down to stay.
Ice-storms do that. Often you must have seen them
Loaded with ice a sunny winter morning
After a rain. They click upon themselves
As the breeze rises, and turn many-coloured
As the stir cracks and crazes their enamel.
Soon the sun's warmth makes them shed crystal shells
Shattering and avalanching on the snow-crust—
Such heaps of broken glass to sweep away
You'd think the inner dome of heaven had fallen.
They are dragged to the withered bracken by the load,
And they seem not to break; though once they are
    bowed
So low for so long, they never right themselves:
You may see their trunks arching in the woods
Years afterwards, trailing their leaves on the ground
Like girls on hands and knees that throw their hair
Before them over their heads to dry in the sun.
But I was going to say when Truth broke in
With all her matter-of-fact about the ice-storm
I should prefer to have some boy bend them
As he went out and in to fetch the cows—
Some boy too far from town to learn baseball,
Whose only play was what he found himself,
Summer or winter, and could play alone.
One by one he subdued his father's trees

ROBERT FROST

By riding them down over and over again
Until he took the stiffness out of them,
And not one but hung limp, not one was left
For him to conquer. He learned all there was
To learn about not launching out too soon
And so not carrying the tree away
Clear to the ground. He always kept his poise
To the top branches, climbing carefully
With the same pains you use to fill a cup
Up to the brim, and even above the brim.
Then he flung outward, feet first, with a swish,
Kicking his way down through the air to the ground.

So was I once myself a swinger of birches;
And so I dream of going back to be.
It's when I'm weary of considerations,
And life is too much like a pathless wood
Where your face burns and tickles with the cobwebs
Broken across it, and one eye is weeping
From a twig's having lashed across it open.
I'd like to get away from earth awhile
And then come back to it and begin over.
May no fate wilfully misunderstand me
And half grant what I wish and snatch me away
Not to return. Earth's the right place for love:
I don't know where it's likely to go better.
I'd like to go by climbing a birch tree,
And climb black branches up a snow-white trunk
Toward heaven, till the tree could bear no more,
But dipped its top and set me down again.
That would be good both going and coming back.
One could do worse than be a swinger of birches.

ROBERT FROST

98 Stopping by Woods on a Snowy Evening

WHOSE woods these are I think I know.
His house is in the village though;
He will not see me stopping here
To watch his woods fill up with snow.

My little horse must think it queer
To stop without a farmhouse near
Between the woods and frozen lake
The darkest evening of the year.

He gives his harness bells a shake
To ask if there is some mistake.
The only other sound's the sweep
Of easy wind and downy flake.

The woods are lovely, dark and deep,
But I have promises to keep,
And miles to go before I sleep,
And miles to go before I sleep.

99   *The Pasture*

I'M going out to clean the pasture spring;
I'll only stop to rake the leaves away
(And wait to watch the water clear, I may):
I shan't be gone long.—You come too.

I'm going out to fetch the little calf
That's standing by the mother. It's so young
It totters when she licks it with her tongue.
I shan't be gone long.—You come too.

ROBERT FROST

Come In

As I came to the edge of the woods,
Thrush music—hark!
Now if it was dusk outside,
Inside it was dark.

Too dark in the woods for a bird
By sleight of wing
To better its perch for the night,
Though it still could sing.

The last of the light of the sun
That had died in the west
Still lived for one song more
In a thrush's breast.

Far in the pillared dark
Thrush music went—
Almost like a call to come in
To the dark and lament.

But no, I was out for stars:
I would not come in.
I meant not even if asked,
And I hadn't been.

WILFRID GIBSON
1878-

The Ice Cart

PERCHED on my city office-stool
  I watched with envy, while a cool
And lucky carter handled ice . . .
And I was wandering in a trice,
Far from the grey and grimy heat
Of that intolerable street,
O'er sapphire berg and emerald floe,
Beneath the still, cold ruby glow
Of everlasting Polar night,
Bewildered by the queer half-light,
Until I stumbled, unawares,
Upon a creek, where big white bears
Plunged headlong down with flourished heels,
And floundered after shining seals
Through shivering seas of blinding blue.
And as I watched them, ere I knew,
I'd stripped, and I was swimming too,
Among the seal-pack, young and hale,
And thrusting on with threshing tail,
With twist and twirl and sudden leap
Through crackling ice and salty deep—
Diving and doubling with my kind,
Until, at last, we left behind
Those big, white, blundering bulks of death,
And lay, at length, with panting breath,
Upon a far untravelled floe,
Beneath a gentle drift of snow—
Snow drifting gently, fine and white,
Out of the endless Polar night.
Falling and falling evermore

WILFRID GIBSON

Upon that far untravelled shore,
Till I was buried fathoms deep
Beneath that cold, white drifting sleep—
Sleep drifting deep,
Deep drifting sleep . . .

The carter cracked a sudden whip:
I clutched my stool with startled grip,
Awakening to the grimy heat
Of that intolerable street.

Rupert Brooke
II

ONCE in my garret—you being far away
  Tramping the hills and breathing upland air,
Or so I fancied—brooding in my chair,
I watched the London sunshine feeble and grey
Dapple my desk, too tired to labour more,
When, looking up, I saw you standing there,—
Although I'd caught no footstep on the stair,—
Like sudden April at my open door.

Though now beyond earth's farthest hills you fare,
Song-crowned, immortal, sometimes it seems to me
That, if I listen very quietly,
Perhaps I'll hear a light foot on the stair,
And see you standing with your angel air,
Fresh from the uplands of eternity.

WILFRID GIBSON

103 *Before Action*

I SIT beside the brazier's glow,
   And, drowsing in the heat,
I dream of daffodils that blow
   And lambs that frisk and bleat—

Black lambs that frolic in the snow
   Among the daffodils,
In a far orchard that I know
   Beneath the Malvern hills.

Next year the daffodils will blow
   And lambs will frisk and bleat;
But I'll not feel the brazier's glow,
   Nor any cold or heat.

104 *The Return*

HE went, and he was gay to go;
   And I smiled on him as he went.
My son—'twas well he couldn't know
My darkest dread, nor what it meant—

Just what it meant to smile and smile
And let my son go cheerily—
My son . . . and wondering all the while
What stranger would come back to me.

WILFRID GIBSON

Lament

WE who are left, how shall we look again
  Happily on the sun, or feel the rain,
Without remembering how they who went
Ungrudgingly, and spent
Their all for us, loved too the sun and rain?

A bird among the rain-wet lilac sings—
But we, how shall we turn to little things
And listen to the birds and winds and streams
Made holy by their dreams,
Nor feel the heart-break in the heart of things?

ROBERT GRAVES
1895-

Star-Talk

'ARE you awake, Gemelli,
  This frosty night?'
'We'll be awake till reveille,
Which is sunrise,' say the Gemelli,
'It's no good trying to go to sleep:
If there's wine to be got we'll drink it deep,
  But rest is hopeless tonight,
  But rest is hopeless tonight.'

'Are you cold too, poor Pleiads,
  This frosty night?'
'Yes, and so are the Hyads:
See us cuddle and hug,' say the Pleiads,

ROBERT GRAVES

'All six in a ring: it keeps us warm:
We'll huddle together like birds in a storm:
  It's bitter weather tonight,
  It's bitter weather tonight.'

'What do you hunt, Orion,
  This starry night?'
'The Ram, the Bull, and the Lion
And the Great Bear,' says Orion,
'With my starry quiver and beautiful belt
I am trying to find a good thick pelt
  To warm my shoulders tonight,
  To warm my shoulders tonight.'

'Did you hear that, Great She-bear,
  This frosty night?'
'Yes, he's talking of stripping *me* bare
Of my own big fur,' says the She-bear.
'I'm afraid of the man and his terrible arrow:
The thought of it chills my bones to the marrow,
  And the frost so cruel tonight!
  And the frost so cruel tonight!'

'How is your trade, Aquarius,
  This frosty night?'
'Complaints are many and various,
And my feet are cold,' says Aquarius,
'There's Venus objects to Dolphin-scales,
And Mars to Crab-spawn found in my pails,
  And the pump has frozen tonight,
  And the pump has frozen tonight.'

ROBERT GRAVES

Babylon

THE child alone a poet is:
Spring and fairyland are his.
Truth and Reason show but dim,
And all's poetry with him.
Rhyme and music flow in plenty
For the lad of one and twenty,
But Spring for him is no more now
Than daisies to a munching cow;
Just a cheery pleasant season,
Daisy buds to live at ease on.
He's forgotten how he smiled
And shrieked at snowdrops when a child,
Or wept one evening secretly
For April's glorious misery.
Wisdom made him old and wary
Banishing the Lords of Faery.
Wisdom made a breach and battered
Babylon to bits: she scattered
To the hedges and ditches
All our nursery gnomes and witches.
Lob and Puck, poor frantic elves,
Drag their treasures from the shelves.
Jack the Giant-killer's gone,
Mother Goose and Oberon.
Bluebeard and Red Riding Hood
Take together to the wood,
And Sir Galahad lies hid
In a cave with Captain Kidd.
None of all the magic hosts,
None remain but a few ghosts
Of timorous heart, to linger on
Weeping for lost Babylon.

JULIAN GRENFELL
1888-1915

Into Battle
1915

THE naked earth is warm with Spring,
    And with green grass and bursting trees
Leans to the sun's gaze glorying,
    And quivers in the sunny breeze;
And Life is Colour and Warmth and Light
    And a striving evermore for these;
And he is dead who will not fight;
    And who dies fighting has increase.

The fighting man shall from the sun
    Take warmth, and life from the glowing earth;
Speed with the light-foot winds to run,
    And with the trees to newer birth;
And find, when fighting shall be done,
    Great rest, and fullness after dearth.

All the bright company of Heaven
    Hold him in their high comradeship,
The Dog-Star and the Sisters Seven,
    Orion's Belt and sworded hip.

The woodland trees that stand together,
    They stand to him each one a friend;
They gently speak in the windy weather;
    They guide to valley and ridge's end.

The kestrel hovering by day,
    And the little owls that call by night,
Bid him be swift and keen as they,
    As keen of ear, as swift of sight.

JULIAN GRENFELL

The blackbird sings to him, 'Brother, brother,
  If this be the last song you shall sing,
Sing well, for you may not sing another;
  Brother, sing.'

In dreary, doubtful, waiting hours,
  Before the brazen frenzy starts,
The horses show him nobler powers;
  O patient eyes, courageous hearts!

And when the burning moment breaks,
  And all things else are out of mind,
And only Joy of Battle takes
  Him by the throat, and makes him blind—

Through joy and blindness he shall know,
  Not caring much to know, that still
Nor lead nor steel shall reach him, so
  That it be not the Destined Will.

The thundering line of battle stands,
  And in the air Death moans and sings;
But Day shall clasp him with strong hands,
  And night shall fold him in soft wings.

RALPH GUSTAFSON
1909-

109   *'This Speaking were Enough'*

THIS speaking were enough
  If words were true—
And every action its own end
  That compassed you.

RALPH GUSTAFSON

I would not need the grace
Of more than this,
To say 'I love'—and then have done
With emphasis.

To tell in other terms
What I have told—
Predict the gold or silver moon
As silver? gold?

I could protest again
And it would be
That I should measure north and south
My apogee.

But I have need, oh I
Have need of more—
Than synonym of love and love,
Before, before,

Who know this traffic false,
The telling cheat,
And every word before the saying
Obsolete.

Dedication

'THEY shall not die in vain,' we said.
   'Let us impose, since we forget
The hopeless giant alphabet,
Great stones above the general dead,'
The living said.

RALPH GUSTAFSON

'They shall not be outdone in stones.
Generously, sculptured grief shall stand
In general over numbered bones
With book and index near at hand
For particular sons.

'And we the living left in peace
Will set aside such legal date
At such and suchlike time or state
Or place as meet and fitting is
Respecting this.'

O boy, locked in the grisly hollow,
You who once idly peeled a willow-
switch, whistling, wondering at the stick
Of willow's whiteness clean and slick,
Do not believe that we shall bury
You with words: aptly carry
Cloth flowers, proxy for love.
O we have done with granite grief
And silk denials: summing you
Within the minutes' silence—two!
More than you had need to target
Hate, against the pitiless bullet's
Calculated greed oppose
Heart's anger: falling, gave to us
What power to lance the pocket of
An easy past, what use of love
Teaching children's laughter loud
On shutters in an evil street,
What edge, O death, of days, delight?

RALPH GUSTAFSON

What linch of love, spate of sun?
And shall we with a sedentary noun
Signature receipt, having had read
The catechism of the generous dead?

You who live, see! These,
These were his hills where laughter was
And counted years of longing, grain
And wintry apples scorched in sun,
Of corded hemlock deep in snow.
Here at his seven birches growing
Oblique by the boulder the fence has stopped—
Rusted wire, posts lopped
For staking. To circle love, he said.
And there are other fables made:
Of plough and intricate loom; the broken
Soldier on the sill; and latin
Parchment framed, conferring letters
On hooded death; the axe the motto
Against the wall; abandoned hills.

Fables for stout reading. Tales
Listened to by twice-told death.
Our tongue how silent, muscles lithe
O land, hoist by the lag-end of little
Deeds? What lack of monstrous metal,
Monumental mouths; over
This land what love, wheel, lever
Of God, anchorage, pivot of days,
Remembering?

RALPH GUSTAFSON

Old and certain the sea,
The mountain-tilted sky, old,
Older than words, than you are old,
Boy, who never thought to point the hill
With dawn! Only as these, our telling:
As men labour: as harvest done:
At dusk a joyful walking home.
Of nearer things: how he was young,
And died, a silent writing down.

H. D. (HILDA DOOLITTLE)
1886-

III   *Evening*

THE light passes
   from ridge to ridge,
from flower to flower—
the hepaticas, wide-spread
under the light
grow faint—
the petals reach inward,
the blue tips bend
toward the bluer heart
and the flowers are lost.

The cornel-buds are still white,
but shadows dart
from the cornel-roots—
black creeps from root to root,

H. D. (HILDA DOOLITTLE)

each leaf
cuts another leaf on the grass,
shadow seeks shadow,
then both leaf
and leaf-shadow are lost.

Cuckoo Song

AH, bird,
our love is never spent
with your clear note,
nor satiate our soul;
not song, not wail, not hurt,
but just a call summons us
with its simple top-note
and soft fall;

not to some rarer heaven
of lilies over-tall,
nor tuberose set against
some sun-lit wall,
but to a gracious
cedar-palace hall;

not marble set with purple
hung with roses and tall
sweet lilies—such
as the nightingale
would summon for us
with her wail—

H. D. (HILDA DOOLITTLE)

(surely only unhappiness
could thrill
such a rich madrigal!)
not she, the nightingale,
can fill our souls
with such a wistful joy as this:
nor, bird, so sweet
was ever a swallow note—
not hers, so perfect
with the wing of lazuli
and bright breast—
nor yet the oriole
filling with melody
from her fiery throat
some island-orchard
in a purple sea.

Ah, dear, ah, gentle bird,
you spread warm length
of crimson wool
and tinted woven stuff
for us to rest upon,
nor numb with ecstasy
nor drown with death:
only you soothe, make still
the throbbing of our brain:
so through her forest trees,
when all her hope was gone
and all her pain,
Calypso heard your call—
across the gathering drift

H. D. (HILDA DOOLITTLE)

of burning cedar-wood,
across the low-set bed
of wandering parsley and violet,
when all her hope was dead.

From 'Songs from Cyprus'

I

GATHER for festival,
bright weed and purple shell;
make, on the holy sand,
pattern as one might make
who treads, with rose-red heel,
a measure
pleasureful;

such as those songs we made
in rose and myrtle shade,
where rose and myrtle fell
(shell-petal or rose-shell),
on just such holy sand;
ah, the song
musical;

give me white rose and red;
find me, in citron glade,
citron of precious weight;
spread gold before her feet;
ah, weave the citron-flower;
hail goddess,
beautiful.

H. D. (HILDA DOOLITTLE)
IV

Where is the nightingale,
in what myrrh-wood and dim?
ah, let the night come black
for we would conjure back
all that enchanted him,
all that enchanted him.

Where is the bird of fire?
in what packed hedge or rose?
in what roofed ledge of flower?
no other creature knows
what magic lurks within,
what magic lurks within.

Bird, bird, bird, bird, we cry,
hear, pity us in pain:
hearts break in the sunlight,
hearts break in daylight rain,
only night heals again,
only night heals again.

V

Bring myrrh and myrtle bud,
bell of the snowy head
of the first asphodel;

frost of the citron flower,
petal on petal, white
wax of faint love-delight;

H. D. (HILDA DOOLITTLE)

flower, flower and little head
of tiny meadow-floret,
white, where no bee has fed;

full of its honey yet
spilling its scented sweet;
spread them before her feet;

white citron, whitest rose,
(myrrh leaves, myrrh leaves enclose),
and the white violet.

Fragment Thirty-six

I know not what to do: my mind is divided.
                                        SAPPHO

I KNOW not what to do,
my mind is reft:
is song's gift best?
is love's gift loveliest?
I know not what to do,
now sleep has pressed
weight on your eyelids.

Shall I break your rest,
devouring, eager?
is love's gift best?
nay, song's the loveliest:
yet, were you lost,
what rapture
could I take from song?
what song were left?

H. D. (HILDA DOOLITTLE)

I know not what to do:
to turn and slake
the rage that burns,
with my breath burn
and trouble your cool breath?
so shall I turn and take
snow in my arms?
(is love's gift best?)
yet flake on flake
of snow were comfortless,
did you lie wondering,
wakened yet unawake.

Shall I turn and take
comfortless snow within my arms?
press lips to lips
that answer not,
press lips to flesh
that shudders not nor breaks?

Is love's gift best?
shall I turn and slake
all the wild longing?
O I am eager for you!
as the Pleiads shake
white light in whiter water
so shall I take you?

My mind is quite divided,
my minds hesitate,

H. D. (HILDA DOOLITTLE)

so perfect matched,
I know not what to do:
each strives with each
as two white wrestlers
standing for a match,
ready to turn and clutch
yet never shake muscle nor nerve nor tendon;
so my mind waits
to grapple with my mind,
yet I lie quiet,
I would seem at rest.

I know not what to do:
strain upon strain,
sound surging upon sound
makes my brain blind;
as a wave-line may wait to fall
yet (waiting for its falling)
still the wind may take
from off its crest,
white flake on flake of foam,
that rises,
seeming to dart and pulse
and rend the light,
so my mind hesitates
above the passion
quivering yet to break,
so my mind hesitates
above my mind,
listening to song's delight.

H. D. (HILDA DOOLITTLE)

I know not what to do:
will the sound break,
rending the night
with rift on rift of rose
and scattered light?
will the sound break at last
as the wave hesitant,
or will the whole night pass
and I lie listening awake?

THOMAS HARDY
1840-1928

115 *The Last Chrysanthemum*

WHY should this flower delay so long
    To show its tremulous plumes?
Now is the time of plaintive robin-song,
    When flowers are in their tombs.

Through the slow summer, when the sun
    Called to each frond and whorl
That all he could for flowers was being done,
    Why did it not uncurl?

It must have felt that fervid call
    Although it took no heed,
Waking but now, when leaves like corpses fall,
    And saps all retrocede.

THOMAS HARDY

Too late its beauty, lonely thing,
  The season's shine is spent,
Nothing remains for it but shivering
  In tempests turbulent.

Had it a reason for delay,
  Dreaming in witlessness
That for a bloom so delicately gay
  Winter would stay its stress?

—I talk as if the thing were born
  With sense to work its mind;
Yet it is but one mask of many worn
  By the Great Face behind.

The Darkling Thrush

I LEANT upon a coppice gate
  When Frost was spectre-gray,
And Winter's dregs made desolate
  The weakening eye of day.
The tangled bine-stems scored the sky
  Like strings of broken lyres,
And all mankind that haunted nigh
  Had sought their household fires.

The land's sharp features seemed to be
  The Century's corpse outleant,
His crypt the cloudy canopy,
  The wind his death-lament.

THOMAS HARDY

The ancient pulse of germ and birth
  Was shrunken hard and dry,
And every spirit upon earth
  Seemed fervourless as I.

At once a voice arose among
  The bleak twigs overhead
In a full-hearted evensong
  Of joy illimited;
An aged thrush, frail, gaunt, and small,
  In blast-beruffled plume,
Had chosen thus to fling his soul
  Upon the growing gloom.

So little cause for carolings
  Of such ecstatic sound
Was written on terrestrial things
  Afar or nigh around,
That I could think there trembled through
  His happy good-night air
Some blessèd Hope, whereof he knew
  And I was unaware.

117   *Beyond the Last Lamp*
(Near Tooting Common)

I

WHILE rain, with eve in partnership,
  Descended darkly, drip, drip, drip,
Beyond the last lone lamp I passed,
  Walking slowly, whispering sadly,
Two linked loiterers, wan, downcast:
Some heavy thought constrained each face,
And blinded them to time and place.

THOMAS HARDY

II

The pair seemed lovers, yet absorbed
In mental scenes no longer orbed
By love's young rays. Each countenance
　As it slowly, as it sadly
　Caught the lamplight's yellow glance,
Held in suspense a misery
At things which had been or might be.

III

When I retrod that watery way
Some hours beyond the droop of day,
Still I found pacing there the twain
　Just as slowly, just as sadly,
　Heedless of the night and rain.
One could but wonder who they were,
And what wild woe detained them there.

IV

Though thirty years of blur and blot
Have slid since I beheld that spot,
And saw, in curious converse there,
　Moving slowly, moving sadly,
　That mysterious tragic pair,
Its olden look may linger on—
All but the couple; they have gone.

V

Whither? Who knows, indeed. . . . And yet
To me, when nights are weird and wet,
Without those comrades there at tryst

Creeping slowly, creeping sadly,
That lone lane does not exist.
There they seem brooding on their pain,
And will, while such a lane remain.

118   *'When I Set out for Lyonnesse'*

WHEN I set out for Lyonnesse,
    A hundred miles away,
The rime was on the spray,
And starlight lit my lonesomeness
When I set out for Lyonnesse
    A hundred miles away.

What would bechance at Lyonnesse
    While I should sojourn there
    No prophet durst declare,
Nor did the wisest wizard guess
What would bechance at Lyonnesse
    While I should sojourn there.

When I came back from Lyonnesse
    With magic in my eyes,
    All marked with mute surmise
My radiance rare and fathomless,
When I came back from Lyonnesse
    With magic in my eyes!

THOMAS HARDY
Afterwards

WHEN the Present has latched its postern behind my tremulous stay,
And the May month flaps its glad green leaves like wings,
Delicate-filmed as new-spun silk, will the neighbours say,
   'He was a man who used to notice such things'?

If it be in the dusk when, like an eyelid's soundless blink,
The dewfall-hawk comes crossing the shades to alight
Upon the wind-warped upland thorn, a gazer may think,
   'To him this must have been a familiar sight.'

If I pass during some nocturnal blackness, mothy and warm,
When the hedgehog travels furtively over the lawn,
One may say, 'He strove that such innocent creatures should come to no harm,
   But he could do little for them; and now he is gone.'

If, when hearing that I have been stilled at last, they stand at the door,
Watching the full-starred heavens that winter sees,
Will this thought rise on those who will meet my face no more,
   'He was one who had an eye for such mysteries'?

THOMAS HARDY

And will any say when my bell of quittance is heard in the gloom,
And a crossing breeze cuts a pause in its outrollings,
Till they rise again, as they were a new bell's boom,
'He hears it not now, but used to notice such things'?

120   In Time of 'The Breaking of Nations'

I

ONLY a man harrowing clods
In a slow silent walk
With an old horse that stumbles and nods
Half asleep as they stalk.

II

Only thin smoke without flame
From the heaps of couch grass;
Yet this will go onward the same
Though Dynasties pass.

III

Yonder a maid and her wight
Come whispering by;
War's annals will fade into night
Ere their story die.

121   The Oxen

CHRISTMAS Eve, and twelve of the clock.
  'Now they are all on their knees,'
An elder said as we sat in a flock
  By the embers in hearthside ease.

THOMAS HARDY

We pictured the meek mild creatures where
   They dwelt in their strawy pen,
Nor did it occur to one of us there
   To doubt they were kneeling then.

So fair a fancy few would weave
   In these years! Yet, I feel,
If someone said on Christmas Eve,
   'Come; see the oxen kneel

'In the lonely barten by yonder coomb
   Our childhood used to know,'
I should go with him in the gloom,
   Hoping it might be so.

Transformations

PORTION of this yew
   Is a man my grandsire knew,
Bosomed here at its foot:
This branch may be his wife,
A ruddy human life
Now turned to a green shoot.

These grasses must be made
Of her who often prayed,
Last century, for repose;
And the fair girl long ago
Whom I often tried to know
May be entering this rose.

So, they are not underground
But as nerves and veins abound
In the growths of upper air,
And they feel the sun and rain,
And the energy again
That made them what they were!

Life Laughs Onward

RAMBLING I looked for an old abode
Where, years back, one had lived I knew;
Its site a dwelling duly showed,
    But it was new.

I went where, not so long ago,
The sod had riven two breasts asunder;
Daisies throve gaily there, as though
    No grave were under.

I walked along a terrace where
Loud children gambolled in the sun:
The figure that had once sat there
    Was missed by none.

Life laughed and moved on unsubdued,
I saw that Old succumbed to Young:
'Twas well. My too regretful mood
    Died on my tongue.

THOMAS HARDY

An Ancient to Ancients

WHERE once we danced, where once we sang,
   Gentlemen,
The floors are sunken, cobwebs hang,
And cracks creep; worms have fed upon
The doors. Yea, sprightlier times were then
Than now, with harps and tabrets gone,
   Gentlemen!

Where once we rowed, where once we sailed
   Gentlemen,
And damsels took the tiller, veiled
Against too strong a stare (God wot
Their fancy, then or anywhen!)
Upon that shore we are clean forgot,
   Gentlemen!

We have lost somewhat, afar and near,
   Gentlemen,
The thinning of our ranks each year
Affords a hint we are nigh undone,
That we shall not be ever again
The marked of many, loved of one,
   Gentlemen.

In dance the polka hit our wish,
   Gentlemen,
The paced quadrille, the spry schottische,
'Sir Roger.'—And in opera spheres
The 'Girl' (the famed 'Bohemian'),
And 'Trovatore' held the ears,
   Gentlemen.

THOMAS HARDY

This season's paintings do not please,
   Gentlemen,
Like Etty, Mulready, Maclise;
Throbbing romance has waned and wanned:
No wizard wields the witching pen
Of Bulwer, Scott, Dumas, and Sand,
   Gentlemen.

The bower we shrined to Tennyson,
   Gentlemen,
Is roof-wrecked; damps there drip upon
Sagged seats, the creeper-nails are rust,
The spider is sole denizen;
Even she who voiced those rhymes is dust,
   Gentlemen!

We who met sunrise sanguine-souled,
   Gentlemen,
Are wearing weary. We are old;
These younger press; we feel our rout
Is imminent to Aïdes' den,—
That evening shades are stretching out,
   Gentlemen!

And yet, though ours be failing frames,
   Gentlemen,
So were some others history names,
Who trod their track light-limbed and fast
As these youth, and not alien
From enterprise, to their long last,
   Gentlemen.

THOMAS HARDY

Sophocles, Plato, Socrates,
  Gentlemen,
Pythagoras, Thucydides,
Herodotus, and Homer,—yea,
Clement, Augustin, Origen,
Burnt brightlier towards their setting day,
  Gentlemen.

And ye, red-lipped and smooth-browed, list,
  Gentlemen;
Much is there waits you we have missed;
Much lore we leave you worth the knowing,
Much, much has lain outside our ken:
Nay, rush not: time serves: we are going,
  Gentlemen.

RALPH HODGSON
1871-

125 'Time, You Old Gypsy Man'

TIME, you old gypsy man,
  Will you not stay,
Put up your caravan
  Just for one day?

All things I'll give you
Will you be my guest,
Bells for your jennet
Of silver the best,
Goldsmiths shall beat you
A great golden ring,

RALPH HODGSON

Peacocks shall bow to you,
Little boys sing,
Oh, and sweet girls will
Festoon you with may,
Time, you old gypsy,
Why hasten away?

Last week in Babylon,
Last night in Rome,
Morning, and in the crush
Under Paul's dome;
Under Paul's dial
You tighten your rein—
Only a moment,
And off once again;
Off to some city
Now blind in the womb,
Off to another
Ere that's in the tomb.

Time, you old gypsy man,
　Will you not stay,
Put up your caravan
　Just for one day?

126 *The Bells of Heaven*

'TWOULD ring the bells of Heaven
　　The wildest peal for years,
If Parson lost his senses
And people came to theirs,
And he and they together
Knelt down with angry prayers

RALPH HODGSON

For tamed and shabby tigers,
And dancing dogs and bears,
And wretched blind pit ponies,
And little hunted hares.

127   *Stupidity Street*

I SAW with open eyes
   Singing birds sweet
Sold in the shops
   For the people to eat,
Sold in the shops of
   Stupidity Street.

I saw in vision
   The worm in the wheat,
And in the shops nothing
   For people to eat;
Nothing for sale in
   Stupidity Street.

128   *From 'The Song of Honour'*

I HEARD it all, each, every note
   Of every lung and tongue and throat,
Ay, every rhythm and rhyme
Of everything that lives and loves
And upward, ever upward moves
From lowly to sublime!
Earth's multitudinous Sons of Light,
I heard them lift their lyric might
With each and every chanting sprite
That lit the sky that wondrous night
As far as eye could climb!

RALPH HODGSON

I heard it all, I heard the whole
Harmonious hymn of being roll
Up through the chapel of my soul
And at the altar die,
And in the awful quiet then
Myself I heard, Amen, Amen,
Amen I heard me cry!
I heard it all, and then although
I caught my flying senses, Oh,
A dizzy man was I!
I stood and stared; the sky was lit,
The sky was stars all over it,
I stood, I knew not why,
Without a wish, without a will,
I stood upon that silent hill
And stared into the sky until
My eyes were blind with stars, and still
I stared into the sky.

GERARD MANLEY HOPKINS
1844-1889

129 *God's Grandeur*

THE world is charged with the grandeur of God.
  It will flame out, like shining from shook foil;
  It gathers to a greatness, like the ooze of oil
Crushed. Why do men then now not reck his rod?
Generations have trod, have trod, have trod;
  And all is seared with trade; bleared, smeared with
    toil;

GERARD MANLEY HOPKINS

And wears man's smudge and shares man's smell; the soil
Is bare now, nor can foot feel, being shod.

And for all this, nature is never spent;
   There lives the dearest freshness deep down things;
And though the last lights off the black West went
   Oh, morning, at the brown brink Eastward, springs—
Because the Holy Ghost over the bent
   World broods with warm breast and with ah! bright wings.

130   *Felix Randal*

FELIX RANDAL the farrier, O he is dead then? my duty all ended,
Who have watched his mould of man, big-boned and hardy-handsome
Pining, pining, till time when reason rambled in it and some
Fatal four disorders, fleshed there, all contended?

Sickness broke him. Impatient he cursed at first, but mended
Being anointed and all; though a heavenlier heart began some
Months earlier, since I had our sweet reprieve and ransom
Tendered to him. Ah well, God rest him all road ever he offended!

This seeing the sick endears them to us, us too it endears.
My tongue had taught thee comfort, touch had quenched thy tears,
Thy tears that touched my heart, child, Felix, poor Felix Randal;

How far from then forethought of, all thy more boisterous years,
When thou at the random grim forge, powerful amidst peers,
Didst fettle for the great grey drayhorse his bright and battering sandal!

131 *The Leaden Echo and the Golden Echo*

(Maidens' song from St. Winefred's Well)

THE LEADEN ECHO

HOW to kéep—is there ány any, is there none such, nowhere known some, bow or brooch or braid or brace, láce, latch or catch or key to keep
Back beauty, keep it, beauty, beauty, beauty, . . . from vanishing away?
Ó is there no frowning of these wrinkles, rankèd wrinkles deep,
Dówn? no waving off of these most mournful messengers, still messengers, sad and stealing messengers of grey?
No there's none, there's none, O no there's none,
Nor can you long be, what you are now, called fair,

GERARD MANLEY HOPKINS

Do what you may do, what, do what you may,
And wisdom is early to despair:
Be beginning; since, no, nothing can be done
To keep at bay
Age and age's evils, hoar hair,
Ruck and wrinkle, drooping, dying, death's worst,
  winding sheets, tombs and worms and tumbling
  to decay;
So be beginning, be beginning to despair.
O there's none; no no no there's none:
Be beginning to despair, to despair,
Despair, despair, despair, despair.

THE GOLDEN ECHO
  Spare!
There ís one, yes I have one (Hush there!);
Only not within seeing of the sun,
Not within the singeing of the strong sun,
Tall sun's tingeing, or treacherous the tainting of the
  earth's air,
Somewhere elsewhere there is ah well where! one,
Ońe. Yes I can tell such a key, I do know such a place,
Where whatever's prized and passes of us, everything
  that's fresh and fast flying of us, seems to us
  sweet of us and swiftly away with, done away
  with, undone,
Undone, done with, soon done with, and yet dearly
  and dangerously sweet
Of us, the wimpled-water-dimpled, not-by-morning-
  matchèd face,

GERARD MANLEY HOPKINS

The flower of beauty, fleece of beauty, too too apt to,
 ah! to fleet,
Never fleets móre, fastened with the tenderest truth
To its own best being and its loveliness of youth: it is
 an everlastingness of, O it is an all youth!
Come then, your ways and airs and looks, locks,
 maiden gear, gallantry and gaiety and grace,
Winning ways, airs innocent, maiden manners, sweet
 looks, loose locks, long locks, lovelocks, gay-
 gear, going gallant, girlgrace—
Resign them, sign them, seal them, send them, motion
 them with breath,
And with sighs soaring, soaring síghs deliver
Them; beauty-in-the-ghost, deliver it, early now, long
 before death
Give beauty back, beauty, beauty, beauty, back to
God, beauty's self and beauty's giver.
See; not a hair is, not an eyelash, not the least lash
 lost; every hair
Is, hair of the head, numbered.
Nay, what we had lighthanded left in surly the mere
 mould
Will have waked and have waxed and have walked
 with the wind what while we slept,
This side, that side hurling a heavyheaded hundred-
 fold
What while we, while we slumbered.
O then, weary then whý should we tread? O why
 are we so haggard at the heart, so care-coiled,
 care-killed, so fagged, so fashed, so cogged, so
 cumbered,

When the thing we freely fórfeit is kept with fonder
     a care,
Fonder a care kept than we could have kept it, kept
Far with fonder a care (and we, we should have lost
     it) finer, fonder
A care kept.—Where kept? Do but tell us where
     kept, where.—
Yonder.—What high as that! We follow, now we
     follow.—Yonder, yes yonder, yonder,
Yonder.

132   *Binsey Poplars*
              felled 1879

MY aspens dear, whose airy cages quelled,
   Quelled or quenched in leaves the leaping sun,
All felled, felled, are all felled;
     Of a fresh and following folded rank
          Not spared, not one
          That dandled a sandalled
       Shadow that swam or sank
On meadow and river and wind-wandering weed-
     winding bank.

  O if we but knew what we do
       When we delve or hew—
     Hack and rack the growing green!
       Since country is so tender
     To touch, her being só slender,
     That, like this sleek and seeing ball
     But a prick will make no eye at all,

Where we, even where we mean
    To mend her we end her,
    When we hew or delve:
After-comers cannot guess the beauty been.
  Ten or twelve, only ten or twelve
    Strokes of havoc únselve
      The sweet especial scene,
  Rural scene, a rural scene,
  Sweet especial rural scene.

133   *Spring*

NOTHING is so beautiful as spring—
  When weeds, in wheels, shoot long and lovely and lush;
Thrush's eggs look little low heavens, and thrush
Through the echoing timber does so rinse and wring
The ear, it strikes like lightnings to hear him sing;
  The glassy peartree leaves and blooms, they brush
  The descending blue; that blue is all in a rush
With richness; the racing lambs too have fair their fling.

What is all this juice and all this joy?
  A strain of the earth's sweet being in the beginning
In Eden garden.—Have, get, before it cloy,
  Before it cloud, Christ, lord, and sour with sinning,
Innocent mind and Mayday in girl and boy,
  Most, O maid's child, thy choice and worthy the winning.

A. E. HOUSMAN
1859-1936

Bredon Hill

IN summertime on Bredon[1]
  The bells they sound so clear;
Round both the shires they ring them
  In steeples far and near,
    A happy noise to hear.

Here of a Sunday morning
  My love and I would lie,
And see the coloured counties,
  And hear the larks so high
    About us in the sky.

The bells would ring to call her
  In valleys miles away:
'Come all to church, good people;
  Good people, come and pray.'
    But here my love would stay.

And I would turn and answer
  Among the springing thyme,
'Oh, peal upon our wedding,
  And we will hear the chime,
    And come to church in time.'

But when the snows at Christmas
  On Bredon top were strown,
My love rose up so early
  And stole out unbeknown
    And went to church alone.

[1] Pronounced Breedon.

A. E. HOUSMAN

They tolled the one bell only,
  Groom there was none to see,
The mourners followed after,
  And so to church went she,
  And would not wait for me.

The bells they sound on Bredon,
  And still the steeples hum.
'Come all to church, good people,'—
  Oh, noisy bells, be dumb;
  I hear you, I will come.

'Tell me not here'

TELL me not here, it needs not saying,
  What tune the enchantress plays
In aftermaths of soft September
  Or under blanching mays,
For she and I were long acquainted
  And I knew all her ways.

On russet floors, by waters idle,
  The pine lets fall its cone;
The cuckoo shouts all day at nothing
  In leafy dells alone;
And traveller's joy beguiles in autumn
  Hearts that have lost their own.

A. E. HOUSMAN

On acres of the seeded grasses
  The changing burnish heaves;
Or marshalled under moons of harvest
  Stand still all night the sheaves;
Or beeches strip in storms for winter
  And stain the wind with leaves.

Possess, as I possessed a season,
  The countries I resign,
Where over elmy plains the highway
  Would mount the hills and shine,
And full of shade the pillared forest
  Would murmur and be mine.

For nature, heartless, witless nature,
  Will neither care nor know
What stranger's feet may find the meadow
  And trespass there and go,
Nor ask amid the dews of morning
  If they are mine or no.

136   *'As I Gird on for Fighting'*

AS I gird on for fighting
  My sword upon my thigh,
I think on old ill fortunes
  Of better men than I.

Think I, the round world over,
  What golden lads are low
With hurts not mine to mourn for
  And shames I shall not know.

A. E. HOUSMAN

What evil luck soever
  For me remains in store,
'Tis sure much finer fellows
  Have fared much worse before.

So here are things to think on
  That ought to make me brave,
As I strap on for fighting
  My sword that will not save.

137   *Reveille*

WAKE: the silver dusk returning
  Up the beach of darkness brims,
And the ship of sunrise burning
  Strands upon the eastern rims.

Wake: the vaulted shadow shatters,
  Trampled to the floor it spanned,
And the tent of night in tatters
  Straws the sky-pavilioned land.

Up, lad, up, 'tis late for lying:
  Hear the drums of morning play;
Hark, the empty highways crying
  'Who'll beyond the hills away?'

Towns and countries woo together,
  Forelands beacon, belfries call;
Never lad that trod on leather
  Lived to feast his heart with all.

A. E. HOUSMAN

Up, lad: thews that lie and cumber
  Sunlit pallets never thrive;
Morns abed and daylight slumber
  Were not meant for man alive.

Clay lies still, but blood's a rover;
  Breath's a ware that will not keep.
Up, lad: when the journey's over
  There'll be time enough to sleep.

138   *'Loveliest of trees'*

LOVELIEST of trees, the cherry now
  Is hung with bloom along the bough,
And stands about the woodland ride
Wearing white for Eastertide.

Now, of my threescore years and ten,
Twenty will not come again,
And take from seventy springs a score,
It only leaves me fifty more.

And since to look at things in bloom
Fifty springs are little room,
About the woodlands I will go
To see the cherry hung with snow.

139 *'Oh see how thick the goldcup flowers'*

OH see how thick the goldcup flowers
  Are lying in field and lane,
With dandelions to tell the hours
  That never are told again.

A. E. HOUSMAN

Oh may I squire you round the meads
　　And pick you posies gay?
—'Twill do no harm to take my arm.
　　'You may, young man, you may.'

Ah, spring was sent for lass and lad,
　　'Tis now the blood runs gold,
And man and maid had best be glad
　　Before the world is old.
What flowers to-day may flower to-morrow,
　　But never as good as new.
—Suppose I wound my arm right round—
　　' 'Tis true, young man, 'tis true.'

Some lads there are, 'tis shame to say,
　　That only court to thieve,
And once they bear the bloom away
　　'Tis little enough they leave.
Then keep your heart for men like me
　　And safe from trustless chaps.
My love is true and all for you.
　　'Perhaps, young man, perhaps.'

Oh, look in my eyes then, can you doubt?
　　—Why, 'tis a mile from town.
How green the grass is all about!
　　We might as well sit down.
—Ah, life, what is it but a flower?
　　Why must true lovers sigh?
Be kind, have pity, my own, my pretty,—
　　'Good-bye, young man, good-bye.'

A. E. HOUSMAN

Fancy's Knell

WHEN lads were home from labour
    At Abdon under Clee,
A man would call his neighbour
    And both would send for me.
And where the light in lances
    Across the mead was laid,
There to the dances
    I fetched my flute and played.

Ours were idle pleasures,
    Yet oh, content we were,
The young to wind the measures,
    The old to heed the air;
And I to lift with playing
    From tree and tower and steep
The light delaying,
    And flute the sun to sleep.

The youth toward his fancy
    Would turn his brow of tan,
And Tom would pair with Nancy
    And Dick step off with Fan;
The girl would lift her glances
    To his, and both be mute:
Well went the dances
    At evening to the flute.

Wenlock Edge was umbered,
    And bright was Abdon Burf,
And warm between them slumbered

A. E. HOUSMAN

  The smooth green miles of turf;
Until from grass and clover
  The upshot beam would fade,
And England over
  Advanced the lofty shade.

The lofty shade advances,
  I fetch my flute and play:
Come, lads, and lead the dances
  And praise the tune today.
Tomorrow, more's the pity,
  Away we both must hie,
To air the ditty,
  And to earth I.

ALDOUS HUXLEY
1894-

141 *The Cicadas*

SIGHTLESS, I breathe and touch; this night
    of pines
Is needly, resinous and rough with bark.
Through every crevice in the tangible dark
The moonlessness above it all but shines.

Limp hangs the leafy sky; never a breeze
Stirs, nor a foot in all this sleeping ground;
And there is silence underneath the trees—
The living silence of continuous sound.

ALDOUS HUXLEY

For like inveterate remorse, like shrill
Delirium throbbing in the fevered brain,
An unseen people of cicadas fill
Night with their one harsh note, again, again.

Again, again, with what insensate zest!
What fury of persistence, hour by hour!
Filled with what devil that denies them rest,
Drunk with what source of pleasure and of power!

Life is their madness, life that all night long
Bids them to sing and sing, they know not why;
Mad cause and senseless burden of their song;
For life commands, and Life! is all their cry.

I hear them sing, who in the double night
Of clouds and branches fancied that I went
Through my own spirit's dark discouragement,
Deprived of inward as of outward sight:

Who, seeking, even as here in the wild wood,
A lamp to beckon through my tangled fate,
Found only darkness and, disconsolate,
Mourned the lost purpose and the vanished good.

Now in my empty heart the crickets' shout
Re-echoing denies and still denies
With stubborn folly all my learned doubt,
In madness more than I in reason wise.

ALDOUS HUXLEY

Life, life! The word is magical. They sing,
And in my darkened soul the great sun shines;
My fancy blossoms with remembered spring,
And all my autumns ripen on the vines.

Life! and each knuckle of the fig-tree's pale
Dead skeleton breaks out with emerald fire.
Life! and the tulips blow, the nightingale
Calls back the rose, calls back the old desire:

And old desire that is for ever new,
Desire, life's earliest and latest birth,
Life's instrument to suffer and to do,
Springs with the roses from the teeming earth;

Desire that from the world's bright body strips
Deforming time and makes each kiss the first;
That gives to hearts, to satiated lips
The endless bounty of to-morrow's thirst.

Time passes, and the watery moonrise peers
Between the tree-trunks. But no outer light
Tempers the chances of our groping years,
No moon beyond our labyrinthine night.

Clueless we go; but I have heard thy voice,
Divine Unreason! harping in the leaves,
And grieve no more; for wisdom never grieves,
And thou hast taught me wisdom; I rejoice.

ALDOUS HUXLEY

Song of Poplars

SHEPHERD, to yon tall poplars tune your flute:
Let them pierce keenly, subtly shrill,
The slow blue rumour of the hill;
Let the grass cry with an anguish of evening gold,
And the great sky be mute.

Then hearken how the poplar trees unfold
Their buds, yet close and gummed and blind,
In airy leafage of the mind,
Rustling in silvery whispers the twin-hued scales
That fade not nor grow old.

'Poplars and fountains and you cypress spires
Springing in dark and rusty flame,
Seek you aught that hath a name?
Or say, say: Are you all an upward agony
Of undefined desires?

'Say, are you happy in the golden march
Of sunlight all across the day?
Or do you watch the uncertain way
That leads the withering moon on cloudy stairs
Over the heaven's wide arch?

'Is it towards sorrow or towards joy you lift
The sharpness of your trembling spears?
Or do you seek, through the grey tears
That blur the sky, in the heart of the triumphing blue,
A deeper, calmer rift?'

ALDOUS HUXLEY

So; I have tuned my music to the trees,
And there were voices, dim below
Their shrillness, voices swelling slow
In the blue murmur of hills, and a golden cry
And then vast silence.

ROBINSON JEFFERS
1887-

143 *Suicide's Stone*

PEACE is the heir of dead desire,
  Whether abundance killed the cormorant
In a happy hour, or sleep or death
Drowned him deep in dreamy waters,
Peace is the ashes of that fire,
  The heir of that king, the inn of that journey.

This last and best and goal: we dead
Hold it so tight you are envious of us
And fear under sunk lids contempt.
Death-day greetings are the sweetest.
Let trumpets roar when a man dies
And rockets fly up, he has found his fortune.

Yet hungering long and pitiably
That way, you shall not reach a finger
To pluck it unripe and before dark
Creep to cover: life broke ten whipstocks
Over my back, broke faith, stole hope,
  Before I denounced the covenant of courage.

ROBINSON JEFFERS

144 *Birds*

THE fierce musical cries of a couple of sparrow-
    hawks hunting on the headland,
Hovering and darting, their heads northwestward,
Prick like silver arrows shot through a curtain the
    noise of the ocean
Trampling its granite; their red backs gleam
Under my window around the stone corners; nothing
    gracefuller, nothing
Nimbler in the wind. Westward the wave-gleaners,
The old gray sea-going gulls are gathered together,
    the northwest wind wakening
Their wings to the wild spirals of the wind-dance.
Fresh as the air, salt as the foam, play birds in the
    bright wind, fly falcons
Forgetting the oak and the pinewood, come gulls
From the Carmel sands and the sands at the river-
    mouth, from Lobos and out of the limitless
Power of the mass of the sea, for a poem
Needs multitude, multitudes of thoughts, all fierce,
    all flesh-eaters, musically clamorous
Bright hawks that hover and dart headlong, and
    ungainly
Gray hungers fledged with desire of transgression,
    salt slimed beaks, from the sharp
Rock-shores of the world and the secret waters.

JAMES JOYCE

1882-1940

145 *A Flower given to my Daughter*

FRAIL the white rose and frail are
   Her hands that gave
Whose soul is sere and paler
Than time's wan wave.

Rosefrail and fair—yet frailest
A wonder wild
In gentle eyes thou veilest,
My blueveined child.

146 *On the Beach at Fontana*

WIND whines and whines the shingle,
   The crazy pierstakes groan;
A senile sea numbers each single
Slimesilvered stone.

From whining wind and colder
Grey sea I wrap him warm
And touch his trembling fineboned shoulder
And boyish arm.

Around us fear, descending
Darkness of fear above
And in my heart how deep unending
Ache of love!

JAMES JOYCE
Chamber Music

V

Lean out of the window,
   Goldenhair,
I heard you singing
   A merry air.

My book is closed;
   I read no more,
Watching the fire dance
   On the floor.

I have left my book:
   I have left my room:
For I heard you singing
   Through the gloom,

Singing and singing
   A merry air.
Lean out of the window,
   Goldenhair.

XXXVI

I hear an army charging upon the land
   And the thunder of horses plunging, **foam about
   their knees.**
Arrogant, in black armour, behind them stand,
   Disdaining the reins, with fluttering whips, the
   chariofeers.

JAMES JOYCE

They cry unto the night their battlename:
  I moan in sleep when I hear afar their whirling laughter.
They cleave the gloom of dreams, a blinding flame,
  Clanging, clanging upon the heart as upon an anvil.

They come shaking in triumph their long green hair:
  They come out of the sea and run shouting by the shore.
My heart, have you no wisdom thus to despair?
  My love, my love, my love, why have you left me alone?

RUDYARD KIPLING
1865-1936

Cities and Thrones and Powers

CITIES and Thrones and Powers
  Stand in Time's eye,
Almost as long as flowers
  Which daily die:
But as new buds put forth,
  To glad new men,
Out of the spent and unconsidered earth
  The cities rise again.

RUDYARD KIPLING

The season's Daffodil,
  She never hears
What change, what chance, what chill,
  Cut down last year's:
But with bold countenance
  And knowledge small,
Esteems her seven days' continuance
  To be perpetual.

So time that is o'er-kind
  To all that be,
Ordains us e'en as blind,
  As bold as she:
That in our very death
  And burial sure,
Shadow to shadow, well persuaded, saith,
  'See how our works endure!'

Recessional
1897

GOD of our fathers, known of old,
  Lord of our far-flung battle-line,
Beneath whose awful Hand we hold
  Dominion over palm and pine—
Lord God of Hosts, be with us yet,
Lest we forget—lest we forget!

The tumult and the shouting dies;
  The captains and the kings depart:
Still stands Thine ancient sacrifice,

RUDYARD KIPLING

An humble and a contrite heart.
Lord God of Hosts, be with us yet,
Lest we forget—lest we forget!

Far-called, our navies melt away;
  On dune and headland sinks the fire:
Lo, all our pomp of yesterday
  Is one with Nineveh and Tyre!
Judge of the Nations, spare us yet,
Lest we forget—lest we forget!

If, drunk with sight of power, we loose
  Wild tongues that have not Thee in awe,
Such boastings as the Gentiles use,
  Or lesser breeds without the Law—
Lord God of Hosts, be with us yet,
Lest we forget—lest we forget!

For heathen heart that puts her trust
  In reeking tube and iron shard,
All valiant dust that builds on dust
  And, guarding, calls not Thee to guard,
For frantic boast and foolish word—
Thy Mercy on Thy People, Lord! Amen.

150   *Harp Song of the Dane Women*

WHAT is a woman that you forsake her,
    And the hearth-fire and the home-acre,
To go with the old grey Widow-maker?

RUDYARD KIPLING

She has no house to lay a guest in—
But one chill bed for all to rest in,
That the pale suns and the stray bergs nest in.

She has no strong white arms to fold you,
But the ten-times-fingering weed to hold you
Bound on the rocks where the tide has rolled you.

Yet, when the signs of summer thicken,
And the ice breaks, and the birch-buds quicken,
Yearly you turn from our side, and sicken—

Sicken again for the shouts and the slaughters,—
You steal away to the lapping waters,
And look at your ship in her winter quarters.

You forget our mirth, and talk at the tables,
The kine in the shed and the horse in the stables—
To pitch her sides and go over her cables.

Then you drive out where the storm-clouds swallow;
And the sound of your oar-blades falling hollow,
Is all we have left through the months to follow.

Ah, what is Woman that you forsake her,
And the hearth-fire and the home-acre,
To go with the old grey Widow-maker?

151 *The Way through the Woods*

THEY shut the road through the woods
   Seventy years ago.
Weather and rain have undone it again,
   And now you would never know

RUDYARD KIPLING

There was once a road through the woods
  Before they planted the trees.
It is underneath the coppice and heath
  And the thin anemones.
  Only the keeper sees
That, where the ring-dove broods,
  And the badgers roll at ease,
There was once a road through the woods.

Yet, if you enter the woods
  Of a summer evening late,
When the night-air cools on the trout-ringed pools
Where the otter whistles his mate,
(They fear not men in the woods
  Because they see so few.)
You will hear the beat of a horse's feet
And the swish of a skirt in the dew,
  Steadily cantering through
    The misty solitudes,
  As though they perfectly knew
The old lost road through the woods . . .
But there is no road through the woods.

ARCHIBALD LAMPMAN
1861-1899

152 *A Summer Evening*

THE clouds grow clear, the pine-wood glooms
    and stills
With brown reflections in the silent bay,
And far beyond the pale blue-misted hills
The rose and purple evening dreams away.
The thrush, the veery, from mysterious dales
Rings his last round; and outward like a sea
The shining, shadowy heart of heaven unveils
The starry legend of eternity.
The day's long troubles lose their sting and pass.
Peaceful the world, and peaceful grows my heart.
The gossip cricket from the friendly grass
Talks of old joys and takes the dreamer's part.
Then night, the healer, with unnoticed breath,
And sleep, dark sleep, so near, so like to death.

153 *A January Morning*

THE glittering roofs are still with frost; each worn
    Black chimney builds into the quiet sky
Its curling pile to crumble silently.
Far out to westward, on the edge of morn,
The slender misty city towers up-borne
Glimmer faint rose against the pallid blue;
And yonder on those northern hills, the hue
Of amethyst, hang fleeces dull as horn.
And here behind me come the woodmen's sleighs
With shouts and clamorous squeakings; might and
    main

ARCHIBALD LAMPMAN

Up the steep slope the horses stamp and strain,
Urged on by hoarse-tongued drivers—cheeks ablaze,
Iced beards and frozen eyelids—team by team,
With frost-fringed flanks, and nostrils jetting steam.

154   *Evening*

FROM upland slopes I see the cows file by,
   Lowing, great-chested, down the homeward trail,
By dusking fields and meadows shining pale
With moon-tipped dandelions. Flickering high,
A peevish night-hawk in the western sky
Beats up into the lucent solitudes,
Or drops with griding wing. The stilly woods
Grow dark and deep and gloom mysteriously.
Cool night winds creep, and whisper in mine ear.
The homely cricket gossips at my feet.
From far-off pools and wastes of reeds I hear,
Clear and soft-piped, the chanting frogs break sweet
In full Pandean chorus. One by one
Shine out the stars, and the great night comes on.

155   *Midnight*

FROM where I sit, I see the stars,
   And down the chilly floor
The moon between the frozen bars
   Is glimmering dim and hoar.

Without in many a peakèd mound
   The glinting snowdrifts lie;
There is no voice or living sound;
   The embers slowly die.

ARCHIBALD LAMPMAN

Yet some wild thing is in mine ear;
   I hold my breath and hark;
Out of the depth I seem to hear
   A crying in the dark;

No sound of man or wife or child,
   No sound of beast that groans,
Or of the wind that whistles wild,
   Or of the tree that moans:

I know not what it is I hear;
   I bend my head and hark;
I cannot drive it from mine ear,
   That crying in the dark.

156   *Late November*

THE far-off leafless forests slowly yield
   To the thick-driving snow. A little while
And night shall darken down. In shouting file
The woodsmen's carts go by me homeward-wheeled
Past the thin fading stubbles, half concealed,
Now golden-gray, sowed softly through with snow,
Where the last ploughman follows still his row,
Turning black furrows through the whitening field.

Far off the village lamps begin to gleam,
Fast drives the snow, and no man comes this way;
The hills grow wintry white, and bleak winds moan
About the naked uplands. I alone
Am neither sad, nor shelterless, nor gray,
Wrapped round with thought, content to watch and
      dream.

D. H. LAWRENCE

1885-1931

157 *Humming-Bird*

I CAN imagine, in some other world
Primeval-dumb, far back
In that most awful stillness, that only gasped and hummed,
Humming-birds raced down the avenues.

Before anything had a soul,
While life was a heave of Matter, half inanimate,
This little bit chipped off in brilliance
And went whizzing through the slow, vast, succulent stems.

I believe there were no flowers then,
In the world where the humming-bird flashed ahead of creation.
I believe he pierced the slow vegetable veins with his long beak.

Probably he was big
As mosses, and little lizards, they say, were once big.
Probably he was a jabbing, terrifying monster.

We look at him through the wrong end of the long telescope of Time,
Luckily for us.

158 *Snake*

A SNAKE came to my water-trough
On a hot, hot day, and I in pyjamas for the heat,
To drink there.

D. H. LAWRENCE

In the deep, strange-scented shade of the great carob-tree
I came down the steps with my pitcher
And must wait, must stand and wait, for there he was at the trough before me.

He reached down from a fissure in the earth-wall in the gloom
And trailed his yellow-brown slackness soft-bellied down, over the edge of the stone trough
And rested his throat upon the stone bottom,
And where the water had dripped from the tap, in a small clearness,
He sipped with his straight mouth,
Softly drank through his straight gums, into his slack long body,
Silently.

Someone was before me at my water trough,
And I, like a second comer, waiting.

He lifted his head from his drinking, as cattle do,
And looked at me vaguely, as drinking cattle do,
And flickered his two-forked tongue from his lips, and mused a moment,
And stooped and drank a little more,
Being earth-brown, earth-golden from the burning bowels of the earth
On the day of Sicilian July, with Etna smoking.

D. H. LAWRENCE

The voice of my education said to me
He must be killed,
For in Sicily the black, black snakes are innocent, the gold are venomous.

And voices in me said, If you were a man
You would take a stick and break him now, and finish him off.

But must I confess how I liked him,
How glad I was he had come like a guest in quiet, to drink at my water-trough
And depart peaceful, pacified, and thankless,
Into the burning bowels of this earth?

Was it cowardice, that I dared not kill him?
Was it perversity, that I longed to talk to him?
Was it humility, to feel so honoured?
I felt so honoured.

And yet those voices:
If you were not afraid, you would kill him!

And truly I was afraid, I was most afraid,
But even so, honoured still more
That he should seek my hospitality
From out the dark door of the secret earth.

He drank enough
And lifted his head, dreamily, as one who has drunken,

And flickered his tongue like a forked night on the air, so black,
Seeming to lick his lips,
And looked around like a god, unseeing, into the air,

And slowly turned his head,
And slowly, very slowly, as if thrice adream,
Proceeded to draw his slow length curving round
And climb again the broken bank of my wall-face.

And as he put his head into that dreadful hole,
And as he slowly drew up, snake-easing his shoulders, and entered farther,
A sort of horror, a sort of protest against his withdrawing into that horrid black hole,
Deliberately going into the blackness, and slowly drawing himself after,
Overcame me now his back was turned.

I looked round, I put down my pitcher,
I picked up a clumsy log
And threw it at the water-trough with a clatter.

I think it did not hit him,
But suddenly that part of him that was left behind convulsed in undignified haste,
Writhed like lightning, and was gone
Into the black hole, the earth-lipped fissure in the wall-front,
At which, in the intense still noon, I stared with fascination.

D. H. LAWRENCE

And immediately I regretted it.
I thought how paltry, how vulgar, what a mean act!
I despised myself and the voices of my accursed human education.

And I thought of the albatross,
And I wished he would come back, my snake.

For he seemed to me again like a king,
Like a king in exile, uncrowned in the underworld,
Now due to be crowned again.

And so, I missed my chance with one of the lords
Of life.
And I have something to expiate;
A pettiness.

159 *Work*

THERE is no point in work
    unless it absorbs you
    like an absorbing game.

If it doesn't absorb you,
if it's never any fun,
    don't do it.

When a man goes out into his work
he is alive like a tree in spring,
he is living, not merely working.

D. H. LAWRENCE

When the Hindus weave thin wool into long, long
    lengths of stuff
with their thin dark hands and their wide dark eyes
    and their still souls absorbed
they are like slender trees putting forth leaves, a long
    white web of living leaf,
        the tissue they weave,
and they clothe themselves in white as a tree clothes
    itself in its own foliage.

As with cloth, so with houses, ships, shoes, wagons or
    cups or loaves.
Men might put them forth as a snail its shell, as a
    bird that leans
        its breast against its nest, to make it
        round,
as the turnip models his round root, as the bush makes
    flowers and gooseberries,
        putting them forth, not manufacturing
        them,
and cities might be as they once were, bowers grown
    out from the busy bodies of people.
And so it will be again, men will smash the machines.

At last, for the sake of clothing himself in his own
    leaf-like cloth
        tissued from his own life,
and dwelling in his own bowery house, like a beaver's
    nibbled mansion
and drinking from cups that came off his fingers like
    flowers off their five-fold stem,
he will cancel the machines we have got.

D. H. LAWRENCE

Bavarian Gentians

NOT every man has gentians in his house
in Soft September, at slow, Sad Michaelmas.

Bavarian gentians, big and dark, only dark
darkening the day-time torch-like with the smoking
    blueness of Pluto's gloom,
ribbed and torch-like, with their blaze of darkness
    spread blue
down flattening into points, flattened under the sweep
    of white day,
torch-flower of the blue smoking darkness, Pluto's
    dark-blue daze,
black lamps from the halls of Dis, burning dark blue,
giving off darkness, blue darkness, as Demeter's pale
    lamps give off light,
lead me then, lead me the way.

Reach me a gentian, give me a torch,
let me guide myself with the blue, forked torch of
    this flower
down the darker and darker stairs, where blue is
    darkened on blueness,
even where Persephone goes, just now, from the
    frosted September
to the sightless realm where darkness is awake upon
    the dark
and Persephone herself is but a voice
or a darkness invisible enfolded in the deeper dark
of the arms Plutonic, and pierced with the passion
    of dense gloom,
among the splendour of torches of darkness, shedding
    darkness on the lost bride and groom.

CECIL DAY LEWIS
1905-

161 *'You that love England'*

YOU that love England, who have an ear for her
    music,
The slow movement of clouds in benediction,
Clear arias of light thrilling over her uplands,
Over the chords of summer sustained peacefully;
Ceaseless the leaves' counterpoint in a west wind
    lively,
Blossom and river rippling loveliest allegro,
And the storms of wood strings brass at year's finale:
Listen. Can you not hear the entrance of a new
    theme?

You who go out alone, on tandem or on pillion,
Down arterial roads riding in April,
Or sad beside lakes where hill-slopes are reflected
Making fires of leaves, your high hopes fallen:
Cyclists and hikers in company, day excursionists,
Refugees from cursed towns and devastated areas;
Know you seek a new world, a saviour to establish
Long-lost kinship and restore the blood's fulfilment.

You who like peace, good sticks, happy in a small way
Watching birds or playing cricket with schoolboys,
Who pay for drinks all round, whom disaster chose
    not;
Yet passing derelict mills and barns roof-rent
Where despair has burnt itself out—hearts at a stand-
    still,
Who suffer loss, aware of lowered vitality;
We can tell you a secret, offer a tonic; only
Submit to the visiting angel, the strange new healer.

CECIL DAY LEWIS

You above all who have come to the far end, victims
Of a run-down machine, who can bear it no longer;
Whether in easy chairs chafing at impotence
Or against hunger, bullies and spies preserving
The nerve for action, the spark of indignation—
Need fight in the dark no more, you know your enemies.
You shall be leaders when zero hour is signalled,
Wielders of power and welders of a new world.

162   'I've heard them lilting at Loom and Belting'

I'VE heard them lilting at loom and belting,
   Lasses lilting before dawn of day:
But now they are silent, not gamesome and gallant—
The flowers of the town are rotting away.

There was laughter and loving in the lanes at evening;
Handsome were the boys then, and girls were gay.
But lost in Flanders by medalled commanders
The lads of the village are vanished away.

Cursed be the promise that takes our men from us—
All will be champion if you choose to obey:
They fight against hunger but still it is stronger—
The prime of our land grows cold as the clay.

The women are weary, once lilted so merry,
Waiting to marry for a year and a day:
From wooing and winning, from owning or earning
The flowers of the town are all turned away.

CECIL DAY LEWIS

163   'Suppose that we, to-morrow or the next day'

SUPPOSE that we, to-morrow or the next day,
Came to an end—in storm the shafting broken,
Or a mistaken signal, the flange lifting—
Would that be premature, a text for sorrow?

Say what endurance gives or death denies us.
Love's proved in its creation, not eternity:
Like leaf or linnet the true heart's affection
Is born, dies later, asks no reassurance.

Over dark wood rises one dawn felicitous,
Bright through awakened shadows fall her crystal
Cadenzas, and once for all the wood is quickened.
So our joys visit us, and it suffices.

Nor fear we now to live who in the valley
Of the shadow of life have found a causeway;
For love restores the nerve and love is under
Our feet resilient. Shall we be weary?

Some say we walk out of Time altogether
This way into a region where the primrose
Shows an immortal dew, sun at meridian
Stands up for ever and in scent the lime tree.

This is a land which later we may tell of.
Here-now we know, what death cannot diminish
Needs no replenishing; yet certain are, though
Dying were well enough, to live is better.

CECIL DAY LEWIS

Passion has grown full man by his first birthday.
Running across the bean-fields in a south wind,
Fording the river mouth to feel the tide-race—
Child's play that was, though proof of our possessions.

Now our research is done, measured the shadow,
The plains mapped out, the hills a natural bound'ry.
Such and such is our country. There remains to
Plough up the meadowland, reclaim the marshes.

164 A Time to Dance

FOR those who had the power
    of the forest fires that burn
Leaving their source in ashes
    to flush the sky with fire:
Those whom a famous urn
    could not contain, whose passion
Brimmed over the deep grave
    and dazzled epitaphs:
For all that have won us wings
    to clear the tops of grief,
My friend who within me laughs
    bids you dance and sing.

Some set out to explore
    earth's limit, and little they recked if
Never their feet came near it,
    outgrowing the need for glory:
Some aimed at a small objective
    but the fierce updraught of their spirit

CECIL DAY LEWIS

Forced them to the stars.
    Are honoured in public who built
The dam that tamed a river;
    or holding the salient for hours
Against odds, cut off and killed,
    are remembered by one survivor.

All these. But most for those
    whom accident made great,
As a radiant chance encounter
    of cloud and sunlight grows
Immortal on the heart:
    whose gift was the sudden bounty
Of a passing moment, enriches
    the fulfilled eye for ever.
Their spirits float serene
    above time's roughest reaches,
But their seed is in us and over
    our lives they are evergreen.

VACHEL LINDSAY
1879-1932

*165   General William Booth enters
            into Heaven*

*(To be sung to the tune of "The Blood of the Lamb"
    with indicated instruments)*

I

(Bass drum beaten loudly)

BOOTH led boldly with his big bass drum—
    (Are you washed in the blood of the Lamb?)
The Saints smiled gravely and they said: "He's come."
(Are you washed in the blood of the Lamb?)
Walking lepers followed, rank on rank,
Lurching bravoes from the ditches dank,
Drabs from the alley-ways and drug fiends pale—
Minds still passion-ridden, soul-powers frail:—
Vermin-eaten saints with mouldy breath,
Unwashed legions with the ways of Death—
(Are you washed in the blood of the Lamb?)

(Banjos)

Every slum had sent its half-a-score
The round world over. (Booth had groaned for more.)
Every banner that the wide world flies
Bloomed with glory and transcendent dyes.
Big-voiced lasses made their banjos bang,
Tranced, fanatical, they shrieked and sang:
"Are you washed in the blood of the Lamb?"
Hallelujah! It was queer to see
Bull-necked convicts with that land make free.
Loons with trumpets blowed a blare, blare, blare,
On, on upward thro' the golden air!
(Are you washed in the blood of the Lamb?)

VACHEL LINDSAY

II

(Bass drum slower and softer)
Booth died blind and still by faith he trod,
Eyes still dazzled by the ways of God.
Booth led boldly, and he looked the chief,
Eagle countenance in sharp relief,
Beard a-flying, air of high command
Unabated in that holy land.

(Sweet flute music)
Jesus came from out the court-house door,
Stretched his hands above the passing poor.
Booth saw not, but led his queer ones there
Round and round the mighty court-house square.
Then in an instant all that blear review
Marched on spotless, clad in raiment new.
The lame were straightened, withered limbs uncurled
And blind eyes opened on a new, sweet world.

(Bass drum louder)
Drabs and vixens in a flash made whole!
Gone was the weasel-head, the snout, the jowl!
Sages and sybils now, and athletes clean,
Rulers of empires, and of forests green!

*(Grand chorus of all instruments; tambourines
to the foreground)*
The hosts were sandalled, and their wings were fire!
(Are you washed in the blood of the Lamb?)
But their noise played havoc with the angel-choir.
(Are you washed in the blood of the Lamb?)
Oh, shout Salvation! It was good to see

VACHEL LINDSAY

Kings and Princes by the Lamb set free.
The banjos rattled and the tambourines
Jing-jing-jingled in the hands of Queens.

(Reverently sung, no instruments)
And when Booth halted by the curb for prayer
He saw his Master thro' the flag-filled air.
Christ came gently with a robe and crown
For Booth the soldier, while the throng knelt down.
He saw King Jesus. They were face to face,
And he knelt a-weeping in that holy place.
Are you washed in the blood of the Lamb?

DOROTHY LIVESAY

1909-

166   *Prelude for Spring*

THESE dreams abound:
   Foot's leap to shore
Above the sound
Of river's roar—
Disabled door
Banged and barricaded.
Then on, on
Furrow, Fawn
Through wall and wood,
So fast no daring could
Tear off the hood
Unmask the soul pursued.

DOROTHY LIVESAY

Slash underbrush
Tear bough and branch
Seek cover, rabbits' burrow—
Hush!

He comes. Insistent, sure
Proud prowler, this pursuer comes
Noiseless, no wind-stir
No leaf-turn over;
Together quiet creeps on twig,
Hush hovers in his hands.

> How loud heart's thump—
> Persistent pump
> Sucks down, down sap
> Then up in surge
> (Axe striking stump).
>
> How breezy breath—
> Too strong a wind
> Scatters a stir
> Where feathers are,
> Bustles a bough.
>
> How blind two eyes
> Shuttling to-fro
> Not weaving light
> Nor sight . . .
> In darkness flow.
>
> (Only the self is loud;
> Worlds whisperless.)

DOROTHY LIVESAY

Dive down then, scuttle under:
Run, fearless of feet's thunder.
Somehow, the road rolls back in mist;
Here is the meadow where we kissed
And here the horses, galloping
We rode upon in spring ...

    O beat of air, wing beat
    Scatter of rain, sleet
    Resisting leaves,
    Retarding feet

    And drip of rain, leaf drip
    Sting on cheek and lip
    Tearing pores
    With lash of whip

    And hoof's away, heart's hoof
    Down greening lanes, with roof
    Of cherry blow
    And apple puff—

    O green wet, sun lit
    Soaked earth's glitter!
    Down mouth, to munch
    Up hoof, to canter

    Through willow lanes
    A gold-shaft shower,
    Embracing elms
    That lack leaf-lustre

DOROTHY LIVESAY

    And copse' cool bed
    All lavendered
    With scentless, sweet
    Hepatica—

    Till side by side
    In fields' brown furrow
    Swathe sunlight over
    Every shadow!

But still
On heart's high hill
And summit of
A day's delight
Still will he swoop
From heaven's height
Soaring unspent,
Still will he stoop to brush
Wing tip on hair,
Fan mind with fear.

    And now the chill
    Raw sun
    Goes greener still—
    The sky
    Cracks like an icicle:

    Frozen, foot-locked
    Heart choked and chafed
    Wing-battered and unsafe,
    Grovel to ground!
    A cry
    Lashes the sky—

These dreams abound.

DOROTHY LIVESAY
Fantasia

AND I have learned how diving's done
How breathing air, cool wafted trees
Clouds massed above the man-made tower
How these
Can live no more in mind and ear:
And mind be dumb
To all save Undine and her comb.

Imagination's underworld! where child goes down
Light as a feather. Water pressure
Hardly holds him, diving's easy
As the flight of bird in air
Or bomber drumming to his lair.

Child goes down, and laughingly
(He's not wanted yet, you see)
Catches fishes in his hand
Burrows toe in sifting sand
Seizes all the weeds about
To make a small sub-rosa boat.

Then up he bobs, as easily
As any blown balloon
To greet the bosky, brooding sky
And hunger for the sun.

. . . .

And child grown taller, clothed in man's
Long limbs, and shaggy hair, his chin outthrust
Searches for years the rounded world
Climbs to its peaks, falls to its valleys green

DOROTHY LIVESAY

Striding the trim and trailing towns
Fingering the fond arteries
Possessing things, and casting them
Cloakwise to earth for sleeping time.

But sometime the lust wanderer
Will sleep, will pause; will dream of plunging deep
Below it all, where he will need
No clock companion, thorn in flesh, no contact man
To urge him from the ground.
For flying's easy, if you do it diving
And diving is the self unmoored
Ranging and roving—man alone.

. . . .

And I have learned how diving's done
Wherefore the many, many
Chose the watery stair
Down, down Virginia
With your fêted hair
Following after Shelley
Or wordcarvers I knew
(Bouchette; and Raymond, you)—
Here is the fascination
Of the salty stare:
And death is here.

Death courteous and calm, glass-smooth
His argument so suave, so water-worn
A weighted stone.
And death's deliberation, his
Most certain waiting-room
His patience with the patient, who will be
His for infinity. . . .

DOROTHY LIVESAY

So no astounded peerers
On the surface craft
No dragging nets, no cranes
No gnarled and toughened rope
Not any prayer nor pulley man-devised
Will shake the undersea
Or be
More than a brief torpedo, children's arrow
More than a gaudy top outspun
Its schedule done.

. . . . .

Wise to have learned: how diving's done
How breathing air, cool wafted trees
Clouds massed above the man-made tower
How these
Can live no more in eye and ear:
And mind be dumb
To all save Undine and her comb.

AMY LOWELL

1874-1925

168 *Purple Grackles*

THE grackles have come.
   The smoothness of the morning is puckered with their incessant chatter.
A sociable lot, these purple grackles,
Thousands of them strung across a long run of wind,
Thousands of them beating the airways with quick
      wing-jerks,

AMY LOWELL

Spinning down the currents of the South.
Every year they come;
My garden is a place of solace and recreation
    evidently,
For they always pass a day with me.
With high good nature they tell me what I do not
    want to hear.
The grackles have come.

I am persuaded that grackles are birds;
But when they are settled in the trees,
I am inclined to declare them fruits
And the trees turned hybrid blackberry vines.
Blackness shining and bulging under leaves,
Does not that mean blackberries, I ask you?
Nonsense! The grackles have come.

Nonchalant highwaymen, pickpockets, second-story
    burglars,
Stealing away my little hope of Summer.
There is no stealthy robbing in this.
Whoever heard such a gabble of thieves' talk!
It seems they delight in unmasking my poor pretense.
Yes, now I see that the hydrangea blooms are rusty;
That the hearts of the golden-glow are ripening to
    lustreless seeds;
That the garden is dahlia-coloured,
Flaming with its last over-hot hues;
That the sun is pale as a lemon too small to fill the
    picking-ring.
I did not see this yesterday,
But today the grackles have come.

AMY LOWELL

They drop out of the trees
And strut in companies over the lawn,
Tired of flying, no doubt;
A grand parade to limber legs and give wings a rest.
I should build a great fish-pond for them,
Since it is evident that a bird-bath, meant to accommodate two goldfinches at most,
Is slight hospitality for these hordes.
Scarcely one can get in,
They all peck and scrabble so,
Crowding, pushing, chasing one another up the bank with spread wings.

'Are we ducks, you owner of such inadequate comforts,
That you offer us lily-tanks where one must swim or drown,
Not stand and splash like a gentleman?'
I feel the reproach keenly, seeing them perch on the edges of the tanks, trying the depth with a chary foot,
And hardly able to get their wings under water in the bird-bath.
But there are resources I had not considered,
If I am bravely ruled out of count.
What is that thudding against the eaves just beyond my window?
What is that spray of water blowing past my face?
Two—three—grackles bathing in the gutter,
The gutter providentially choked with leaves.
I pray they think I put the leaves there on purpose;

AMY LOWELL

I would be supposed thoughtful and welcoming
To all guests, even thieves.
But considering that they are going South and I am not,
I wish they would bathe more quietly:
It is unmannerly to flaunt one's good fortune.

They rate me of no consequence,
But they might reflect that it is my gutter.
I know their opinion of me,
Because one is drying himself on the window-sill
Not two feet from my hand.
His purple neck is sleek with water,
And the fellow preens his feathers for all the world as if I were a fountain statue.
If it were not for the window,
I am convinced he would light on my head.
Tyrian-feathered freebooter,
Appropriating my delightful gutter with so extravagant an ease,
You are as cool a pirate as ever scuttled a ship,
And are you not scuttling my Summer with every peck of your sharp bill?

But there is a cloud over the beech-tree,
A quenching cloud for lemon-livered suns.
The grackles are all swinging in the tree-tops,
And the wind is coming up, mind you.
That boom and reach is no Summer gale;
I know that wind;
It blows the Equinox over seeds and scatters them,

AMY LOWELL

It rips petals from petals, and tears off half-turned
    leaves.
There is rain on the back of that wind.
Now I would keep the grackles,
I would plead with them not to leave me.
I grant their coming, but I would not have them go.
It is a milestone, this passing of grackles.
A day of them, and it is a year gone by.
There is magic in this and terror,
But I only stare stupidly out of the window.
The grackles have come.

Come! Yes, they surely came.
But they have gone.
A moment ago the oak was full of them,
They are not there now.
Not a speck of a black wing,
Not an eye-peep of a purple head.
The grackles have gone,
And I watch an Autumn storm
Stripping the garden,
Shouting black rain challenges to an old, limp Summer
Laid down to die in the flower-beds.

WILSON MACDONALD
1880-

Exit

EASILY to the old
Opens the hard ground:
But when youth grows cold,
And red lips have no sound,
Bitterly does the earth
Open to receive
And bitterly do the grasses
In the churchyard grieve.

Cold clay knows how to hold
An agèd hand;
But how to comfort youth
It does not understand.
Even the gravel rasps
In a dumb way
When youth comes homing
Before its day.

Elizabeth's hair was made
To warm a man's breast,
Her lips called like roses
To be caressed;
But grim the Jester
Who gave her hair to lie
On the coldest lover
Under the cold sky.

WILSON MACDONALD

But Elizabeth never knew,
Nor will learn now,
How the long wrinkle comes
On the white brow;
Nor will she ever know,
In her robes of gloom,
How chill is a dead child
From a warm womb.

O clay, so tender
When a flower is born!
Press gently as she dreams
In her bed forlorn.
They who come early
Must weary of their rest—
Lie softly, then, as light
On her dear breast.

Unflowered is her floor,
Her roof is unstarred.
Is this then the ending—
Here, shuttered and barred?
Nay, not the ending;
She will awake
Or the heart of the earth
That enfolds her will break.

Easily to the old
Opens the hard ground:
But when youth grows cold,
And red lips have no sound,

WILSON MACDONALD

Bitterly does the earth
Open to receive
And bitterly do the grasses
In the churchyard grieve.

L. A. MACKAY
1901-

170   *Admonition for Spring*

LOOK away now from the high lonesome hills
So hard on the hard sky since the swift shower;
See where among the restless daffodils
The hyacinth sets his melancholy tower.

Draw in your heart from vain adventurings;
Float slowly, swimmer, slowly drawing breath.
See, in this wild green foam of growing things
The heavy hyacinth remembering death.

171   *Non Nobis*
(For Paul McGillicuddy)

NOT for our sake your life was ended thus,
In the red air, by the white metal flying.
You died for yourself; you did not die for us.
What have we ever done that was worth your dying?

You were no scapegoat of the bungled past,
No dupe of any politician's scheming.
Your own hand staked your own life on the cast,
For you were awake when most of us were dreaming.

L. A. MACKAY

Honestly, simply, almost without emotion
You matched the risk with what there was to lose,
And chanced a death you never would have chosen
Rather than risk a life you could not choose.

Your free mind saw the end from the beginning.
We will not shame it now with fawning breath.
Your fight is fought. Our freedom waits our winning.
We have no claim, no proxy in your death.

172 Rend your Heart and not your Garments

PITY the innocent. There are none innocent, none.
  Not all the quiet kindly men of good will.
We were weak who should have been strong, we were disunited,
We were smug, and lazy, and gullible, and short-sighted.
Whatever we did, there was more we should have done
Before there was nothing left to do but kill.

Now we squeal and squirm, and shift and shuffle blame
On the paltry paladins that hold command
Because we let them. But God is not mocked;
Hell-gates are open; we could have kept them locked.
If it be shame to slay, on us the shame,
And if we die, we die by our own hand.

ARCHIBALD MACLEISH
1892-

173 *Immortal Autumn*

I SPEAK this poem now with grave and level voice
In praise of autumn of the far-horn-winding fall
I praise the flower-barren fields the clouds the tall
Unanswering branches where the wind makes sullen noise

I praise the fall it is the human season now
No more the foreign sun does meddle at our earth
Enforce the green and bring the fallow land to birth
Nor winter yet weigh all with silence the pine bough.

But now in autumn with the black and outcast crows
Share we the spacious world the whispering year is gone
There is more room to live now the once secret dawn
Comes late by daylight and the dark unguarded goes

Between the mutinous brave burning of the leaves
And winter's covering of our hearts with his deep snow
We are alone there are no evening birds we know
The naked moon the tame stars circle at our eaves

It is the human season on this sterile air
Do words outcarry breath the sound goes on and on
I hear a dead man's cry from autumn long since gone

I cry to you beyond this bitter air.

ARCHIBALD MACLEISH
Memorial Rain

AMBASSADOR PUSER the ambassador
Reminds himself in French, felicitous tongue,
What these (young men no longer) lie here for
In rows that once, and somewhere else, were young—

> All night in Brussels the wind had tugged at my
>   door:
> I had heard the wind at my door and the trees
>   strung
> Taut, and to me who had never been before
> In that country it was a strange wind blowing
> Steadily, stiffening the walls, the floor,
> The roof of my room. I had not slept for knowing
> He too, dead, was a stranger in that land
> And felt beneath the earth in the wind's flowing
> A tightening of roots and would not understand,
> Remembering lake winds in Illinois,
> That strange wind. I had felt his bones in the
>   sand
> Listening.

—Reflects that these enjoy
Their country's gratitude, that deep repose,
That peace no pain can break, no hurt destroy,
That rest, that sleep—

> At Ghent the wind rose.
> There was a smell of rain and a heavy drag
>   Of wind in the hedges but not as the wind blows

ARCHIBALD MACLEISH

Over fresh water when the waves lag
Foaming and the willows huddle and it will rain:
I felt him waiting.

                —Indicates the flag
Which (may he say) enisles in Flanders' plain
This little field these happy, happy dead
Have made America—

                In the ripe grain
The wind coiled glistening, darted, fled,
Dragging its heavy body: at Waereghem
The wind coiled in the grass above his head:
Waiting—listening—

                —Dedicates to them
This earth their bones have hallowed, this last gift
A grateful country—

                Under the dry grass stem
The words are blurred, are thickened, the words sift
Confused by the rasp of the wind, by the thin grating
Of ants under the grass, the minute shift
And tumble of dusty sand separating
From dusty sand. The roots of the grass strain,
Tighten, the earth is rigid, waits—he is waiting—

And suddenly, and all at once the rain!

ARCHIBALD MACLEISH

The living scatter, they run into houses, the wind
Is trampled under the rain, shakes free, is again
Trampled. The rain gathers, running in thinned
Spurts of water that ravel in the dry sand
Seeping in the sand under the grass roots, seeping
Between cracked boards to the bones of a
    clenched hand:
The earth relaxes, loosens; he is sleeping,
He rests, he is quiet, he sleeps in a strange land.

175   1933

'The first I knew was the spirit of my fellow, Elpenor, whose body was not yet interred under the ample ground. We had left him unwept and unburied in the halls of Circe, for that these other labours came upon us urgently. When I saw him I had compassion and sharply cried across to him: "Elpenor, how come you here into the gloomy shades? Your feet have been quicker than my ship." He ... answered me:'—From Book XI of the Odyssey: Lawrence's translation.

IT is I, Odysseus—Elpenor:
Oarsman: death is between us:

Three days I have waited you
Coming my own way
Not your way

(The oar-handle hard to the nipple)
Not being come in the ship:

ARCHIBALD MACLEISH

Neither by dry earth
There being no dry earth

But roundabout: by an art:
By the deft-in-air-darting

Way of an art severing
Earth or air or whatever:

And the place I believe to be Hell from the
Many dead and the pelts of

Great captains: emperors:
Princes: leaders of men:

Their rumps turned round to the wind:
And the rich with their eyes hidden:

And the redblooded twofisted gogetting
He-ghosts froghonking wretchedly:

And from cairns and from creeks and from rock
    piles
And out of the holes of foxes

Fools booming like oracles:
Philosophers promising more

And worse to come of it yet
And proving it out of the textbooks:

ARCHIBALD MACLEISH

Also the young men
Their rears strung out on the fences

Watching for shifts in the breeze:
And beyond under the lee are the

Actual dead: the millions
Only a god could have killed—

Millions starving for corn with
Mountains of waste corn and

Millions cold for a house with
Cities of empty houses and

Millions naked for cloth and the
Looms choked with the cloth-weave:

The place I believe to be Hell from the
Cold and the cries and the welter of

Kings dukes dictators
Heroes headmen of cities

Ranting orations from balconies
Boasting to lead us back to the

Other days: to the odour of
Cooked leeks in the cold and our

ARCHIBALD MACLEISH

Wives and the well-known landmarks—
To the normal life of a man as in

Old days and in sun:
The noon's work done

And the butterflies in their pairs
Under the beams of the areas:

Is it to these shores
Odysseus contriver of horses
You of all men born

Come—and alive—demanding
The way back to your land—
The way back to the sands and the

Boat-grooved beaches of years
Before the war and the spear-handling?

Wishful still to return
Do you ask way by the earth or by

Dark sea to a country
Known under other suns?

Roads on the sea fade:
And only the old ladies

ARCHIBALD MACLEISH

Remembering red coats
Hope to return to the lotuses:

Let tit-formed Tiresias tell you
Tasting the bloody helm
The way back by the fells and the

Hate and the wars and the envy of
Men aroused against men—
With a Heaven-on-earth at the end of it!

For myself—if you ask me—
There's no way back over sea water

Nor by earth's oaks nor beyond them:
There is only the way on:

You had best—if you ask me—
Push on from this place to the seaward

Laying your course close in
Where Tiresias' sirens sing of the

Dialectical hope
And the kind of childish utopia

Found in a small boys' school—
Destiny written in Rules:

Life as the Teacher left it:
Work as the answer to everything—

ARCHIBALD MACLEISH

Driving her on through
Till you hear the words of that music:

Till you see well how the white and
Grey of those rocks is the white and

Grey not of dead men's ribs
But the stain of the seagulls' dribblings:

You had best—trusting neither to
Charts nor to prophets but seamanship—

You had best—if you ask me—
Sail on by the sun to the seaward

Till you come to a clean place
With the smell of the pine in your faces and

Broom and a bitter turf
And the larks blown over the surf and the

Rocks red to the wave-height:
No sound but the wave's:

No call of a cock from the
Windward shore nor of oxen—

Gull's shadow for hawk's:
Gull's cry for the hawk's cry—

On by the open sea
To a land with a clean beach

ARCHIBALD MACLEISH

An unploughed country
Pure under cleansing sun

With the dung burned dry on the gravel
And only the sand to have

And begin it again: start over
Forgetting the raised loaves and the

Fat cows and the larders of
Sweating stone—the arms of a

Naked girl under lamb-skins:
Begin it again with the hammer of

Hard rain on your heads and the
Raw fern for your bedding and

Thirst and the thorn to grow—
Bringing yourselves to a home
By your own arms and the boat in

Spite of gods and the prophecy:
Who here of the soft and the

Boneless dead will hinder you?
Rich men? wise ones? kings?

Dictators? adolescents
Screaming from well-lined nests?

ARCHIBALD MACLEISH

Or Tiresias: he that in Hell
Drunken with blood: foretelling the

Future day by the past:
Serving time for a master:

Teaches your living selves
That the dooms of the Fates are inevitable?

You have only to push on
To whatever it is that's beyond us

Showing the flat of your sword and they'll
Lick sand from before you!

You have only to cross this place
And launch ship and get way on her

Working her out with the oars to the
Full wind and go forward and

Bring yourselves to a home:
To a new land: to an ocean

Never sailed: not to Ithaca:
Not to your beds—but the withering

Seaweed under the thorn and the
Gulls and another morning. . . .

ARCHIBALD MACLEISH

As long as you bury me there on the beach
With my own oar stuck in the sand
So that ships standing along in
May see the stick of it straighter (though
    grey) than the
Olives: and ease all: and say—
'There is some man dead there that once pulled
'Water as we do with these and the thing is his
'Oarsweep': as long as you bury me there
What will it matter to me if my name
Lacks and the fat-leaved beach-plants cover my
Mound and the wood of the oar goes silver as
Drift sea wood goes silver—

JOHN GILLESPIE MAGEE

1923-1942

176 *High Flight*

OH, I have slipped the surly bonds of earth
  And danced the skies on laughter-silvered wings;
Sunward I've climbed and joined the tumbling mirth
Of sun-split clouds—and done a hundred things
You have not dreamed of—wheeled and soared and
    swung
High in the sunlit silence. Hov'ring there,
I've chased the shouting wind along and flung
My eager craft through footless halls of air.

JOHN GILLESPIE MAGEE

Up, up the long delirious, burning blue
I've topped the wind-swept heights with easy grace,
Where never lark, or even eagle, flew;
And, while with silent, lifting mind I've trod
The high untrespassed sanctity of space,
Put out my hand and touched the face of God.

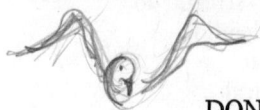

DON MARQUIS

1878-1937

177 *the hen and the oriole*

well boss did it
ever strike you that a
hen regrets it just as
much when they wring her
neck as an oriole but
nobody has any
sympathy for a hen because
she is not beautiful
while everyone gets
sentimental over the
oriole and says how
shocking to kill the
lovely thing this thought
comes to my mind
because of the earnest
endeavour of a
gentleman to squash me
yesterday afternoon when i

DON MARQUIS

was riding up in the
elevator if i had been a
butterfly he would have
said how did that
beautiful thing happen to
find its way into
these grimy city streets do
not harm the splendid
creature but let it
fly back to its rural
haunts again beauty always
gets the best of
it be beautiful boss
a thing of beauty is a
joy for ever
be handsome boss and let
who will be clever is
the sad advice
of your ugly little friend

                      archy

ANNE MARRIOTT

1913-

The Wind our Enemy

I

Wind
flattening its gaunt furious self against
the naked siding, knifing in the wounds
of time, pausing to tear aside the last
old scab of paint.

ANNE MARRIOTT

Wind
surging down the cocoa-coloured seams
of summer-fallow, darting in about
white hoofs and brown, snatching the sweaty cap
shielding red eyes.

Wind
filling the dry mouth with bitter dust
whipping the shoulders worry-bowed too soon,
soiling the water pail, and in grim prophecy
graying the hair.

II

The wheat in spring was like a giant's bolt of silk
Unrolled over the earth.
When the wind sprang
It rippled as if a great broad snake
Moved under the green sheet
Seeking its outward way to light.
In autumn it was an ocean of flecked gold
Sweet as a biscuit, breaking in crisp waves
That never shattered, never blurred in foam.
That was the last good year. . . .

. . . . . .

VI

Relief
  'God, we tried so hard to stand alone!'

Relief
  'Well, we can't let the kids go cold.'
  They trudge away to school swinging half-empty
    lard-pails,

to shiver in the schoolhouse (unpainted seven
>   years),
learning from a blue-lipped girl
almost as starved as they.

Relief cars
>   'Apples, they say, and clothes!'
>   The folks in town get their pick first,
>   Then their friends—
>   'Eight miles for us to go so likely we
>   won't get much—'
>   'Maybe we'll get the batteries charged up and
>   have
>   the radio to kind of brighten things—'

Insurgents march in Spain

Japs bomb Chinese

Airliner lost

'Maybe we're not as badly off as some—'
>   'Maybe there'll be a war and we'll get paid to
>   fight—'
>   'Maybe—'
>   'See if Eddie Cantor's on tonight!'

VII
>   People grew bored
>   Well-fed in the east and west
>   By stale, drought-area tales,
>   Bored by relief whinings,

ANNE MARRIOTT

Preferred their own troubles.
So those who still had stayed
On the scorched prairie,
Found even sympathy
Seeming to fail them
Like their own rainfall.

'Well—let's forget politics,
Forget the wind, our enemy!
Let's forget farming, boys,
Let's put on a dance tonight!
Mrs. Smith'll bring a cake.
Mrs. Olsen's coffee's swell!'

The small uneven schoolhouse floor
Scraped under big work-boots
Cleaned for the evening's fun,
Gasoline lamps whistled.
One Hungarian boy
Snapped at a shrill guitar,
A Swede from out north of town
Squeezed an acordion dry,
And a Scotchwoman from Ontario
Made the piano dance
In time to 'The Mocking Bird'
And 'When I Grow too Old to Dream,'
Only taking time off
To swing in a square-dance,
Between ten and half-past three.

ANNE MARRIOTT

Yet in the morning
Air peppered thick with dust,
All the night's happiness
Seemed far away, unreal
Like a lying mirage,
Or the icy-white glare
Of the alkali slough.

VIII

Presently the dark dust seemed to build a wall
That cut them off from east and west and north;
Kindness and honesty, things they used to know,
Seemed blown away and lost
In frantic soil.
At last they thought
Even God and Christ were hidden
By the false clouds.
—Dust-blinded to the staring parable,
Each wind-splintered timber like a pain-bent Cross.
Calloused, groping fingers, trembling
With overwork and fear,
Ceased trying to clutch at some faith in the dark,
Thin sick courage fainted, lacking hope.
But tightened, tangled nerves scream to the brain
If there is no hope, give them forgetfulness!
The cheap light of the beer-parlour grins out,
Promising shoddy security for an hour.
The Finn who makes bad liquor in his barn
Grows fat on groaning emptiness of souls.

ANNE MARRIOTT

IX

The sun goes down. Earth like a thick black coin
Leans its round rim against the yellowed sky.
The air cools. Kerosene lamps are filled and lit
In dusty windows. Tired bodies crave to lie
In bed for ever. Chores are done at last.
A thin horse neighs drearily. The chickens drowse,
Replete with grasshoppers that have gnawed and scraped
Shrivelled garden-leaves. No sound from the gaunt cows.

Poverty, hand in hand with fear, two great
Shrill-jointed skeletons stride loudly out
Across the pitiful fields, none to oppose.
Courage is roped with hunger, chained with doubt.
Only against the yellow sky, a part
Of the jetty silhouette of barn and house
Two figures stand, heads close, arms locked,
And suddenly some spirit seems to rouse
And gleam, like a thin sword, tarnished, bent,
But still shining in the spared beauty of moon,
As his strained voice says to her, 'We're not licked yet!
It must rain again—it *will*! Maybe—soon—'

X

Wind
in a lonely laughterless shrill game
with broken wash-boiler, bucket without
a handle, Russian thistle, throwing up
sections of soil.

ANNE MARRIOTT

God, will it never rain again? What about
those clouds out west? No, that's just dust, as
    thick
and stifling now as winter underwear.
No rain, no crop, no feed, no faith, only
wind.

179   Woodyards in Rain

THE smell of woodyards in the rain is strong
like six-foot lumberjacks with hairy chests
and thick axe-leathered hands.
The scent is raw and slices through
pale drizzle and dull mist
biting the sense.
I like to watch piled wetness dripping off
the yellow-brown stacked shingles,
while behind
the smoke churns up in black revolving towers
from lean mill chimneys.
Now the broad-hipped tugs
sniff through the squall and swing the oblong booms
by tar-stained wharves,
as with a last fierce gesture rain
small-pocks the oil-green water with a hurled
ten million wire nails.

180   Sandstone

IN this buff-gray cliff
Ash-crumbling under rock-blow,
Gouged by the sea's claws,
See the prints of the old generations.

ANNE MARRIOTT

Slice the stone cleanly, see
Webbed beech-leaf signature,
Ribbed shell-mark where now no shell is,
Soft wood time-turned flinty,
Bone of the unknown, unvisioned creature
Once as your bone.

Wind sucks broken sand with a terrible breathing,
Stone that shattered bone by bone is shattered,
Sea snatches out taloned green fingers
To shatter all;
Outjut of sandstone falls and is crumb and is dust.

See the path, upward in stone,
To where strong trees bind encouraged soil together.
On atrophied fallen, forgotten,
Stands steady the supple new growth
Beyond the strained stretch of the clutching tide.

JOHN MASEFIELD
1878-

181 *Sea-Fever*

I MUST go down to the seas again, to the lonely sea
    and the sky,
And all I ask is a tall ship, and a star to steer her by,
And the wheel's kick and the wind's song and the white
    sail's shaking,
And a grey mist on the sea's face and a grey dawn
    breaking.

JOHN MASEFIELD

I must go down to the seas again, for the call of the running tide
Is a wild call and a clear call that may not be denied;
And all I ask is a windy day with the white clouds flying,
And the flung spray and the blown spume, and the seagulls crying.

I must go down to the seas again, to the vagrant gypsy life,
To the gull's way and the whale's way where the wind's like a whetted knife;
And all I ask is a merry yarn from a laughing fellow-rover,
And quiet sleep and a sweet dream when the long trick's over.

The Passing Strange

OUT of the earth to rest or range
Perpetual in perpetual change,
The unknown passing through the strange.

Water and saltness held together
To tread the dust and stand the weather
And plough the field and stretch the tether,

To pass the wine-cup and be witty,
Water the sands and build the city,
Slaughter like devils and have pity,

JOHN MASEFIELD

Be red with rage and pale with lust,
Make beauty come, make peace, make trust,
Water and saltness mixed with dust;

Drive over earth, swim under sea,
Fly in the eagle's secrecy,
Guess where the hidden comets be;

Know all the deathy seeds that still
Queen Helen's beauty, Caesar's will,
And slay them even as they kill;

Fashion an altar for a rood,
Defile a continent with blood,
And watch a brother starve for food;

Love like a madman, shaking, blind,
Till self is burnt into a kind
Possession of another mind;

Brood upon beauty, till the grace
Of beauty with the holy face
Brings peace into the bitter place;

Probe in the lifeless granites, scan
The stars for hope, for guide, for plan;
Live as a woman or a man;

Fasten to lover or to friend,
Until the heart break at the end
The break of death that cannot mend;

JOHN MASEFIELD

Then to lie useless, helpless, still,
Down in the earth, in dark, to fill
The roots of grass or daffodil.

Down in the earth, in dark, alone,
A mockery of the ghost in bone,
The strangeness, passing the unknown.

Time will go by, that outlasts clocks,
Dawn in the thorps will rouse the cocks,
Sunset be glory on the rocks:

But it, the thing, will never heed
Even the rootling from the seed
Thrusting to suck it for its need.

. . . . . .

Since moons decay and suns decline,
How else should end this life of mine?
Water and saltness are not wine.

But in the darkest hour of night
When even the foxes peer for sight,
The byre-cock crows; he feels the light.

So, in this water mixed with dust,
The byre-cock spirit crows from trust
That death will change because it must;

For all things change, the darkness changes,
The wandering spirits change their ranges,
The corn is gathered to the granges.

JOHN MASEFIELD

The corn is sown again, it grows;
The stars burn out, the darkness goes;
The rhythms change, they do not close.

They change, and we, who pass like foam,
Like dust blown through the streets of Rome,
Change ever, too; we have no home,

Only a beauty, only a power,
Sad in the fruit, bright in the flower,
Endlessly erring for its hour,

But gathering, as we stray, a sense
Of Life, so lovely and intense,
It lingers when we wander hence,

That those who follow feel behind
Their backs, when all before is blind,
Our joy, a rampart to the mind.

Sonnet XXIX

IF I could come again to that dear place
Where once I came, where Beauty lived
    and moved,
Where, by the sea, I saw her face to face,
That soul alive by which the world has loved;
If, as I stood at gaze among the leaves,
She would appear again as once before,
While the red herdsman gathered up his sheaves
And brimming waters trembled up the shore;

JOHN MASEFIELD

If, as I gazed, her Beauty that was dumb
In that old time, before I learned to speak,
Would lean to me and revelation come,
Words to the lips and colour to the cheek,
Joy with its searing-iron would burn me wise;
I should know all, all powers, all mysteries.

GEORGE MEREDITH
1828-1909

184   *Lucifer in Starlight*

ON a starred night Prince Lucifer uprose.
   Tired of his dark dominion swung the fiend
Above the rolling ball in cloud part screened,
Where sinners hugged their spectre of repose.
Poor prey to his hot fit of pride were those.
And now upon his western wing he leaned,
Now his huge bulk o'er Afric's sands careened,
Now the black planet shadowed Arctic snows.

Soaring through wider zones that pricked his scars
With memory of the old revolt from Awe,
He reached a middle height, and at the stars,
Which are the brain of heaven, he looked, and sank.
Around the ancient track marched, rank on rank,
The army of unalterable law.

GEORGE MEREDITH

185 *Dirge in Woods*

A WIND sways the pines,
   And below
Not a breath of wild air;
Still as the mosses that glow
On the flooring and over the lines
Of the roots here and there.
The pine-tree drops its dead;
They are quiet, as under the sea.
Overhead, overhead
Rushes life in a race,
As the clouds the clouds chase;
   And we go,
As we drop like the fruits of the tree,
   Even we,
   Even so.

186 *Woodland Peace*

SWEET as Eden is the air,
   And Eden-sweet the ray.
No paradise is lost for them
Who foot by branching root and stem,
And lightly with the woodland share
   The change of night and day.

Here all say,
We serve her, even as I:
We brood, we strive to sky,
We gaze upon decay,

GEORGE MEREDITH

We wot of life through death,
How each feeds each we spy;
And is a tangle round,
Are patient; what is dumb
We question not, nor ask
The silent to give sound,
The hidden to unmask,
The distant to draw near.

And this the woodland saith:
I know not hope or fear;
I take whate'er may come:
I raise my head to aspects fair,
From foul I turn away.

Sweet as Eden is the air,
    And Eden-sweet the ray.

CHARLOTTE MEW
1870-1928

187   *In the Fields*

LORD, when I look at lovely things which pass,
    Under old trees the shadow of young leaves
Dancing to please the wind along the grass,
    Or the gold stillness of the August sun on the
        August sheaves;
Can I believe there is a heavenlier world than this?
    And if there is

Will the strange heart of any everlasting thing
    Bring me these dreams that take my breath away?
They come at evening with the home-flying rooks and
        the scent of hay,
    Over the fields. They come in Spring.

188   *Moorland Night*

MY face is against the grass—the moorland grass
    is wet—
    My eyes are shut against the grass, against my lips
        there are the little blades,
        Over my head the curlews call,
    And now there is the night wind in my hair;
My heart is against the grass and the sweet earth;—
    it has gone still, at last.
        It does not want to beat any more,
            And why should it beat?
        This is the end of the journey;
            The Thing is found.

        This is the end of all the roads—
    Over the grass there is the night-dew
And the wind that drives up from the sea along the
        moorland road;
    I hear a curlew start out from the heath
    And fly off, calling through the dusk,
        The wild, long, rippling call.
    The Thing is found and I am quiet with the earth.
Perhaps the earth will hold it, or the wind, or that
        bird's cry,

But it is not for long in any life I know. This cannot stay,
Not now, not yet, not in a dying world, with me, for very long.
    I leave it here:
      And one day the wet grass may give it back—
      One day the quiet earth may give it back—
    The calling birds may give it back as they go by—
To someone walking on the moor who starves for love and will not know
    Who gave it to all these to give away;
    Or, if I come and ask for it again,
      Oh! then, to me.

189   *I Have been through the Gates*

HIS heart, to me, was a place of palaces and pinnacles and shining towers;
I saw it then as we see things in dreams,—I do not remember how long I slept;
I remember the trees, and the high, white walls, and how the sun was always on the towers;
The walls are standing today, and the gates: I have been through the gates, I have groped, I have crept
Back, back. There is dust in the streets, and blood; they are empty; darkness is over them;
His heart is a place with the lights gone out, forsaken by great winds and the heavenly rain, unclean and unswept,
Like the heart of the holy city, old, blind, beautiful Jerusalem,
Over which Christ wept.

EDNA ST. VINCENT MILLAY
1892-

190 *'Love is not all'*

LOVE is not all; it is not meat nor drink
Nor slumber nor a roof against the rain,
Nor yet a floating spar to men that sink
And rise and sink and rise and sink again;
Love can not fill the thickened lung with breath,
Nor clean the blood, nor set the fractured bone;
Yet many a man is making friends with death
Even as I speak, for lack of love alone.
It well may be that in a difficult hour,
Pinned down by pain and moaning for release,
Or nagged by want past resolution's power,
I might be driven to sell your love for peace,
Or trade the memory of this night for food.
It well may be. I do not think I would.

191 *'I know I am but Summer'*

I KNOW I am but summer to your heart,
And not the full four seasons of the year;
And you must welcome from another part
Such noble moods as are not mine, my dear.
No gracious weight of golden fruits to sell
Have I, nor any wise and wintry thing;
And I have loved you all too long and well
To carry still the high sweet breast of Spring.
Wherefore I say: O love, as summer goes,
I must be gone, steal forth with silent drums,
That you may hail anew the bird and rose
When I come back to you, as summer comes.
Else will you seek, at some not distant time,
Even your summer in another clime.

EDNA ST. VINCENT MILLAY

192 Anselmo Speaks
(From 'Conversation at Midnight')

THERE is no peace on earth today save the peace in the heart
At home with God. From that sure habitation
The heart looks forth upon the sorrows of the savage world
And pities them, and ministers to them; but is not implicated.
All else has failed, as it must always fail.
No man can be at peace with his neighbour who is not at peace
With himself; the troubled mind is a trouble maker.

There is no freedom like the freedom of a man who sees his duty plain
And does it without demur; the edges of the torn brain
In him knit properly and heal;
The jangled bells are tuned, and peal
Once more from the sunny belfry in a morning clear and mild
Like to those mornings when he woke and wondered
What rapture was in store,—and it was only the simple day!
Bright mornings when he was a child.

How sweet when the battle is lost to unbuckle from the weary shoulders
The straps that cut and gall,

And let the heavy armour fall;
Let clatter to the floor and abandon where it lies
The shield whereon he took
All day shock upon shock
Of the opposing lance, his angel in disguise.

The act of complete submission to the Divine Will
Is to you an ignominious act,
An expedient of the cruelly pressed, an ugly pact
To save the soul at the expense of the soul's pride:
A mess of pottage in exchange for a princely heritage
  denied.
Can you not see that to surrender darkness to light is
  to be still
Valiant, and more valiant than before, and at length
  victor?
Or do you think so ill
Of light, as such, that it must walk in your Triumph
  as planned, and the way for it cleared
By a blind lictor?

   * * *

Anselmo said, and took in his brown hands
Quietly the small ebony crucifix
That hung between his knees, 'Knowledge expands,
And men grow canny; yet if they cannot mix
Science and Jesus, they leave Jesus out—
Though Science, like the ogre on the mat,
Turns into fog, snake, demon, leaves in doubt
His face for ever; and Christ has not done that.

EDNA ST. VINCENT MILLAY

Out of such peace as can be troubled only
By your distress, I spoke; and I have erred.
You heard me through with deference; I saw plainly
You strove to get my drift—and got no word.
I am chagrined, like one who has defined
The colours of sunset to a friend born blind.'

After a solemn pause, Anselmo said,
'I think I'll play some Bach, if you can stand
My noise. Go right on talking, please!' and spread
Over the pedals of the concert grand
Ricardo could not play, but kept in tune
Always, in hope someone might call who could,
His broad black boots, twitched up his gown, and soon
Built Peace—from felt, wire, ivory, and wood.

Nobody talked, although it seemed that some
Preferred to talk, were cowed into this hush;
Ricardo not—he cared not whence might come
This beauty, so it came; the mutinous flush
Of John said, Jesus had a champion there
Unjustly come by, tricky, not quite fair.

Anselmo closed the piano. 'I'm afraid I must go,
Ricardo,' he said; 'I have some work to do.
Good-night to you all.'
Ricardo went with him into the hall.
At the door Anselmo turned and said gently, in his
    fine voice free from unction and warm,

EDNA ST. VINCENT MILLAY

'*Dominus vobiscum;*' then looked at Ricardo with a
    look both quizzical and sad.
Ricardo, returning the look with deep affection,
    gravely replied,
'*Et cum spiritu tuo.*'

HAROLD MONRO
1879-1932

193   *Children of Love*

THE holy boy
Went from his mother out in the cool of the day
Over the sun-parched fields
And in among the olives shining green and shining
    grey.

There was no sound,
No smallest voice of any shivering stream.
Poor sinless little boy,
He desired to play, and to sing; he could only sigh
    and dream.

Suddenly came
Running along to him naked, with curly hair,
That rogue of the lovely world,
That other beautiful child whom the virgin Venus
    bare.

HAROLD MONRO

The holy boy
Gazed with those sad blue eyes that all men know.
Impudent Cupid stood
Panting, holding an arrow and pointing his bow.

(Will you not play?
Jesus, run to him, run to him, swift for our joy.
Is he not holy like you?
Are you afraid of his arrows, O beautiful dreaming
    boy?)

And now they stand
Watching one another with timid gaze;
Youth has met youth in the wood,
But holiness will not change its melancholy ways.

Cupid at last
Draws his bow and softly lets fly a dart.
Smile for a moment, sad world!—
It has grazed the white skin and drawn blood from
    the sorrowful heart.

Now, for delight,
Cupid tosses his locks and goes wantonly near;
But the child that was born to the cross
Has let fall on his cheek, for the sadness of life, a
    compassionate tear.

Marvellous dream!
Cupid has offered his arrows for Jesus to try:
He has offered his bow for the game,
But Jesus went weeping away, and left him there
    wondering why.

HAROLD MONRO

194 *The Nightingale near the House*

HERE is the soundless cypress on the lawn:
　　It listens, listens. Taller trees beyond
Listen. The moon at the unruffled pond
　　Stares. And you sing, you sing.

That star-enchanted song falls through the air
From lawn to lawn down terraces of sound,
Darts in white arrows on the shadowed ground;
　　While all the night you sing.

My dreams are flowers to which you are a bee,
As all night long I listen, and my brain
Receives your song, then loses it again
　　In moonlight on the lawn.

Now is your voice a marble high and white,
Then like a mist on fields of paradise;
Now is a raging fire, then is like ice,
　　Then breaks, and it is dawn.

195 *Milk for the Cat*

WHEN the tea is brought at five o'clock,
　　And all the neat curtains are drawn with care,
The little black cat with bright green eyes
Is suddenly purring there.

At first she pretends, having nothing to do,
She has come in merely to blink by the grate,
But, though tea may be late or the milk may be sour,
She is never late.

HAROLD MONRO

And presently her agate eyes
Take a soft large milky haze,
And her independent casual glance
Becomes a stiff, hard gaze.

Then she stamps her claws or lifts her ears,
Or twists her tail and begins to stir,
Till suddenly all her lithe body becomes
One breathing, trembling purr.

The children eat and wriggle and laugh,
The two old ladies stroke their silk:
But the cat is grown small and thin with desire,
Transformed to a creeping lust for milk.

The white saucer like some full moon descends
At last from the clouds of the table above;
She sighs and dreams and thrills and glows,
Transfigured with love.

She nestles over the shining rim,
Buries her chin in the creamy sea;
Her tail hangs loose; each drowsy paw
Is doubled under each bending knee.

A long dim ecstasy holds her life;
Her world is an infinite shapeless white,
Till her tongue has curled the last holy drop,
Then she sinks back into the night,

HAROLD MONRO

Draws and dips her body to heap
Her sleepy nerves in the great arm-chair,
Lies defeated and buried deep
Three or four hours unconscious there.

196 *From 'Trees'*

THERE are some men, of course, some men, I know,
Who, when they pass,
Seem like trees walking, and to grow
From earth, and, native in the grass,
(So taut their muscles) move on gliding roots.
They blossom every day: their fruits
Are always new and cover the happy ground.
Wherever they may stand
You hear inevitable sound
Of birds and branches, harvest and all delights
Of pastured and wooded land.
For them it is not dangerous to go
Each side that barrier moving to and fro:
They without trepidation undertake
Excursions into sleep, and safely come awake.

But it is different, different for me,
(Also for you I fear)
To whom a tree seems something more than tree,
And when we see,
Clustered together, two or three,
We almost are afraid to pass them near.
How beautifully they grow,

HAROLD MONRO

Above their stiles and lanes and watery places,
Crowding the brink of silence everywhere,
With branches dipping low
To smile toward us or to stroke our faces.
They drown us in their summer, and swirl round,
Leaving us faint: so nobody is free,
But always some surrounding ground
Is swamped and washed and covered in by tree.

They follow us and haunt us. We must build
Houses of wood. Our evening rooms are filled
With fragments of the forest: chairs and tables.
We swing our wooden doors;
Pile up, divide our sheds, byres, stables
With logs, make wooden stairs, lay wooden floors,
Sit, move and sleep among the limbs of trees,
Rejoicing to be near them. How men saw,
Chisel and hammer, carve and tease
All timber to their purpose, modelling
The forest in their chambers. And the raw
Wild stuff, built like a cupboard or a shelf,
Will crack and shiver in the night, and sing,
Reminding everybody of itself;
Out of decayed old centuries will bring
A sudden memory
Of growing tree.

SIR HENRY NEWBOLT
1862-1938

197 *Drake's Drum*

DRAKE he's in his hammock an' a thousand mile away,
  (Capten, art tha sleepin' there below?)
Slung atween the round shot in Nombre Dios Bay,
  An' dreamin' arl the time o' Plymouth Hoe.
Yarnder lumes the Island, yarnder lie the ships,
  Wi' sailor-lads a-dancin' heel-an'-toe,
An' the shore-lights flashin', an' the night-tide dashin',
  He sees et arl so plainly as he saw et long ago.

Drake he was a Devon man, an' ruled the Devon seas,
  (Capten, art tha sleepin' there below?)
Rovin' tho' his death fell, he went wi' heart at ease,
  An' dreamin' arl the time o' Plymouth Hoe.
'Take my drum to England, hang et by the shore,
  Strike et when your powder's runnin' low;
If the Dons sight Devon, I'll quit the port o' Heaven,
  An' drum them up the Channel as we drummed them long ago.'

Drake he's in his hammock till the great Armadas come,
  (Capten, art tha sleepin' there below?)
Slung atween the round shot, listenin' for the drum,
  An' dreamin' arl the time o' Plymouth Hoe.
Call him on the deep sea, call him up the Sound,
  Call him when ye sail to meet the foe;
Where the old trade's plyin' an' the old flag flyin'
  They shall find him ware an' wakin', as they found him long ago!

SIR HENRY NEWBOLT

'He Fell among Thieves'

'YE have robb'd,' said he, 'ye have slaughter'd and made an end,
 Take your ill-got plunder, and bury the dead:
What will ye more of your guest and sometime friend?'
 'Blood for our blood,' they said.

He laugh'd: 'If one may settle the score for five,
 I am ready; but let the reckoning stand till day:
I have loved the sunlight as dearly as any alive.'
 'You shall die at dawn,' said they.

He flung his empty revolver down the slope,
 He climb'd alone to the Eastward edge of the trees;
All night long in a dream untroubled of hope
 He brooded, clasping his knees.

He did not hear the monotonous roar that fills
 The ravine where the Yassin river sullenly flows;
He did not see the starlight on the Laspur hills,
 Or the far Afghan snows.

He saw the April noon on his books aglow,
 The wistaria trailing in at the window wide;
He heard his father's voice from the terrace below
 Calling him down to ride.

He saw the gray little church across the park,
 The mounds that hid the loved and honour'd dead;
The Norman arch, the chancel softly dark,
 The brasses black and red.

SIR HENRY NEWBOLT

He saw the School Close, sunny and green,
   The runner beside him, the stand by the parapet wall,
The distant tape, and the crowd roaring between,
   His own name over all.

He saw the dark wainscot and timber'd roof,
   The long tables, and the faces merry and keen,
The College Eight and their trainer dining aloof,
   The Dons on the dais serene.

He watch'd the liner's stem ploughing the foam,
   He felt her trembling speed and the thrash of her screw;
He heard her passengers' voices talking of home,
   He saw the flag she flew.

And now it was dawn. He rose strong on his feet,
   And strode to his ruin'd camp below the woods;
He drank the breath of the morning cool and sweet,
   His murderers round him stood.

Light on the Laspur hills was broadening fast,
   The blood-red snow-peaks chill'd to a dazzling white;
He turn'd, and saw the golden circle at last,
   Cut by the Eastern height.

'O glorious Life, Who dwellest in earth and sun,
   I have lived, I praise and adore Thee.' A sword swept.
Over the pass the voices one by one
   Faded, and the hill slept.

SIR HENRY NEWBOLT
Clifton Chapel

THIS is the Chapel: here, my son,
　　Your father thought the thoughts of youth,
And heard the words that one by one
　　The touch of Life has turned to truth.
Here in a day that is not far
　　You too may speak with noble ghosts
Of manhood and the vows of war
　　You made before the Lord of Hosts.

To set the cause above renown,
　　To love the game beyond the prize,
To honour, while you strike him down,
　　The foe that comes with fearless eyes;
To count the life of battle good,
　　And dear the land that gave you birth,
And dearer yet the brotherhood
　　That binds the brave of all the earth—

My son, the oath is yours: the end
　　Is His, Who built the world of strife,
Who gave His children Pain for friend,
　　And Death for surest hope of life.
Today and here the fight's begun,
　　Of the great fellowship you're free;
Henceforth the School and you are one,
　　And what You are, the race shall be.

God send you fortune: yet be sure,
Among the light that gleam and pass,
You'll live to follow none more pure
　　Than that which glows on yonder brass.

SIR HENRY NEWBOLT

'Qui procul hinc,' the legend's writ,—
 The frontier-grave is far away—
'Qui ante diem periit:
 'Sed miles, sed pro patria.'

ROBERT NICHOLS
1893-

200   *The Sprig of Lime*

HE lay, and those who watched him were amazed
 To see unheralded beneath the lids
Twin tears, new-gathered at the price of pain,
Start and at once run crookedly athwart
Cheeks channelled long by pain, never by tears.
So desolate, too, the sigh next uttered
They had wept also, but his great lips moved,
And bending down one heard, *'A sprig of lime;
Bring me a sprig of lime.'* Whereat she stole
With dumb sign forth to pluck the thing he craved.

So lay he till a lime-twig had been snapped
From some still branch that swept the outer grass
Far from the silver pillar of the bole,
Which mounting past the house's crusted roof
Split into massy limbs, crossed boughs, a maze
Of close-compacted intercontorted staffs
Bowered in foliage, wherethrough the sun
Shot sudden showers of light or crystal spars,
Or wavered in a green and vitreous flood.

ROBERT NICHOLS

And all the while in faint and fainter tones,
Scarce audible on deepened evening's hush,
He framed his curious and last request
For *'lime, a sprig of lime'*. Her trembling hand
Closed his loose fingers on the awkward stem
Covered with gentle heart-shaped leaves
And under dangling, pale as honey-wax,
Square clusters of sweet-scented starry flowers.

She laid his bent arm back upon his breast,
Then watched above white knuckles clenched in prayer.
He never moved. Only at last his eyes
Opened, then brightened in such avid gaze
She feared the coma mastered him again . . .
But no; strange sobs rose chuckling in his throat,
A stranger ecstasy suffused the flesh
Of that just mask so sun-dried, gouged and old,
Which few—too few!—had loved, too many feared.
'Father!' she cried; 'Father!'
                       He did not hear.

She knelt and kneeling drank the scent of limes,
Blown round the slow blind by a vesperal gust,
Till the room swam. So the lime-incense blew
Into her life as once it had in his,
Though how and when and with what ageless charge
Of sorrow and deep joy how could she know?

Sweet lime that often at the height of noon
Diffusing dizzy fragrance from your boughs
Tasselled with blossoms more innumerable

ROBERT NICHOLS

Than the black bees, the uproar of whose toil
Filled your green vaults, winning such metheglin
As clouds their sappy cells, distil, as once
Ye used, your sunniest emanations
Toward the window where a woman kneels—
She who within that room in childish hours
Lay through the lasting murmur of blanch'd noon
Behind the sultry blind, now full, now flat,
Drinking anew of every odorous breath,
Supremely happy in her ignorance
Of Time that hastens hourly and of Death
Who need not haste. Scatter your fumes, O lime,
Loose from each hispid star of citron bloom,
Tangled beneath the labyrinthine boughs,
Cloud on such stinging cloud of exhalation
As reeks of youth, fierce life and summer's prime,
Though hardly now shall he in that dusk room
Savour your sweetness, since the very sprig,
Profuse of blossom and of essences,
He smells not, who in a paltering hand
Clasps it laid close his peaked and gleaming face
Propped in the pillow. Breathe silent, lofty lime,
Your curfew secrets out in fervid scent
To the attendant shadows! Tinge the air
Of the midsummer night that now begins,
At an owl's oaring flight from dusk to dusk
And downward caper of the giddy bat
Hawking against the lustre of bare skies,
With something of th' unfathomable bliss
He, who lies dying there, knew once of old
In the serene trance of a summer night,
When with th' abundance of his young bride's hair

ROBERT NICHOLS

Loosed on his breast he lay and dared not sleep,
Listening for the scarce motion of your boughs,
Which sighed with bliss as she with blissful sleep,
And drinking desperately each honied wave
Of perfume wafted past the ghostly blind,
Knew first th' implacable and bitter sense
Of Time that hastes and Death who need not haste.
Shed your last sweetness, limes!
       But now no more.
She, fruit of that night's love, she heeds you not,
Who bent, compassionate, to the dim floor,
Takes up the sprig of lime and presses it
In pain against the stumbling of her heart,
Knowing, untold, he cannot need it now.

ALFRED NOYES
1880-

The Barrel-Organ

THERE'S a barrel-organ carolling across a golden street
 In the City as the sun sinks low;
And the music's not immortal; but the world has made it sweet
 And fulfilled it with the sunset glow;
And it pulses through the pleasures of the City and the pain
 That surround the singing organ like a large eternal light;
And they've given it a glory and a part to play again
 In the Symphony that rules the day and night.

ALFRED NOYES

And now it's marching onward through the realms of
 old romance,
 And trolling out a fond familiar tune,
And now it's roaring cannon down to fight the King
 of France,
 And now it's prattling softly to the moon.
And all around the organ there's a sea without a shore
 Of human joys and wonders and regrets;
To remember and to recompense the music evermore
 For what the cold machinery forgets. . . .

    Yes; as the music changes,
      Like a prismatic glass,
    It takes the light and ranges
      Through all the moods that pass;
    Dissects the common carnival
      Of passions and regrets,
    And gives the world a glimpse of all
      The colours it forgets.

    And there *La Traviata* sighs
      Another sadder song;
    And there *Il Trovatore* cries
      A tale of deeper wrong;
    And bolder knights to battle go
      With sword and shield and lance,
    Than ever here on earth below
      Have whirled into—*a dance!*—

Go down to Kew in lilac-time, in lilac-time, in lilac-
 time;
 Go down to Kew in lilac-time (it isn't far from
 London!)

ALFRED NOYES

And you shall wander hand in hand with love in
summer's wonderland;
   Go down to Kew in lilac-time (it isn't far from
London!)

The cherry-trees are seas of bloom and soft perfume
and sweet perfume,
   The cherry trees are seas of bloom (and oh, so near
to London!)
And there, they say, when dawn is high and all the
world's a blaze of sky
   The cuckoo, though he's very shy, will sing a song
for London.

The Dorian nightingale is rare and yet they say
you'll find him there
   At Kew, at Kew in lilac-time (and oh, so near to
London!)
The linnet and the throstle, too, and after dark the
long halloo
   And golden-eyed *tu-whit, tu-whoo* of owls that ogle
London.

For Noah hardly knew a bird of any kind that isn't
heard
   At Kew, at Kew in lilac-time (and oh, so near to
London!)
And when the rose begins to pout and all the chestnut
spires are out
   You'll hear the rest without a doubt, all chorusing
for London:—

ALFRED NOYES

Come down to Kew in lilac-time, in lilac-time, in lilac-time;
  Come down to Kew in lilac-time (it isn't far from London!)
And you shall wander hand in hand with love in summer's wonderland;
  Come down to Kew in lilac-time (it isn't far from London!).

And then the troubadour begins to thrill the golden street
  In the City as the sun sinks low;
And in all the gaudy busses there are scores of weary feet
Marking time, sweet time, with a dull mechanic beat,
And a thousand hearts are plunging to a love they'll never meet,
Through the meadows of the sunset, through the poppies and the wheat,
  In the land where the dead dreams go.

Verdi, Verdi, when you wrote Il Trovatore did you dream
  Of the City when the sun sinks low,
Of the organ and the monkey and the many-coloured stream
On the Piccadilly pavement, of the myriad eyes that seem
To be litten for a moment with a wild Italian gleam
As *A che la morte* parodies the world's eternal theme
  And pulses with the sunset-glow?

ALFRED NOYES

There's a thief, perhaps, that listens with a face of
 frozen stone
  In the City as the sun sinks low;
There's a portly man of business with a balance of
 his own,
There's a clerk and there's a butcher of a soft repose-
 ful tone.
And they're all of them returning to the heavens they
 have known:
They are crammed and jammed in busses and—
 they're each of them alone
  In the land where the dead dreams go.

There's a very modish woman and her smile is very
 bland
  In the City as the sun sinks low;
And her hansom jingles onward, but her little jewelled
 hand
Is clenched a little tighter and she cannot understand
What she wants or why she wanders to that undis-
 covered land,
For the parties there are not at all the sort of thing
 she planned,
  In the land where the dead dreams go.

There's a rowing man that listens and his heart is
 crying out
  In the City as the sun sinks low;
For the barge, the eight, the Isis, and the coach's
 whoop and shout,

ALFRED NOYES

For the minute-gun, the counting and the long dishevelled rout,
For the howl along the tow-path and a fate that's still in doubt,
For a roughened oar to handle and a race to think about
In the land where the dead dreams go.

There's a labourer that listens to the voices of the dead
  In the City as the sun sinks low;
And his hand begins to tremble and his face to smoulder red
As he sees a loafer watching him and—there he turns his head
And stares into the sunset where his April love is fled,
For he hears her softly singing and his lonely soul is led
  Through the land where the dead dreams go.

There's an old and haggard demi-rep, it's ringing in her ears,
  In the City as the sun sinks low;
With the wild and empty sorrow of the love that blights and sears,
Oh, and if she hurries onward, then be sure, be sure she hears,
Hears and bears the bitter burden of the unforgotten years,
And her laugh's a little harsher and her eyes are brimmed with tears
  For the land where the dead dreams go.

ALFRED NOYES

There's a barrel-organ carolling across a golden street
  In the City as the sun sinks low;
Though the music's only Verdi there's a world to make it sweet
Just as yonder yellow sunset where the earth and heaven meet
Mellows all the sooty City! Hark, a hundred thousand feet
Are marching on to glory through the poppies and the wheat
  In the land where the dead dreams go.

    So it's Jeremiah, Jeremiah,
      What have you to say
    When you meet the garland girls
      Tripping on their way?

    All around my gala hat
      I wear a wreath of roses
    (A long and lonely year it is
      I've waited for the May!)
    If anyone should ask you,
      The reason why I wear it is—
    My own love, my true love,
      Is coming home today.

And it's, Buy a bunch of violets for the lady
  (It's lilac-time in London; it's lilac-time in London!)
Buy a bunch of violets for the lady
  While the sky burns blue above:

ALFRED NOYES

On the other side the street you'll find it shady
  (It's lilac-time in London; it's lilac-time in London!)
But buy a bunch of violets for the lady
  And tell her she's your own true love.

There's a barrel-organ carolling across a golden street
  In the City as the sun sinks glittering and slow;
And the music's not immortal; but the world has made it sweet
And enriched it with the harmonies that make a song complete
In the deeper heavens of music where the night and morning meet,
  As it dies into the sunset-glow;

And it pulses through the pleasures of the City and the pain
  That surround the singing organ like a large eternal light,
And they've given it a glory and a part to play again
  In the Symphony that rules the day and night.

> And there, as the music changes,
>   The song runs round again.
> Once more it turns and ranges
>   Through all its joy and pain,
> Dissects the common carnival
>   Of passions and regrets;
> And the wheeling world remembers all
>   The wheeling song forgets.

ALFRED NOYES

>Once more *La Traviata* sighs
>   Another sadder song:
>Once more *Il Trovatore* cries
>   A tale of deeper wrong;
>Once more the knights to battle go
>   With sword and shield and lance,
>Till once, once more, the shattered foe
>   Has whirled into—*a dance*!

Come down to Kew in lilac-time, in lilac-time, in lilac-time;
   Come down to Kew in lilac-time (it isn't far from London!)
And you shall wander hand in hand with love in summer's wonderland;
   Come down to Kew in lilac-time (it isn't far from London!)

202   *The Highwayman*

I

THE wind was a torrent of darkness among the gusty trees,
The moon was a ghostly galleon tossed upon cloudy seas,
The road was a ribbon of moonlight over the purple moor,
And the highwayman came riding—
      Riding—riding—
The highwayman came riding, up to the old inn-door.

ALFRED NOYES

He'd a French cocked-hat on his forehead, a bunch of lace at his chin,
A coat of the claret velvet, and breeches of brown doeskin;
They fitted with never a wrinkle: his boots were up to the thigh!
And he rode with a jewelled twinkle,
      His pistol butts a-twinkle,
His rapier hilt a-twinkle, under the jewelled sky.

Over the cobbles he clattered and clashed in the dark inn-yard,
And he tapped with his whip on the shutters, but all was locked and barred;
He whistled a tune to the window, and who should be waiting there
But the landlord's black-eyed daughter,
      Bess, the landlord's daughter,
Plaiting a dark red love-knot into her long black hair.

And dark in the dark old inn-yard a stable-wicket creaked
Where Tim the ostler listened; his face was white and peaked;
His eyes were hollows of madness, his hair like mouldy hay,
But he loved the landlord's daughter,
      The landlord's red-lipped daughter;—
Dumb as a dog he listened, and he heard the robber say—

ALFRED NOYES

'One kiss, my bonny sweetheart, I'm after a prize
    to-night,
But I shall be back with the yellow gold before the
    morning light;
Yet, if they press me sharply, and harry me through
    the day,
Then look for me by moonlight,
        Watch for me by moonlight,
I'll come to thee by moonlight, though hell should bar
    the way.'

He rose upright in the stirrups; he scarce could reach
    her hand,
But she loosened her hair i' the casement! His face
    burnt like a brand
As the black cascade of perfume came tumbling over
    his breast;
And he kissed its waves in the moonlight,
        (Oh, sweet black waves in the moonlight!)
Then he tugged at his rein in the moonlight, and
    galloped away to the West.

II

He did not come in the dawning; he did not come at
    noon;
And out o' the tawny sunset, before the rise o' the
    moon,
When the road was a gypsy's ribbon, looping the
    purple moor,
A red-coat troop came marching—
        Marching—marching—
King George's men came marching, up to the old
    inn-door.

ALFRED NOYES

They said no word to the landlord, they drank his ale instead,
But they gagged his daughter and bound her to the foot of her narrow bed;
Two of them knelt at her casement, with muskets at their side!
There was death at every window,
        And hell at one dark window,
For Bess could see, through her casement, the road that *he* would ride.

They had tied her up to attention, with many a sniggering jest;
They had bound a musket beside her, with the barrel beneath her breast!
'Now keep good watch!' and they kissed her.
She heard the dead man say—
Look for me by moonlight;
        Watch for me by moonlight;
I'll come to thee by moonlight, though hell should bar the way!

She twisted her hands behind her; but all the knots held good!
She writhed her hands till her fingers were wet with sweat or blood!
They stretched and strained in the darkness, and the hours crawled by like years,
Till now, on the stroke of midnight,
        Cold, on the stroke of midnight,
The tip of one finger touched it! The trigger at least was hers!

ALFRED NOYES

The tip of one finger touched it; she strove no more for the rest!
Up, she stood up to attention, with the barrel beneath her breast;
She would not risk their hearing; she would not strive again;
For the road lay bare in the moonlight,
    Blank and bare in the moonlight,
And the blood of her veins in the moonlight throbbed to her love's refrain.

Tlot-tlot; tlot-tlot! Had they heard it? The horse-hoofs ringing clear;
Tlot-tlot, tlot-tlot in the distance? Were they deaf that they did not hear?
Down the ribbon of moonlight, over the brow of the hill,
The highwayman came riding,
    Riding, riding!
The red-coats looked to their priming! She stood up, straight and still!

Tlot-tlot, in the frosty silence! *Tlot-tlot*, in the echoing night!
Nearer he came and nearer! Her face was like a light!
Her eyes grew wide for a moment; she drew one last deep breath,
Then her finger moved in the moonlight,
    Her musket shattered the moonlight,
Shattered her breast in the moonlight and warned him—with her death.

ALFRED NOYES

He turned; he spurred to the Westward; he did not
    know who stood
Bowed with her head o'er the musket, drenched with
    her own red blood!
Not till the dawn he heard it, and slowly blanched to
    hear
How Bess, the landlord's daughter,
        The landlord's black-eyed daughter,
Had watched for her love in the moonlight, and died
    in the darkness there.

Back he spurred like a madman, shrieking a curse to
    the sky,
With the white road smoking behind him, and his
    rapier brandished high!
Blood-red were his spurs in the golden noon; wine-red
    was his velvet coat,
When they shot him down on the highway,
        Down like a dog on the highway,
And he lay in his blood on the highway, with the
    bunch of lace at his throat.

      . . . . . .

And still of a winter's night, they say, when the wind
    is in the trees,
When the moon is a ghostly galleon tossed upon
    cloudy seas,
When the road is a ribbon of moonlight over the
    purple moor,
A highwayman comes riding—
        Riding—riding—
A highwayman comes riding, up to the old inn-door.

ALFRED NOYES

*Over the cobbles he clatters and clangs in the dark
    inn-yard;
And he taps with his whip on the shutters, but all is
    locked and barred;
He whistles a tune to the window, and who should
    be waiting there
But the landlord's black-eyed daughter,
        Bess; the landlord's daughter,
Plaiting a dark red love-knot into her long black hair.*

WILFRED OWEN
1893-1918

Strange Meeting

IT seemed that out of battle I escaped
Down some profound dull tunnel, long since scooped
Through granites which Titanic wars had groined.
Yet also there encumbered sleepers groaned,
Too fast in thought or death to be bestirred.
Then, as I probed them, one sprang up, and stared
With piteous recognition in fixed eyes,
Lifting distressful hands as if to bless.
And by his smile, I knew that sullen hall;
By his dead smile I knew we stood in Hell.
With a thousand pains that vision's face was grained;
Yet no blood reached there from the upper ground,
And no guns thumped, or down the flues made moan.
'Strange friend,' I said, 'here is no cause to mourn.'

WILFRED OWEN

'None,' said the other, 'save the undone years,
The hopelessness. Whatever hope is yours,
Was my life also; I went hunting wild
After the wildest beauty in the world,
Which lies not calm in eyes, or braided hair,
But mocks the steady running of the hour,
And if it grieves, grieves richlier than here.
For by my glee might many men have laughed,
And of my weeping something has been left,
Which must die now. I mean the truth untold,
The pity of war, the pity war distilled.
Now men will go content with what we spoiled,
Or, discontent, boil bloody, and be spilled.
They will be swift with swiftness of the tigress,
None will break ranks, though nations trek from progress.
Courage was mine, and I had mystery,
Wisdom was mine, and I had mastery;
To miss the march of this retreating world
Into vain citadels that are not walled.
Then, when much blood had clogged their chariot-wheels
I would go up and wash them from sweet wells,
Even with truths that lie too deep for taint.
I would have poured my spirit without stint
But not through wounds; not on the cess of war.
Foreheads of men have bled where no wounds were.
I am the enemy you killed, my friend.
I knew you in this dark; for so you frowned
Yesterday through me as you jabbed and killed.
I parried; but my hands were loath and cold.
Let us sleep now . . .'

WILFRED OWEN
Dulce et Decorum Est

BENT double, like old beggars under sacks,
    Knock-kneed, coughing like hags, we cursed through sludge,
Till on the haunting flares we turned our backs,
And towards our distant rest began to trudge.
Men marched asleep. Many had lost their boots,
But limped on, blood-shod. All went lame, all blind;
Drunk with fatigue; deaf even to the hoots
Of gas-shells dropping softly behind.

Gas! GAS! Quick, boys!—An ecstasy of fumbling
Fitting the clumsy helmets just in time,
But someone still was yelling out and stumbling
And flound'ring like a man in fire or lime.—
Dim through the misty panes and thick green light,
As under a green sea, I saw him drowning.

In all my dreams before my helpless sight
He plunges at me, guttering, choking, drowning.

If in some smothering dreams, you too could pace
Behind the wagon that we flung him in,
And watch the white eyes writhing in his face,
His hanging face, like a devil's sick of sin,
If you could hear, at every jolt, the blood
Come gargling from the froth-corrupted lungs
Bitten as the cud
Of vile, incurable sores on innocent tongues,—
My friend, you would not tell with such high zest
To children ardent for some desperate glory,
The old lie: *Dulce et decorum est
Pro patria mori.*

WILFRED OWEN

205 *The Parable of the Old Men
and the Young*

SO Abram rose, and clave the wood, and went,
And took the fire with him, and a knife.
And as they sojourned both of them together,
Isaac the first-born spake and said, My Father,
Behold the preparations, fire and iron,
But where the lamb for this burnt-offering?
Then Abram bound the youth with belts and straps,
And builded parapets and trenches there,
And stretchèd forth the knife to slay his son.
When lo! an angel called him out of heaven,
Saying, Lay not thy hand upon the lad,
Neither do anything to him. Behold,
A ram, caught in the thicket by its horns;
Offer the Ram of Pride instead of him.
But the old man would not do so, but slew his son,—
And half the seed of Europe, one by one.

206 *Apologia pro Poemate Meo*

I, too, saw God through mud,—
The mud that cracked on cheeks when wretches smiled.
War brought more glory to their eyes than blood,
And gave their laughs more glee than shakes a child.

Merry it was to laugh there—
Where death becomes absurd and life absurder.
For power was on us as we slashed bones bare
Not to feel sickness or remorse of murder.

331

WILFRED OWEN

I, too, have dropped off fear—
   Behind the barrage, dead as my platoon,
   And sailed my spirit surging, light and clear
   Past the entanglement where hopes lay strewn;

And witnessed exultation—
   Faces that used to curse me, scowl for scowl,
   Shine and lift up with passion of oblation,
   Seraphic for an hour; though they were foul.

I have made fellowships—
   Untold of happy lovers in old song,
   For love is not the binding of fair lips
   With the soft silk of eyes that look and long,

By Joy, whose ribbon slips,—
   But wound with war's hard wire whose stakes are strong;
   Bound with the bandage of the arm that drips;
   Knit in the welding of the rifle-thong.

I have perceived much beauty
   In the hoarse oaths that kept our courage straight;
   Heard music in the silentness of duty;
   Found peace where shell-storms spouted reddest spate.

Nevertheless, except you share
   With them in hell the sorrowful dark of hell,
   Whose world is but the trembling of a flare,
   And heaven but as the highway for a shell,

WILFRED OWEN

You shall not hear their mirth:
  You shall not come to think them well content
  By any jest of mine. These men are worth
  Your tears: you are not worth their merriment.

MARJORIE PICKTHALL
1883-1922

207   *Père Lalement*

I LIFT the Lord on high,
  Under the murmuring hemlock boughs, and see
The small birds of the forest lingering by
And making melody.
These are mine acolytes and these my choir,
And this mine altar in the cool green shade,
Where the wild, soft-eyed does draw nigh
  Wondering, as in the byre
Of Bethlehem the oxen heard Thy cry
And saw Thee, unafraid.

My boatmen sit apart,
  Wolf-eyed, wolf-sinewed, stiller than the trees.
Help me, O Lord, for very slow of heart
And hard of faith are these.
Cruel are they, yet Thy children. Foul are they,
Yet wert Thou born to save them utterly.
Then make me as I pray
  Just to their hates, kind to their sorrows, wise
After their speech, and strong before their free
Indomitable eyes.

MARJORIE PICKTHALL

Do the French lilies reign
Over Mont Royal and Stadacona still?
Up the St. Lawrence comes the spring again,
Crowning each southward hill
And blossoming pool with beauty, while I roam
Far from the perilous folds that are my home,
There where we built St. Ignace for our needs,
Shaped the rough roof tree, turned the first sweet sod,
St. Ignace and St. Louis, little beads
On the rosary of God.

Pines shall Thy pillars be,
Fairer than those Sidonian cedars brought
By Hiram out of Tyre, and each birch-tree
Shines like a holy thought.
But come no worshippers; shall I confess,
St. Francis-like, the birds of the wilderness?
Oh, with Thy love my lonely head uphold.
A wandering shepherd I, who hath no sheep;
A wandering soul, who hath no scrip, nor gold,
Nor anywhere to sleep.

My hour of rest is done;
On the smooth ripple lifts the long canoe;
The hemlocks murmur sadly as the sun
Slants his dim arrows through.
Whither I go I know not, nor the way,
Dark with strange passions, vext with heathen charms,
Holding I know not what of life or death;

MARJORIE PICKTHALL

Only be Thou beside me day by day,
Thy rod my guide and comfort, underneath
Thy everlasting arms.

208 *The Lamp of Poor Souls*

In many English churches before the Reformation there was kept a little lamp continually burning, called the Lamp of Poor Souls. People were reminded thereby to pray for the souls of those dead whose kinsfolk were too poor to pay for prayers and masses.

ABOVE my head the shields are stained with rust,
The wind has taken his spoil, the moth his part;
Dust of dead men beneath my knees, and dust,
Lord, in my heart.

Lay Thou the hand of faith upon my fears;
The priest has prayed, the silver bell has rung,
But not for him. O unforgotten tears,
He was so young!

Shine, little lamp, nor let thy light grow dim.
Into what vast, dread dreams, what lonely lands,
Into what griefs hath death delivered him
Far from my hands?

Cradled is he, with half his prayers forgot.
I cannot learn the level way he goes.
He whom the harvest hath remembered not
Sleeps with the rose.

MARJORIE PICKTHALL

Shine, little lamp, fed with sweet oil of prayers,
Shine, little lamp, as God's own eyes may shine,
When He treads softly down His starry stairs
And whispers, 'Thou art Mine.'

Shine, little lamp, for love hath fed thy gleam,
Shine, little soul, by God's own hands set free.
Cling to His arms and sleep, and, sleeping, dream
And, dreaming, look for me.

209 *A Modern Endymion*

YOU!—
    You stealing violets where the snail-tracks glisten
In the dew,
And the little secret roses when the doctor's back is
       turned—
Listen!
Listen, and I'll tell you how my window burned!

Burning silver ran about the pane in fires,
Piercing silver fires, and their points went creeping
All along the sidewalks and the branches and the wires
And the chimneys of the houses where the smoke was
       sleeping.
O, white, white, white,
Was my window of the night,
And the glass was dripping in the old cold flame,
And soon, soon, soon,
Underneath the little bars that barricade it black,

MARJORIE PICKTHALL

With the whiteness and the brightness dripping from
    her back,
The bare moon came,
Came the moon!

They cannot keep her out, O my secret, O my white,
Silver-throated goddess of the night, of the night.
They may stifle me all day, but by night I am free,
Waiting for the goddess to climb the walnut tree
In the gray asylum grounds
Where the watchman goes his rounds.
He never sees her mounting, limb by silver limb.
He never sees her counting the stairway of the stars
With her bright hair twining,—
She's just the moon to him,
Shining,—
Shining through my window with the black strong
    bars.
And close, close, close,
Closer than the dew-shine to the rose,
And near, near, near,
I am holding her all night, my terrible, my dear,
And the four gray walls
Run a drowning sluice of silver, and it falls
Where it will,—
Falls
Fierce and still,
Fierce and still—

Hush!
The little doctor's coming to take away your flowers!
If you run, run, run

MARJORIE PICKTHALL

Round the candleberry bush
In the pathway of the sun,
Maybe he won't find you, he won't follow you for hours.
But he can't touch me.
He can't find her, he can't feel her, he can't see, see, see
Her climbing to my window by the silver fruited tree.

EZRA POUND
1885-

Canto XIII

KUNG walked
    by the dynastic temple
and into the cedar grove,
    and then out by the lower river,
And with him Khieu Tchi
    and Tian the low speaking
And 'we are unknown,' said Kung,
'You will take up charioteering?
    'Then you will become known,
'Or perhaps I should take up charioteering, or archery?
'Or the practice of public speaking?'
And Tseu-lou said, 'I would put the defences in order,'
And Khieu said, 'If I were lord of a province
'I would put it in better order than this is.'

EZRA POUND

And Tchi said, 'I should prefer a small mountain
    temple,
'With order in the observances,
        with a suitable performance of the ritual.'
And Tian said, with his hand on the strings of his lute
The low sounds continuing
        after his hand left the strings,
And the sound went up like smoke, under the leaves,
And he looked after the sound:
        'The old swimming hole
'And the boys flopping off the planks,
'Or sitting in the underbrush playing mandolins.'
        And Kung smiled upon all of them equally.
And Thseng-sie desired to know:
        'Which had answered correctly?'
And Kung said, 'They have all answered correctly,
That is to say, each in his nature.'
And Kung raised his cane against Yuan Jang,
        Yuan Jang being his elder,
For Yuan Jang sat by the roadside pretending to
        be receiving wisdom.
And Kung said,
        'You old fool, come out of it,
Get up and do something useful.'
        And Kung said,
'Respect a child's faculties
'From the moment it inhales the clear air,
'But a man of fifty who knows nothing
        Is worthy of no respect.'
And 'When the prince has gathered about him

All the savants and artists, his riches will be fully
    employed.'
And Kung said, and wrote on the bo leaves:
        'If a man have not order within him
'He cannot spread order about him;
'And if a man have not order within him
'His family will not act with due order;
        'And if the prince have not order within him
'He cannot put order in his dominions.'
And Kung gave the words 'order'
and 'brotherly deference'
And said nothing of the 'life after death'.
And he said,
        'Anyone can run to excesses,
'It is easy to shoot past the mark,
'It is hard to stand firm in the middle.'

And they said, 'If a man commit murder
        'Should his father protect him, and hide him?'
And Kung said,
        'He should hide him.'

And Kung gave his daughter to Kong-Tchang
        Although Kong-Tchang was in prison.
And he gave his niece to Nan-Young
        although Nan-Young was out of office.
And Kung said, 'Wang ruled with moderation,
        'In his day the State was well kept,
'And even I can remember
'A day when the historians left blanks in their writings,
'I mean for things they didn't know,

EZRA POUND

'But that time seems to be passing.'
And Kung said, 'Without character you will
      be unable to play on that instrument
'Or to execute the music fit for the Odes.
'The blossoms of the apricot
      blow from the east to the west,
'And I have tried to keep them from falling.'

211   *'Ione, Dead the Long Year'*

EMPTY are the ways,
    Empty are the ways of this land
And the flowers
      Bend over with heavy heads.
They bend in vain.
Empty are the ways of this land
        where Ione
Walked once, and now does not walk
But seems like a person just gone.

212   *The Coming of War: Actaeon*

AN image of Lethe
      and the fields
Full of faint light
    but golden,
Grey cliffs,
      and beneath them
A sea
Harsher than granite,
      unstill, never ceasing;

EZRA POUND

High forms
      with the movement of gods,
Perilous aspect;
    And one said:
'This is Actaeon.'
         Actaeon of golden greaves!
Over fair meadows,
Over the cool face of that field,
Unstill, ever moving
Hosts of an ancient people,
The silent cortège.

213   *The Return*

SEE, they return; ah, see the tentative
   Movements, and the slow feet,
The trouble in the pace and the uncertain
Wavering!

See, they return, one, and by one,
With fear, as half-awakened;
As if the snow should hesitate
And murmur in the wind,
    and half turn back;
These were the 'Wing'd-with-Awe',
       Inviolable.

Gods of the winged shoe!
With them the silver hounds,
      sniffing the trace of air!

Haie! Haie!
>These were the swift to harry;
These the keen-scented;
These were the souls of blood.

Slow on the leash,
>pallid the leash-men!

Night Litany

O DIEU, purifiez nos coeurs!
>Purifiez nos coeurs!

Yea, the lines hast thou laid unto me
>in pleasant places,
And the beauty of this, thy Venice,
>hast thou shown unto me
Until its loveliness is become unto me
>a thing of tears.

O God, what great kindness
>have we done in times past
>and forgotten it,
That thou givest this wonder unto us,
>O god of waters?

O God of the night,
>What great sorrow
Cometh unto us
>That thou thus repayest us
Before the time of its coming?

EZRA POUND

O God of silence,
   Purifiez nos coeurs,
   Purifiez nos coeurs,
For we have seen
The glory of the shadow of the
   likeness of thine handmaid,
Yea, the glory of the shadow
   of thy Beauty hath walked
Upon the shadow of the waters
In this thy Venice,
     And before the holiness
Of the shadow of thy handmaid
Have I hidden mine eyes,
     O God of waters.

O God of silence,
   Purifiez nos coeurs,
   Purifiez nos coeurs,
O God of waters,
   make clean our hearts within us
And our lips to show forth thy praise,
   For I have seen the
Shadow of this thy Venice
Floating upon the waters,
   And thy stars
Have seen this thing, out of their far courses
Have they seen this thing,
   O God of waters,
Even as are thy stars
Silent unto us in their far coursing,
Even so is mine heart
   become silent within me.

EZRA POUND

Purifiez nos coeurs,
O God of the silence.
Purifiez nos coeurs,
O God of waters.

E. J. PRATT

1883-

The Prize Cat

PURE blood domestic, guaranteed,
Soft-mannered, musical in purr,
The ribbon had declared the breed,
Gentility was in the fur.

Such feline culture in the gads,
No anger ever arched her back—
What distance since those velvet pads
Departed from the leopard's track!

And when I mused how Time had thinned
The jungle strains within the cells,
How human hands had disciplined
Those prowling optic parallels;

I saw the generations pass
Along the reflex of a spring,
A bird had rustled in the grass,
The tab had caught it on the wing:

E. J. PRATT

Behind the leap so furtive-wild
Was such ignition in the gleam,
I thought an Abyssinian child
Had cried out in the whitethroat's scream.

The Decision

(To L.R., a college athlete who died May, 1923)

YOU left the field and no one heard
   A murmur from you. We,
With burning look and stubborn word,
Challenged the Referee—

Why he forbade you to complete
The run, hailing you back
Before your firm and eager feet
Were half-way round the track;

Unless he had contrived, instead,
To start you on a race,
With an immortal course ahead,
And daybreak on your face.

Silences

THERE is no silence upon the earth or under the
   earth like the silence under the sea;
No cries announcing birth,
No sounds declaring death.
There is silence when the milt is laid on the spawn in
   the weeds and fungus of the rock-clefts;
And silence in the growth and struggle for life.

E. J. PRATT

The bonitoes pounce upon the mackerel,
And are themselves caught by the barracudas,
The sharks kill the barracudas
And the great molluscs rend the sharks,
And all noiselessly—
Though swift be the action and final the conflict,
The drama is silent.

There is no fury upon the earth like the fury under the sea.
For growl and cough and snarl are the tokens of spendthrifts who know not the ultimate economy of rage.
Moreover, the pace of the blood is too fast.
But under the waves the blood is sluggard and has the same temperature as that of the sea.

There is something pre-reptilian about a silent kill.

Two men may end their hostilities just with their battle-cries.
'The devil take you,' says one.
'I'll see you in hell first,' says the other.
And these introductory salutes followed by a hail of gutturals and sibilants are often the beginning of friendship, for who would not prefer to be lustily damned than to be half-heartedly blessed?
No one need fear oaths that are properly enunciated, for they belong to the inheritance of just men made perfect, and, for all we know, of such may be the Kingdom of Heaven.

E. J. PRATT

But let silent hate be put away for it feeds upon the
 heart of the hater.
Today I watched two pairs of eyes. One pair was
 black and the other grey. And while the
 owners thereof, for the space of five seconds,
 walked past each other, the grey snapped at
 the black and the black riddled the grey.
One looked to say—'The cat,'
And the other—'The cur.'
But no words were spoken
Not so much as a hiss or a murmur came through the
 perfect enamel of the teeth; not so much as a
 gesture of enmity.
If the right upper lip curled over the canine, it went
 unnoticed.
The lashes veiled the eyes not for an instant in the
 passing.
And as between the two in respect to candour of
 intention or eternity of wish, there was no
 choice, for the stare was mutual and absolute.
A word would have dulled the exquisite edge of the
 feeling,
An oath would have flawed the crystallization of the
 hate.
For only such culture could grow in a climate of
 silence,—
Away back before the emergence of fur or feather,
 back to the unvocal sea and down deep where
 the darkness spills its wash on the threshold of
 light, where the lids never close upon the eyes,
 where the inhabitants slay in silence and are
 as silently slain.

E. J. PRATT

218   Burial at Sea
From 'The Roosevelt and the Antinoe'

WITH separated phrase and smothered word
    An immemorial psalm became a blurred
Bulwark under erosion by the sea.
Beneath the maddening crashes of the wind
Crumbled the grammar of the liturgy.

God of all comfort . . .
                       humbly beseeching thee . . .
We do acknowledge . . . . sinned . . .
Most merciful . . . confess . . . grievously . . .
Who spreadest out the heavens, crownest the years.
. . . . Grant us we pray thee . . . . .
Who commandest the seas and they do obey thee.
Nigh unto all . . . .
. . . . our distresses and fears.
. . . . A father to the fatherless.
Followed the fragments of great passages:
I am the Resurrection. . . . . We
. . . . commit . . . . . bodies to the deep . .
Corruptible . . . . Of those who sleep . . .
. . . . shall put on immortality.

And then brief tributes to the seamen drowned,
While Miller and his men were ranged around,
Bandaged in head and wrist, with arms in sling,
And others who had come, despite the warning,
To take their places were envisaging
The job that lay before them in the morning.

E. J. PRATT

Meanwhile outside, echoing the ritual—
Now unto Him who is able to do . . . . .
Exceeding abundantly . . . a wild antiphonal
Of shriek and whistle from the shrouds broke through,
Blending with thuds as though some throat had laughed
In thunder down the ventilating shaft;
And the benediction ended with the crack
Of a stanchion on the starboard beam, the beat
Of a loose block, with the fast run of feet,
Where a flying guy careered about the stack;
Then following the omen of a lull,
The advent of a wave which like a wall
Crashed down in volleys flush against the hull,
Lifting its white and shafted spume to fall
Across the higher decks; and through it all,
As on the dial of the telegraph,
Governed by derelict and hurricane,
Rang *Stop, Full Speed Astern* or *Slow* or *Half,*
The irregular pulse and cough of the engine strain,
The quick smite of the blades against a wave,
And always threat, escape, threat, then the brave
Lift of the keel, and still that breathless sink,
Dividing up the seconds, nearing the brink
Of a gray, unplumbed precipice and grave.

Within this hour a priest clothed with the whole
Habiliment and dignity of office—
Black cassock, surplice white and purple stole—
Feeling that from an older faith would come

E. J. PRATT

The virtue of a rubric yet unspoken
For the transition of a soul, a crumb
Of favour from a cupboard not bereft
Of all by the night's intercessions, left
His room; climbed up the stairs; pushed through a door
Storm-wedged, and balancing along the floor
Of the deck to where a davit stood, he placed
His grip securely on a guy rope there.
Lifting up a crucifix, he faced
The starboard quarter, looking down the waste
Of the waters casting back the flickering light
Of the steamer, where two bodies without wrap
Of shroud, deprived of their deck funeral rite,
Swung to the rune of the sea's stern foster-lap.

Ego vos absolvo . . . . ab omnibus
Peccatis et censuris . . . .
. in nomine
Patris et Filii et Spiritus . . . . .
Sancti . . . . Attende Domine
. . . . et miserere
Hear . . . O stella maris . . . Mary.

But no Gennesaret of Galilee
Conjured to its level by the sway
Of a hand or a word's magic was this sea,
Contesting with its iron-alien mood,
Its pagan face, its own primordial way,
The pale heroic suasion of a rood.

E. J. PRATT

And the absolving Father, when the ship
Righted her keel between two giant rolls,
Recrossed himself, and letting go his hold,
Returned to berth, murmuring *God rest their souls.*

HERBERT READ

1893-

219   *The Scene of War: Fear*

FEAR is a wave
  Beating through the air
And on taut nerves impingeing
Till there it wins
Vibrating chords.

All goes well
So long as you tune the instrument
To simulate composure.

(So you will become
A gallant gentleman.)

But when the strings are broken ...
Then you will grovel on the earth
And your rabbit eyes
Will fill with the fragments of your shattered soul.

HERBERT READ

220 *The Scene of War: The Happy Warrior*

HIS wild heart beats with painful sobs,
His strained hands clench an ice-cold rifle,
His aching jaws grip a hot parched tongue,
And his wide eyes search unconsciously.
He cannot shriek.

Bloody saliva
Dribbles down his shapeless jacket.

I saw him stab
And stab again
A well-killed Boche.

This is the happy warrior,
This is he . . .

221 *Inbetweentimes*

EMERGING at midnight
to cool my aching eyes with the sight of stars
I hear the nightingale
throbbing in the thicket by my garden gate

and I think:
A poet in the old days would have made a song
of your song and the starlit night
and the scent of wallflowers clinging to the ground.

But now it is different:
You sing but we are silent,
our hearts too sadly patient
all these years. . . .

Sing on; the night is cool.
Morning, and the world will be lit
with whitebeam candles shining and o the frail
and tender daring splendour of wild cherry trees.

222 *September Fires*

HAULMS burn
in distant fields:
reluctantly the plumes of smoke
rise against the haze
of hills blue and clear
but featureless.

Our feet
crush the crinkled beech-leaves.
There is no other life than ours.
God is good to us this September evening
to give us a sun
and a world burning its dross.

Let us burn the twisted years
that have brought us to this meeting.
The crops are culled—
we can expect no other fruit
until another year
brings fire and fealty and the earth in barren stillness.

SIR CHARLES G. D. ROBERTS
1860-1943

223 *Hath Hope Kept Vigil*

FRAIL lilies that beneath the dust so long
　Have lain in cerements of musk and slumber,
While over you hath fled the viewless throng
　Of hours and winds and voices out of number,

Pulseless and dead in that enswathing dark
　Hath hope kept vigil at your core of being?
Did the germ know what unextinguished spark
　Held these white blooms within its heart unseeing?

Once more into the dark when I go down,
　And deep and deaf the black clay seals my prison,
Will the numbed soul foreknow how light shall crown
　With strong young ecstasy its life new risen?

224 *The Solitary Woodsman*

WHEN the grey lake-water rushes
　　Past the dripping alder-bushes,
　And the bodeful autumn wind
In the fir-tree weeps and hushes,—

When the air is sharply damp
Round the solitary camp,
　And the moose-bush in the thicket
Glimmers like a scarlet lamp,—

When the birches twinkle yellow,
And the cornel bunches mellow,
　And the owl across the twilight
Trumpets to his downy fellow,—

SIR CHARLES G. D. ROBERTS

When the nut-fed chipmunks romp
Through the maples' crimson pomp,
   And the slim viburnum flushes
In the darkness of the swamp,—

When the blueberries are dead,
When the rowan clusters red,
   And the shy bear, summer-sleekened,
In the bracken makes his bed,—

On a day there comes once more
To the latched and lonely door,
   Down the wood-road striding silent,
One who has been here before.

Green spruce branches for his head,
Here he makes his simple bed,
   Couching with the sun, and rising
When the dawn is frosty red.

All day long he wanders wide
With the grey moss for his guide,
   And his lonely axe-stroke startles
The expectant forest-side.

Toward the quiet close of day
Back to camp he takes his way,
   And about his sober footsteps
Unafraid the squirrels play.

SIR CHARLES G. D. ROBERTS

On his roof the red leaf falls,
At his door the bluejay calls,
  And he hears the wood-mice hurry
Up and down his rough log-walls;

Hears the laughter of the loon
Thrill the dying afternoon;
  Hears the calling of the moose
Echo to the early moon.

And he hears the partridge drumming,
The belated hornet humming,—
  All the faint, prophetic sounds
That foretell the winter's coming.

And the wind about his eaves
Through the chilly night-wet grieves,
  And the earth's dumb patience fills him,
Fellow to the falling leaves.

225 *Tantramar Revisited*

SUMMERS and summers have come, and gone with the flight of the swallow;
Sunshine and thunder have been, storm, and winter, and frost;
Many and many a sorrow has all but died from remembrance,
Many a dream of joy fall'n in the shadow of pain.
Hands of chance and change have marred, or moulded, or broken,

SIR CHARLES G. D. ROBERTS

Busy with spirit or flesh, all I most have adored;
Even the bosom of Earth is strewn with heavier shadows,—
Only in these green hills, aslant to the sea, no change!
Here where the road that has climbed from the inland valleys and woodlands
Dips from the hilltops down, straight to the base of the hills,—
Here from my vantage-ground, I can see the scattering houses,
Stained with time, set warm in orchards, meadows and wheat,
Dotting the broad bright slopes outspread to southward and eastward,
Wind-swept all day long, blown by the south-east wind.

Skirting the sunbright uplands stretches a riband of meadow,
Shorn of the labouring grass, bulwarked well from the sea,
Fenced on its seaward border with long clay dykes from the turbid
Surge and flow of the tides vexing the Westmoreland shores.
Yonder, toward the left, lie broad the Westmoreland marshes,—
Miles on miles they extend, level, and grassy, and dim,
Clear from the long red sweep of flats to the sky in the distance,
Save for the outlying heights, green-rampired Cumberland Point;

SIR CHARLES G. D. ROBERTS

Miles on miles outrolled, and the river-channels divide them,—
Miles on miles of green, barred by the hurtling gusts.

Miles and miles beyond the tawny bay is Minudie.
There are the low blue hills; villages gleam at their feet.
Nearer a white sail shines across the water, and nearer
Still are the slim, grey masts of fishing boats dry on the flats.
Ah, how well I remember those wide red flats, above tide mark,
Pale with scurf of the salt, seamed and baked in the sun!
Well I remember the piles of blocks and ropes, and the net-reels
Wound with the beaded nets, dripping and dark from the sea!
Now at this season the nets are unwound; they hang from the rafters
Over the fresh-stowed hay in upland barns, and the wind
Blows all day through the chinks, with the streaks of sunlight, and sways them
Softly at will; or they lie heaped in the gloom of a loft.

Now at this season the reels are empty and idle; I see them
Over the lines of the dikes, over the gossiping grass.
Now at this season they swing in the long strong wind, thro' the lonesome

SIR CHARLES G. D. ROBERTS

Golden afternoon, shunned by the foraging gulls.
Near about sunset the crane will journey homeward above them;
Round them, under the moon, all the calm night long,
Winnowing soft grey wings of marsh-owls wander and wander,
Now to the broad, lit marsh, now to the dusk of the dike.
Soon, through their dew-wet frames, in the live keen freshness of morning,
Out of the teeth of the dawn blows back the awakening wind.
Then, as the blue day mounts, and the low-shot shafts of the sunlight
Glance from the tide to the shore, gossamers jewelled with dew
Sparkle and wave, where late sea-spoiling fathoms of drift-net,
Myriad-meshed, uploomed sombrely over the land.

Well I remember it all. The salt, raw scent of the margin;
While, with men at the windlass, groaned each reel, and the net,
Surging in ponderous lengths, uprose and coiled in its station;
Then each man to his home,—well I remember it all!

Yet, as I sit and watch, this present peace of the landscape,—
Stranded boats, these reels empty and idle, the hush,

SIR CHARLES G. D. ROBERTS

One grey hawk slow-wheeling above yon cluster of haystacks,—
More than the old-time stir this stillness welcomes me home.
Ah, the old-time stir, how once it stung me with rapture,—
Old-time sweetness, the winds freighted with honey and salt!
Yet will I stay my steps and not go down to the marshland,—
Muse and recall far off, rather remember than see,—
Lest on too close sight I miss the darling illusion,
Spy at their task even here the hands of chance and change.

VICTORIA SACKVILLE-WEST
1892-

Labour
From 'The Land'

AND since to live men labour, only knowing
Life's little lantern between dark and dark,
The fieldsman in his grave humility
Goes about his centennial concerns,
Bread for his race and fodder for his kine,
Mating and breeding, since he only knows
The life he sees, how it may best endure,
(But on his Sabbath pacifies his God
Blindly, though storm may wreck his urgent crops,)

VICTORIA SACKVILLE-WEST

And sees no beauty in his horny life,
With closer wisdom than soft poets use.
But I, like him, who strive
Closely with earth, and know her grudging mind,
Will sing no songs of bounty, for I see
Only the battle between man and earth,
The sweat, the weariness, the care, the balk;
See earth the slave and tyrant, mutinous,
Turning upon her tyrant and her slave,
Yielding reluctantly her fruits, to none
But most peremptory wooers.
Wherever waste eludes man's vigilance,
There spring the weeds and darnels; where he treads
Through woods a tangle nets and trips his steps;
His hands alone force fruitfulness and tilth;
Strange lovers, man and earth! their love and hate
Braided in mutual need; and of their strife
A tired contentment born.

227 *Vintage*
From 'The Land'

YET I recall
Another harvest, not beneath this sky
So Saxon-fair, so washed by dews and rain;
Another harvest, where the gods still rouse,
And stretch, and waken with the evenfall.
Down from the hill the slow white oxen crawl,
Dragging the purple waggon heaped with must,
Raising on sundered hoofs small puffs of dust,
With scarlet tassels on their milky brows,
Gentle as evening moths. Beneath the yoke

VICTORIA SACKVILLE-WEST

Lounging against the shaft they fitful strain
To draw the waggon on its creaking spoke,
And all the vineyard folk
With staves and shouldered tools surround the wain.
The wooden shovels take the purple stain,
The dusk is heavy with the wine's warm load;
Here the long sense of classic measure cures
The spirit weary of its difficult pain;
Here the old Bacchic piety endures,
Here the sweet legends of the world remain.
Homeric waggons lumbering the road;
Vergilian litanies among the bine;
Pastoral sloth of flocks beneath the pine;
The swineherd watching, propped upon his goad,
Under the chestnut trees the rootling swine.
Who could so stand, and see this evening fall,
This calm of husbandry, this redolent tilth,
This terracing of hills, this vintage wealth,
Without the pagan sanity of blood
Mounting his veins in young and tempered health?
Who could so stand, and watch processional
The vintners, herds and flocks in dusty train
Wend through the molten evening to regain
The terraced farm and trodden threshing-floor
Where late the flail
Tossed high the maize in scud of gritty ore,
And lies half-buried in the heap of grain,—
Who could so watch and not forget the rack
Of wills worn thin and thought become too frail,
Nor roll the centuries back
And feel the sinews of his soul grow hale,
And know himself for Rome's inheritor?

VICTORIA SACKVILLE-WEST

228 *Full Moon*

SHE was wearing the coral taffeta trousers
Someone had brought her from Ispahan,
And the little gold coat with pomegranate blossoms,
And the coral-hafted feather fan;
And she ran down a Kentish lane in the moonlight,
And skipped in the pool of the moon as she ran.

She cared not a rap for all the big planets
For Betelgeuse or Aldebaran,
And all the big planets cared nothing for her,
That small impertinent charlatan;
But she climbed on a Kentish stile in the moonlight,
And laughed at the sky through the sticks of her fan.

CARL SANDBURG
1878-

229 *Chicago*

HOG Butcher for the World,
Tool Maker, Stacker of Wheat,
Player with Railroads and the Nation's
     Freight Handler;
Stormy, husky, brawling,
City of the Big Shoulders:

They tell me you are wicked and I believe them, for I
     have seen your painted women under the gas
     lamps luring the farm boys.

CARL SANDBURG

And they tell me you are crooked and I answer: Yes, it is true I have seen the gunmen kill and go free to kill again.

And they tell me you are brutal and my reply is: On the faces of women and children I have seen the marks of wanton hunger.

And having answered so I turn once more to those who sneer at this my city, and I give them back the sneer and say to them:

Come and show me another city with lifted head singing so proud to be alive and coarse and strong and cunning.

Flinging magnetic curses amid the toil of piling job on job, here is a tall bold slugger set vivid against the little soft cities;

Fierce as a dog with tongue lapping for action, cunning as a savage pitted against the wilderness,
      Bareheaded,
      Shoveling,
      Wrecking,
      Planning,
      Building, breaking, rebuilding.

Under the smoke, dust all over his mouth, laughing with white teeth,

Under the terrible burden of destiny laughing as a young man laughs,

Laughing even as an ignorant fighter laughs who has never lost a battle,

Bragging and laughing that under his wrist is the pulse and under his ribs the heart of the people,
      Laughing!

CARL SANDBURG

Laughing the stormy, husky, brawling Laughter of
Youth, half-naked, sweating, proud to be Hog
Butcher, Tool Maker, Stacker of Wheat, Player
with Railroads and Freight Handler to the
Nation.

230 *Cool Tombs*

WHEN Abraham Lincoln was shoveled into the tombs,
he forgot the copperheads and the assassin . . .
in the dust, in the cool tombs.

And Ulysses Grant lost all thought of con men and
Wall Street, cash and collateral turned ashes
. . . in the dust, in the cool tombs.

Pocahontas's body, lovely as a poplar, sweet as a red
haw in November or a pawpaw in May, did
she wonder? does she remember? . . . in the
dust, in the cool tombs.

Take any streetful of people buying clothes and
groceries, cheering a hero or throwing confetti
and blowing tin horns . . . tell me if the lovers
are losers . . . tell me if any get more than the
lovers . . . in the dust . . . in the cool tombs.

231 *Loam*

IN the loam we sleep,
In the cool moist loam,
To the lull of years that pass
And the break of stars.

CARL SANDBURG

From the loam, then,
The soft warm loam,
  We rise:
To shape of rose leaf,
Of face and shoulder.

We stand, then,
  To a whiff of life,
Lifted to the silver of the sun
Over and out of the loam
  A day.

SIEGFRIED SASSOON
1886-

Grandeur of Ghosts

WHEN I have heard small talk about great men
  I climb to bed; light my two candles; then
Consider what was said; and put aside
What Such-a-one remarked and Someone-else replied.

They have spoken lightly of my deathless friends,
(Lamps for my gloom, hands guiding where I
    stumble,)
Quoting, for shallow conversational ends,
What Shelley shrilled, what Blake once wildly muttered. . . .

SIEGFRIED SASSOON

How can they use such names and be not humble?
I have sat silent; angry at what they uttered.
The dead bequeathed them life; the dead have said
What these can only memorize and mumble.

233   Base Details

IF I were fierce and bald and short of breath,
   I'd live with scarlet Majors at the Base,
And speed glum heroes up the line to death.
   You'd see me with my puffy petulant face,
Guzzling and gulping in the best hotel,
   Reading the Roll of Honour. 'Poor young chap,'
I'd say—'I used to know his father well;
   Yes, we've lost heavily in this last scrap.'
And when the war is done and youth stone dead
I'd toddle safely home and die—in bed.

234   The Glory of Women

YOU love us when we're heroes, home on leave,
   Or wounded in a mentionable place.
You worship decorations; you believe
That chivalry redeems the war's disgrace.
You make us shells. You listen with delight,
By tales of dirt and danger fondly thrilled.
You crown our distant ardours while we fight,
   And mourn our laurelled memories when we're killed.

SIEGFRIED SASSOON

You can't believe that British troops 'retire'
When hell's last horror breaks them, and they run,
Trampling the terrible corpses—blind with blood.
O German mother dreaming by the fire,
While you are knitting socks to send your son
His face is trodden deeper in the mud.

235 *The Heart's Journey* (V)

YOU were glad tonight: and now you've gone away.
   Flushed in the dark you put your dreams to bed;
But as you fall asleep I hear you say
Those tired sweet drowsy words we left unsaid.

Sleep well: for I can follow you to bless
And lull your distant beauty where you roam;
And with wild songs of hoarded loveliness
Recall you to these arms that were your home.

236 *The Heart's Journey* (XXXIV)

A FLOWER has opened in my heart . . .
   What flower is this, what flower of spring,
What simple secret thing?
It is the peace that shines apart,
The peace of daybreak skies that bring
Clear song and wild swift wing.

SIEGFRIED SASSOON

Heart's miracle of inward light,
What powers unknown have sown your seed
And your perfection freed? ...
O flower within me wondrous white,
I know you only as my need
And my unsealèd sight.

237 *Morning Glory*

IN this meadow starred with spring
Shepherds kneel before their king.
Mary throned, with dreaming eyes,
Gowned in blue like rain-washed skies,
Lifts her tiny son that he
May behold their courtesy.
And green-smocked children, awed and good,
Bring him blossoms from the wood.

Clear the sunlit steeples chime
Mary's coronation-time.
Loud the happy children quire
To the golden-windowed morn;
While the lord of their desire
Sleeps below the crimson thorn.

238 *On Reading the War Diary of a Defunct Ambassador*

SO that's your Diary—that's your private mind
Translated into shirt-sleeved History. That
Is what diplomacy has left behind
For after-ages to peruse, and find
What passed beneath your elegant silk-hat.

SIEGFRIED SASSOON

You were a fine old gentleman; compact
Of shrewdness, charm, refinement and finesse.
Impeccable in breeding, taste and dress,
No diplomatic quality you lacked—
No tittle of ambassadorial tact.

I can imagine you among 'the guns',
Urbanely peppering partridge, grouse or pheasant—
Guest of those infinitely privileged ones
Whose lives are padded, petrified, and pleasant.
I visualize you feeding off gold plate
And gossiping on grave affairs of State.

Now you're defunct; your gossip's gravely printed;
The world discovers where you lunched and dined
On such and such a day; and what was hinted
By ministers and generals far behind
The all-important conflict, carnage-tinted.

The world can read the rumours that you gleaned
From various Fronts; the well-known Names you met;
Each conference you attended and convened;
And (at appropriate moments) what you ate.
Thus (if the world's acute) it can derive
Your self, exact, uncensored and alive.

The world will find no pity in your pages;
No exercise of spirit worthy of mention;
Only a public-funeral grief-convention;
And all the circumspection of the ages.
But I, for one, am grateful, overjoyed,

SIEGFRIED SASSOON

And unindignant that your punctual pen
Should have been so constructively employed
In manifesting to unprivileged men
The visionless officialized fatuity
That once kept Europe safe for Perpetuity.

DUNCAN CAMPBELL SCOTT
1862-

239 *After Battle*

WHEN the first larks began to soar,
    They left him wounded there;
Pity unlatched the sun-lit door,
    And smoothed his clotted hair.

But when the larks were still, before
    The mist began to rise,
'Twas Love that latched the star-lit door,
    And closed his dreamless eyes.

240 *The Forsaken*

I

ONCE in the winter
    Out on a lake
In the heart of the north-land,
Far from the Fort
And far from the hunters,
A Chippewa woman
With her sick baby,

DUNCAN CAMPBELL SCOTT

Crouched in the last hours
Of a great storm.
Frozen and hungry,
She fished through the ice
With a line of the twisted
Bark of the cedar
And a rabbit-bone hook
Polished and barbed;
Fished with the bare hook
All through the wild day,
Fished and caught nothing;
While the young chieftain
Tugged at her breasts,
Or slept in the lacings
Of the warm *tikanagan*.
All the lake-surface
Streamed with the hissing
Of millions of iceflakes
Hurled by the wind;
Behind her the round
Of a lonely island
Roared like a fire
With the voice of the storm
In the deeps of the cedars.
Valiant, unshaken,
She took of her own flesh,
Baited the fish-hook,
Drew in a gray-trout,
Drew in his fellows,
Heaped them beside her,
Dead in the snow.

Valiant, unshaken,
She faced the long distance,
Wolf-haunted and lonely,
Sure of her goal
And the life of her dear one:
Tramped for two days,
On the third in the morning,
Saw the strong bulk
Of the Fort by the river,
Saw the wood-smoke
Hang soft in the spruces,
Heard the keen yelp
Of the ravenous huskies
Fighting for whitefish:
Then she had rest.

II

Years and years after,
When she was old and withered,
When her son was an old man
And his children filled with vigour,
They came in their northern tour on the verge of winter,
To an island in a lonely lake.
There one night they camped, and on the morrow
Gathered their kettles and birch-bark,
Their rabbit-skin robes and their mink-traps,
Launched their canoes and slunk away through the islands,
Left her alone for ever,

DUNCAN CAMPBELL SCOTT

Without a word of farewell,
Because she was old and useless,
Like a paddle broken and warped,
Or a pole that was splintered.
Then, without a sigh,
Valiant, unshaken,
She smoothed her dark locks under her kerchief,
Composed her shawl in state,
Then folded her hands ridged with sinews and corded
 with veins,
Folded them across her breasts spent with the nourish-
 ing of children,
Gazed at the sky past the tops of the cedars,
Saw two spangled nights arise out of the twilight,
Saw two days go by filled with the tranquil sunshine,
Saw, without pain, or dread, or even a moment of
 longing:
Then on the third great night there came thronging
 and thronging
Millions of snowflakes out of a windless cloud;
They covered her close with a beautiful crystal shroud,
Covered her deep and silent.
But in the frost of the dawn,
Up from the life below,
Rose a column of breath
Through a tiny cleft in the snow,
Fragile, delicately drawn,
Wavering with its own weakness,
In the wilderness a sign of the spirit,
Persisting still in the sight of the sun

Till day was done.
Then all light was gathered up by the hand of God
    and hid in His breast,
Then there was born a silence deeper than silence,
Then she had rest.

241   *Spring in the Valley*

SPRING has caught up the eager earth
    With her enchanted power;
In rounded drifts of ashy white
    The plum-trees are in flower.

The light is like a fluttering bird
    Caught in a cage of blue;
The warmth is like a beating heart
    Flooding the world through.

No leaves are full upon the woods
    Only a dream of leaves;
The sun, from the hollow to the height,
    A wave of colour weaves.

Groups of black pines like builded piers
    Stand solid in the glow,
As if they held the shimmering tide
    Back from an overflow.

Only two sounds are on the air,
    A snow-brook babbles free,
A blue-bird tries his early note
    In an old apple-tree.

DUNCAN CAMPBELL SCOTT

Under the pines, in the brown shade,
   Two lovers are at rest;
No thoughts disturb the pools of joy
   Tranquil in either breast.

The mist of evening in his eyes,
   The dew of morn in hers,
Between them in the fluttering light
   The breath of beauty stirs.

A Song

IN the air there are no coral-
   Reefs or ambergris,
No rock-pools that hide the lovely
   Sea-anemones,
No strange forms that flow with phosphor
   In a deep-sea night,
No slow fish that float their colour
   Through the liquid light,
No young pearls, like new moons, growing
   Perfect in their shells;
If you be in search of beauty
   Go where beauty dwells.

In the sea there are no sunsets
   Crimson in the west,
No dark pines that hold the shadow
   On the mountain-crest,
There is neither mist nor moonrise
   Rainbows nor rain,
No sweet flowers that in the autumn

Die to bloom again,
Music never moves the silence,—
  Reeds or silver bells;
If you be in search of beauty
  Go where beauty dwells.

243   *Hymn for Those in the Air*
   To The Royal Canadian Air Force

ETERNAL Father by Whose Might
  The firmament was planned,
Who set the stars their paths of light,
  Who made the sea and land,
Thou Who art far yet near,
  In the bright Now and Here,
And where the Void is sleeping,
  Take them who dare to fly
Into Thy keeping.

Guide them who move through dark and cloud
  Parting the pathless sky,
Sustain them when the storm is loud
  Till night and storm are by;
Driving through snow and sleet
  When wild the head winds beat,
Thy sovereign Will commanding
  Bring them who dare to fly
To a safe landing.

Lead them who, dauntless, mount the height
  Of the embattled air,
Through piercing shell, through searching light,
  Hold and be with them there,

DUNCAN CAMPBELL SCOTT

Keep them in life or death
  Mindful of One Who saith,
Where the wild birds shall gather
  Not the least sparrow falls
Without the Father.

Lift up the souls who yet aspire
  To move within Thy will,
Who rise above the World's desire,
  Foiled but unconquered still,
Triumphant in Thy Might,
  Gather them into Light,
The Valiant who have striven,
  Winged with Immortal Joy,
Into Thy Heaven.

244   *Old Olives at Bordighera*

HERE on the valley's slope is the olive grove,
  The trees are gnarled and distorted;
They stand neglected and forgotten,
Ruins of ancient labour;
After bearing through years uncounted
The innumerable olive,
The grove is barren.

Never will the lads beat the trees
To bring down the high, reluctant fruit;
Never will the old crones, crouching here,
Search the grass
For the bronze ovals of the late-fallen;
Or the labourer carry the final sack
To the oil-press.

DUNCAN CAMPBELL SCOTT

Only the idle visit here;
Or at times the shepherd,
In his weathered-saffron cloak,
Drifts here with his sheep.
They come following
With heads drooped to the scant herbage,
Cropping with a whispering sound
As if conferring with bent heads;
Flooding in full tide over the parched grass
They ebb away past the boles of the olives
And draw the shepherd with them.

No fruit from the olives!
But the loiterer idles here
And gathers an immaterial aftermath.
For beauty abides in the olive grove,
In fathomless peace the beauty of quietude:—
The dust-green silver of the leaves,
The silver subdued of the tree-stems,
The branch-screen that draws gold from sunlight
And casts a residue of silver shadow.
Afar from hidden Vallecrosia
Comes the vibration of a silver bell,
And from Vallebona runs a parallel of bell-silver
To join the silver community of olives;
Under the serene element on the high mountain
Shines dim snow-silver;
Below, and beyond the province of the grove,
Trembles a vision of ocean,
Flawed with silver by the west wind.

GEOFFREY SCOTT
1884-1929

Faster

GOD flings
In air His box of things;
He rights them in their race,
Apart, aspin, apace,
Moonsilver, gold and green,
Moon, sun, and earth between.

Night falls at the fair
On three bright balls in air,
Spun by a clown
With dunce's cap for crown:
A powdered Pantaloon
Must pack up soon.

For God and me the same,
Life's game;
'Tis death if hand or will
Sway, falter or lie still;
Juggle, or come to dust,
Man, like his Maker, must.

O turn, O teach and twist,
Sure eye and supple wrist;
Spin faster, Master, spin . . .
But mind and ghost within
They are so still,
Yet laugh, or weep their fill.

GEOFFREY SCOTT

Pack up the fair, put out
Lantern and lamp about;
Hide mask and hoop from sight
Beneath the encrusted night;
So the clown goes;
The ghost, who knows?

246 *All our Joy is enough*

ALL we make is enough
Barely to seem
A bee's din,
A beetle-scheme—
Sleepy stuff
For God to dream:
Begin.

All our joy is enough
At most to fill
A thimble cup
A little wind puff
Can shake, can spill:
Fill it up;
Be still.

All we know is enough;
Though written wide,
Small spider yet
With tangled stride
Will soon be off
The page's side:
Forget.

GEOFFREY SCOTT

The Bridge

HERE was gold,
A moment gone, untold;
Day-fall's gay flare and fiery flying kiss
Was this.

How careful is the dark:
It creeps so slow; a spark
Finds welcome made
In mothering mounting wells of shade:
Star fingers feel the air, and shadow's feet
Meet.
Here on this bridge, this stone
I wait. Dusk leans, leans down
The silvery shy
And leaf-laced listening sky.

Wait longer: what is there
In falling veils of the air? . . .
Quiet. Now blackness is.
No quiet is like this.
Sudden and sharp, what ridge
Looms huge above the bridge?
Night's gentle, . . . No, 'tis icy keen, and why
Is all so changed, pricked, nigh?

I know
How death doth go.
Now, not many a mile
He moves, with a smile;
Near, and nought between, sudden his face unseen
Will peer.
So, . . . 'Twill be so, . . . so:
Here I have been.

FREDEGOND SHOVE
1889-
The Farmer, 1917

I SEE a farmer walking by himself
In the ploughed field, returning like the day
To his dark nest. The plovers circle round
In the gray sky; the blackbird calls; the thrush
Still sings—but all the rest have gone to sleep.
I see the farmer coming up the field,
Where the new corn is sown, but not yet sprung;
He seems to be the only man alive
And thinking through the twilight of this world.
I know that there is war behind those hills,
And I surmise, but cannot see the dead,
And cannot see the living in their midst—
So awfully and madly knit with death.
I cannot feel, but know that there is war,
And has been now for three eternal years,
Behind the subtle cinctures of those hills.
I see the farmer coming up the field,
And as I look, imagination lifts
The sullen veil of alternating cloud,
And I am stunned by what I see behind
His solemn and uncompromising form:
Wide hosts of men who once could walk like him
In freedom, quite alone with night and day,
Uncounted shapes of living flesh and bone,
Worn dull, quenched dry, gone blind and sick, with war;
And they are him and he is one with them;
They see him as he travels up the field.

FREDEGOND SHOVE

O God, how lonely freedom seems today!
O single farmer walking through the world,
They bless the seed in you that earth shall reap,
When they, their countless lives, and all their thoughts,
Lie scattered by the storm: when peace shall come
With stillness, and long shivers, after death.

249 *A Dream in Early Spring*

NOW when I sleep the thrush breaks through
    my dreams
With sharp reminders of the coming day:
After his call, one minute I remain
Unwaked, and on the darkness which is Me
There springs the image of a daffodil,
Growing upon a grassy bank alone,
And seeming with great joy his bell to fill
With drops of golden dew, which on the lawn
He shakes again, where they lie bright and chill.

His head is drooped; the shrouded winds that sing
Bend him which way they will: never on earth
Was there before so beautiful a ghost;
Alas, he had a less than flower-birth,
And like a ghost indeed must shortly glide
From all but the sad cells of memory,
Where he will linger, an imprisoned beam,
Or fallen shadow of the golden world,
Long after this and many another dream.

FREDEGOND SHOVE

The New Ghost

'And he, casting away his garment, rose and came to Jesus.'

AND he cast it down, down, on the green grass,
Over the young crocuses, where the dew was—
He cast the garment of his flesh that was full of death,
And like a sword his spirit showed out of the cold sheath.

He went a pace or two, he went to meet his Lord,
And, as I said, his spirit looked like a clean sword,
And seeing him the naked trees began shivering,
And all the birds cried out aloud as it were late spring,

And the Lord came on, He came down, and saw
That a soul was waiting there for Him, one without flaw,
And they embraced in the churchyard where the robins play,
And the daffodils hang down their heads, as they burn away.

The Lord held his head fast, and you could see
That he kissed the unsheathed ghost that was gone free—
As a hot sun, on a March day, kisses the cold ground;
And the spirit answered, for he knew well that his peace was found.

FREDEGOND SHOVE

The spirit trembled, and sprang up at the Lord's word—
As on a wild April day, springs a small bird—
So the ghost's feet lifting him up, he kissed the Lord's cheek,
And for the greatness of their love neither of them could speak.

But the Lord went then, to show him the way,
Over the young crocuses, under the green may
That was not quite in flower yet—to a far-distant land;
And the ghost followed, like a naked cloud holding the sun's hand.

A. J. M. SMITH

1902-

251 *The Lonely Land*

CEDAR and jagged fir
uplift sharp barbs
against the gray
and cloud-piled sky;
and in the bay
blown spume and windrift
and thin, bitter spray
snap
at the whirling sky;
and the pine trees
lean one way.

A. J. M. SMITH

A wild duck calls
to her mate,
and the ragged
and passionate tones
stagger and fall,
and recover,
and stagger and fall,
on these stones—
are lost
in the lapping of water
on smooth, flat stones.

This is a beauty
of dissonance,
this resonance
of stony strand,
this smoky cry
curled over a black pine
like a broken
and wind-battered branch
when the wind
bends the tops of the pines
and curdles the sky
from the north.

This is the beauty
of strength
broken by strength
and still strong.

A. J. M. SMITH

Ode: On the Death of W. B. Yeats

AN old thorn tree in a stony place
  Where the mountain stream has run dry,
Torn in the black wind under the race
Of the icicle-sharp kaleidoscopic white sky,
  Bursts into sudden flower.

Under the central dome of winter and night
A wild swan spreads his fanatic wing.
Ancestralled energy of blood and power
Beats in his sinewy breast. And now the ravening
Soul, fulfilled, his first-last hour
  Upon him, chooses to exult.

Over the edge of shivering Europe,
Over the chalk front of Kent, over Eire,
Dwarfing the crawling waves' amoral savagery,
Daring the hiding clouds' rhetorical tumult,
  The white swan plummets the mountain top.

The stream has suddenly pushed the papery leaves!
It digs a rustling channel of clear water
On the scarred flank of Ben Bulben.
The twisted tree is incandescent with flowers.
The swan leaps singing into the cold air:
  This is a glory not for an hour:

  Over the Galway shore
  The white bird is flying
  Forever, and crying
  To the tumultuous throng
Of the sky his cold and passionate song.

A. J. M. SMITH
Good Friday

THIS day upon the bitter tree
  Died One who had He willed
Could have dried up the wide sea
  And the wind stilled.

It was about the ninth hour
  He surrenderèd the ghost,
And His face was a faded flower
  Drooping and lost.

Who then was not afraid?
  Targeted, heart and eye,
Struck, as with darts, by godhead
  In human agony.

For Him, who with a cry
  Could shatter if He willed
The sea and earth and sky
  And them rebuild,

Who chose amid the tumult
  Of the darkening sky
A chivalry more difficult—
  As Man to die—

What answering meed of love
  Can finite flesh return
That is not all unworthy of
  The God I mourn?

STEPHEN SPENDER
1909–

254 'I think continually of those who were truly great'

I THINK continually of those who were truly great,
Who, from the womb, remembered the soul's history
Through corridors of light where the hours are suns
Endless and singing. Whose lovely ambition
Was that their lips, still touched with fire,
Should tell of the Spirit clothed from head to foot in song,
And who hoarded from the Spring branches
The desires falling across their bodies like blossoms.

What is precious is never to forget
The essential delight of the blood drawn from ageless springs
Breaking through rocks in worlds before our earth;
Never to deny its pleasure in the morning simple light
Nor its grave evening demand for love,
Never to allow gradually the traffic to smother
With noise and fog the flowering of the spirit.

Near the snow, near the sun, in the highest fields
See how these names are fêted by the waving grass
And by the streamers of white cloud
And whispers of wind in the listening sky.
The names of those who in their lives fought for life
Who wore at their hearts the fire's centre.
Born of the sun they travelled a short while towards the sun,
And left the vivid air signed with their honour.

STEPHEN SPENDER

'After they have tired'

AFTER they have tired of the brilliance of cities
And of striving for office where at last they may languish
Hung round with easy chains until
Death and Jerusalem glorify also the crossing-sweeper:
Then those streets the rich built and their easy love
Fade like old cloths, and it is death stalks through life
Grinning white through all faces
Clean and equal like the shine from snow.
In this time when grief pours freezing over us,
When the hard light of pain gleams at every street corner,
When those who were pillars of that day's gold roof
Shrink in their clothes; surely from hunger
We may strike fire, like fire from flint?
And our strength is now the strength of our bones
Clean and equal like the shine from snow
And the strength of famine and of our enforced idleness,
And it is the strength of our love for each other.

Readers of this strange language,
We have come at last to a country
Where light equal, like the shine from snow, strikes all faces,
Here you may wonder
How it was that works, money, interest, building, could ever hide
The palpable and obvious love of man for man.

STEPHEN SPENDER

O comrades, let not those who follow after
—The beautiful generation that shall spring from our
   sides—
Let them not wonder how after the failure of banks,
The failure of cathedrals and the declared insanity of
   our rulers,
We lacked the Spring-like resources of the tiger
Or of plants who strike out new roots to gushing
   waters.
But through torn-down portions of old fabric let their
   eyes
Watch the admiring dawn explode like a shell
Around us, dazing us with its light like snow.

256   *The Funeral*

DEATH is another milestone on their way.
   With laughter on their lips and with winds
      blowing round them
They record simply
How this one excelled all others in making driving
   belts.

This is festivity; it is the time of statistics
When they record what one unit contributed:
They are glad as they lay him back in the earth
And thank him for what he gave them.

They walk home remembering the straining red flags,
And with pennons of song still fluttering through their
   blood

STEPHEN SPENDER

They speak of the world state
With its towns like brain-centres and its pulsing arteries.

They think how one life hums, revolves and toils,
One cog in a golden and singing hive:
Like spark from fire, its task happily achieved,
It falls away quietly.

No more are they haunted by the individual grief
Nor the crocodile tears of European genius,
The decline of a culture
Mourned by scholars who dream of the ghosts of Greek boys.

257   *'Who Live under the Shadow'*

WHO live under the shadow of a war,
   What can I do that matters?
My pen stops, and my laughter, dancing, stop
Or ride to a gap.
How often, on the powerful crest of pride,
I am shot with thought
That halts the untamed horses of the blood,
The grip on good.

That moving whimpering and mating bear
Tunes to deaf ears:
Stuffed with the realer passions of the earth
Beneath this hearth.

JAMES STEPHENS

1882-

The Goat Paths

THE crooked paths go every way
  Upon the hill—they wind about
  Through the heather, in and out
Of the quiet sunniness.
And there the goats, day after day,
  Stray in sunny quietness,
Cropping here and cropping there,
  As they pause and turn and pass,
Now a bit of heather spray,
  Now a mouthful of the grass.

In the deeper sunniness,
  In the place where nothing stirs,
Quietly in quietness,
  In the quiet of the furze,
For a time they come and lie
Staring on the roving sky.

If you approach they run away,
  They leap and stare, away they bound,
  With a sudden angry sound,
To the sunny quietude;
  Crouching down where nothing stirs
  In the silence of the furze,
Crouching down again to brood
In the sunny solitude.

JAMES STEPHENS

If I were as wise as they,
  I would stray apart and brood,
I would beat a hidden way
Through the quiet heather spray
  To a sunny solitude;

And should you come I'd run away,
  I would make an angry sound,
  I would stare and turn and bound
To the deeper quietude,
  To the place where nothing stirs
  In the silence of the furze.

In that airy quietness
  I would think as long as they;
Through the quiet sunniness
  I would stray away to brood
By a hidden beaten way
  In a sunny solitude.

I would think until I found
  Something I can never find,
Something lying on the ground,
  In the bottom of my mind.

Deirdre

DO not let any woman read this verse!
  It is for men, and after them their sons,
And their sons' sons!

JAMES STEPHENS

The time comes when our hearts sink utterly;
When we remember Deirdre, and her tale,
And that her lips are dust.

Once she did tread the earth: men took her hand;
They looked into her eyes and said their say,
And she replied to them.

More than two thousand years it is since she
Was beautiful: she trod the waving grass;
She saw the clouds.

Two thousand years! The grass is still the same,
The clouds as lovely as they were that time
When Deirdre was alive.

But there has been again no woman born
Who was so beautiful; not one so beautiful
Of all the women born.

Let all men go apart and mourn together!
No man can ever love her! Not a man
Can dream to be her lover!

No man can bend before her! No man say—
What could one say to her? There are no words
That one could say to her!

Now she is but a story that is told
Beside the fire! No man can ever be
The friend of that poor queen!

JAMES STEPHENS

Hate

My enemy came nigh;
And I
Stared fiercely in his face.
My lips went writhing back in a grimace,
And stern I watched him with a narrow eye.
Then, as I turned away, my enemy,
That bitter heart and savage said to me:
'Some day, when this is past,
When all the arrows that we have are cast,
We may ask one another why we hate,
And fail to find a story to relate.
It may seem to us then a mystery
That we could hate each other.'
                         Thus said he,
And did not turn away,
Waiting to hear what I might have to say;
But I fled quickly, fearing if I stayed
I might have kissed him as I would a maid.

What Tomas Said in a Pub

I saw God! Do you doubt it?
Do you dare to doubt it?
I saw the Almighty man! His hand
Was resting on a mountain! And
He looked upon the World, and all about it:
I saw Him plainer than you see me now
—You mustn't doubt it!

JAMES STEPHENS

He was not satisfied!
His look was all dissatisfied!
His beard swung on a wind far out of sight
Behind the world's curve! And there was light
Most fearful from His forehead! And He sighed
—That star went always wrong, and from the start
I was dissatisfied!—

He lifted up His hand!
I say He heaved a dreadful hand
Over the spinning earth! Then I said,—Stay,
You must not strike it, God! I'm in the way!
And I will never move from where I stand!—
He said,—Dear child, I feared that you were dead,—
... And stayed His hand!

JOHN MILLINGTON SYNGE
1871-1909

262 He is Jealous of the Heavens and Earth

WHAT a grudge I am bearing the earth that has
its arms about her, and is holding that face
away from me, where I was finding peace from great
sadness.

What a grudge I am bearing the Heavens that are
after taking her, and shutting her in with their
greediness, the Heavens that do push their bolt
against so many.

JOHN MILLINGTON SYNGE

What a grudge I am bearing the blessed saints that have got her sweet company, that I am always seeking; and what a grudge I am bearing against Death, that is standing in her two eyes, and will not call me with a word.

(From Petrarch.)

263 *He wishes he might die and follow Laura*

IN the years of her age the most beautiful and the most flowery—the time Love has his mastery—Laura, who was my life, has gone away leaving the earth stripped and desolate. She has gone up into the Heavens, living and beautiful and naked, and from that place she is keeping her Lordship and her reign upon me, and I crying out: Ohone, when will I see that day breaking that will be my first day with herself in Paradise?

My thoughts are going after her, and it is that way my soul would follow her, lightly, and airily, and happily, and I would be rid of all my great troubles. But what is delaying me is the proper thing to lose me utterly, to make me a greater weight on my own self.

Oh, what a sweet death I might have died this day three years to-day!

(From Petrarch.)

JOHN MILLINGTON SYNGE

264 *He understands the Great Cruelty of Death*

MY flowery and green age was passing away, and I feeling a chill in the fires had been wasting my heart, for I was drawing near the hillside that is above the grave.

Then my sweet enemy was making a start, little by little, to give over her great wariness, the way she was wringing a sweet thing out of my sharp sorrow. The time was coming when Love and Decency can keep company, and lovers may sit together and say out all the things are in their hearts. But Death had his grudge against me, and he got up in the way, like an armed robber, with a pike in his hand.
(From Petrarch.)

265 *Laura waits for him in Heaven*

THE first day she passed up and down through the Heavens, gentle and simple were left standing, and they in great wonder, saying one to the other:

'What new light is that? What new beauty at all? The like of her hasn't risen up these long years from the common world.'

And herself, well pleased with the Heavens, was going forward, matching herself with the most perfect that were before her, yet one time, and another, waiting a little, and turning her head back to see if myself was coming after her. It's for that I'm lifting up all my thoughts and will into the Heavens, because I do hear her praying that I should be making haste for ever. *(From Petrarch.)*

An Old Woman's Lamentations

THE man I had a love for—a great rascal would kick me in the gutter—is dead thirty years and over it, and it is I am left behind, grey and aged. When I do be minding the good days I had, minding what I was one time, and what it is I'm come to, and when I do look on my own self, poor and dry, and pinched together, it wouldn't be much would set me raging in the streets.

Where is the round forehead I had, and the fine hair, and the two eyebrows, and the eyes with a big gay look out of them would bring folly from a great scholar? Where is my straight, shapely nose, and two ears, and my chin with a valley in it, and my lips were red and open?

Where are the pointed shoulders were on me, and the long arms and nice hands to them? Where is my bosom was as white as any, or my straight rounded sides?

It's the way I am this day—my forehead is gone away into furrows, the hair of my head is grey and whitish, my eyebrows are tumbled from me, and my two eyes have died out within my head—those eyes that would be laughing to the men—my nose has a hook on it, my ears are hanging down, and my lips are sharp and skinny.

That's what's left over from the beauty of a right woman—a bag of bones, and legs the like of two shrivelled sausages going beneath it.

JOHN MILLINGTON SYNGE

It's of the like of that we old hags do be thinking, of
   the good times are gone away from us, and we
   crouching on our hunkers by a little fire of twigs,
   soon kindled and soon spent, we that were the pick
   of many.

                                    (From Villon.)

SARA TEASDALE
                                           1884-1933

267   *'There will be Stars'*

THERE will be stars over the place for ever;
   Though the house we loved and the street we
      loved are lost,
Every time the earth circles her orbit
   On the night the autumn equinox is crossed,
Two stars we knew, poised on the peak of midnight,
   Will reach their zenith; stillness will be deep;
There will be stars over the place for ever,
   There will be stars for ever, while we sleep.

268   *The Fountain*

FOUNTAIN, fountain, what do you say
   Singing at night alone?
'It is enough to rise and fall
Here in my basin of stone.'

But are you content as you seem to be
So near the freedom and rush of the sea?
'I have listened all night to its labouring sound,
It heaves and sags, as the moon runs round;
Ocean and fountain, shadow and tree,
Nothing escapes, nothing is free.'

269 *I shall not Care*

WHEN I am dead and over me bright April
    Shakes out her rain-drenched hair,
Though you should lean above me broken-hearted,
    I shall not care.

I shall have peace, as leafy trees are peaceful
    When rain bends down the bough;
And I shall be more silent and cold-hearted
    Than you are now.

270 *Blue Squills*

HOW many million Aprils came
    Before I ever knew
How white a cherry bough could be,
    A bed of squills, how blue!

And many a dancing April
    When life is done with me,
Will lift the blue flame of the flower
    And the white flame of the tree.

SARA TEASDALE

Oh burn me with your beauty, then,
   Oh hurt me, tree and flower,
Lest in the end death try to take
   Even this glistening hour.

O shaken flowers, O shimmering trees,
   O sunlit white and blue,
Wound me, that I, through endless sleep,
   May bear the scar of you.

271   *Winter Night Song*

WILL you come as of old with singing,
   And shall I hear as of old?
Shall I rush to open the window
   In spite of the arrowy cold?

     Ah no, my dear, ah no,
       I shall sit by the fire reading,
     Though you sing half the night in the snow
       I shall not be heeding.

Though your voice remembers the forest,
   The warm green light and the birds,
Though you gather the sea in your singing
   And pour its sound into words,

     Even so, my dear, even so,
       I shall not heed you at all;
     Though your shoulders are white with snow,
       Though you strain your voice to a call,

SARA TEASDALE

I shall drowse and the fire will drowse,
 The draught will be cold on the floor,
The clock running down,
 Snow banking the door.

EDWARD THOMAS
1878-1917

The New House

Now first, as I shut the door,
 I was alone
In the new house; and the wind
 Began to moan.

Old at once was the house,
 And I was old;
My ears were teased with the dread
 Of what was foretold,

Nights of storm, days of mist, without end;
 Sad days when the sun
Shone in vain: old griefs and griefs
 Not yet begun.

All was foretold me; naught
 Could I foresee;
But I learnt how the wind would sound
 After these things should be.

EDWARD THOMAS

273 *'If I should ever by Chance'*

IF I should ever by chance grow rich
I'll buy Codham, Cockridden, and Childerditch,
Roses, Pyrgo, and Lapwater,
And let them all to my elder daughter.
The rent I shall ask of her will be only
Each year's first violets, white and lonely,
The first primroses and orchises—
She must find them before I do, that is.
But if she finds a blossom on furze
Without rent they shall all for ever be hers,
Codham, Cockridden, and Childerditch,
Roses, Pyrgo, and Lapwater,—
I shall give them all to my elder daughter.

274 *Adlestrop*

YES, I remember Adlestrop—
The name, because one afternoon
Of heat the express-train drew up there
Unwontedly. It was late June.

The steam hissed. Some one cleared his throat.
No one left and no one came
On the bare platform. What I saw
Was Adlestrop—only the name

And willows, willow-herb, and grass,
And meadowsweet, and haycocks dry,
No whit less still and lonely fair
Than the high cloudlets in the sky.

407

EDWARD THOMAS

And for that minute a blackbird sang
Close by, and round him, mistier,
Farther and farther, all the birds
Of Oxfordshire and Gloucestershire.

275   *'Out in the Dark'*

OUT in the dark over the snow
The fallow fawns invisible go
With the fallow doe;
And the winds blow
Fast as the stars are slow.

Stealthily the dark haunts round
And, when a lamp goes, without sound
At a swifter bound
Than the swiftest hound,
Arrives, and all else is drowned;

And I and star and wind and deer
Are in the dark together—near,
Yet far,—and fear
Drums in my ear
In that sage company drear.

How weak and little is the light,
All the universe of sight,
Love and delight,
Before the might,
If you love it not, of night.

W. J. TURNER

Romance

WHEN I was but thirteen or so
   I went into a golden land,
Chimborazo, Cotopaxi
   Took me by the hand.

My father died, my brother too,
   They passed like fleeting dreams,
I stood where Popocatapetl
   In the sunlight gleams.

I dimly heard the Master's voice
   And boys far-off at play,
Chimborazo, Cotopaxi
   Had stolen me away.

I walked in a great golden dream
   To and fro from school—
Shining Popocatapetl
   The dusty streets did rule.

I walked home with a gold dark boy
   And never a word I'd say,
Chimborazo, Cotopaxi
   Had taken my speech away:

I gazed entranced upon his face
   Fairer than any flower—
O shining Popocatapetl
   It was thy magic hour:

W. J. TURNER

The houses, people, traffic seemed
　　Thin fading dreams by day,
Chimborazo, Cotopaxi
　　They had stolen my soul away!

277　　*Ecstasy*

I SAW a frieze on whitest marble drawn
Of boys who sought for shells along the shore,
Their white feet shedding pallor in the sea,
The shallow sea, the spring-time sea of green
That faintly creamed against the cold, smooth pebbles.

The air was thin, their limbs were delicate,
The wind had graven their small eager hands
To feel the forests and the dark nights of Asia
Behind the purple bloom of the horizon,
Where sails would float and slowly melt away.

Their naked, pure and grave, unbroken silence
Filled the soft air as gleaming, limpid water
Fills a spring sky those days when rain is lying
In shattered bright pools on the wind-dried roads,
And their sweet bodies were wind-purified.

One held a shell unto his shell-like ear
And there was music carven in his face,
His eyes half-closed, his lips just breaking open
To catch the lulling, mazy, coralline roar
Of numberless caverns filled with singing seas.

W. J. TURNER

And all of them were hearkening as to singing
Of far-off voices thin and delicate,
Voices too fine for any mortal wind
To blow into the whorls of mortal ears—
And yet those sounds flowed from their grave, sweet
      faces.

And as I looked I heard that delicate music
And I became as grave, as calm, as still
As those carved boys. I stood upon that shore,
I felt the cool sea dream around my feet,
My eyes were staring at the far horizon:

And the wind came and purified my limbs,
And the stars came and set within my eyes,
And snowy clouds rested upon my shoulders,
And the blue sky shimmered deep within me,
And I sang like a carven pipe of music.

ANNA WICKHAM
1884-

Sehnsucht

BECAUSE of body's hunger are we born,
And by contriving hunger are we fed;
Because of hunger is our work well done,
As so are songs well sung, and things well said.
Desire and longing are the whips of God—
God save us all from death when we are fed.

ANNA WICKHAM

279 *The Mummer*

STRICT I walk my ordered way
Through the strait and duteous day;
The hours are nuns that summon me
To offices of huswifry.
Cups and cupboards, flagons, food
Are things of my solicitude.
No elfin Folly haply strays
Down my precise and well-swept ways.

When that compassionate lady Night
Shuts out a prison from my sight,
With other thrift I turn a key
Of the old chest of Memory.
And in my spacious dreams unfold
A flimsy stuff of green and gold,
And walk and wander in the dress
Of old delights, and tenderness.

280 *The Cherry-Blossom Wand*
(To be sung)

I WILL pluck from my tree a cherry-blossom wand,
And carry it in my merciless hand,
So I will drive you, so bewitch your eyes,
With a beautiful thing that can never grow wise.

Light are the petals that fall from the bough,
And lighter the love that I offer you now;
In a spring day shall the tale be told
Of the beautiful things that will never grow old.

ANNA WICKHAM

The blossoms shall fall in the night wind,
And I will leave you so, to be kind:
Eternal in beauty are short-lived flowers,
Eternal in beauty, these exquisite hours.

I will pluck from my tree a cherry-blossom wand,
And carry it in my merciless hand,
So I will drive you, so bewitch your eyes,
With a beautiful thing that shall never grow wise.

HUMBERT WOLFE
The Saint 1885-1940
She

281

Do you remember, Joan, (O vain to wonder
   if you remember how the evening star,
a thousand times you drove the herd home under,
admitted you to vision's Calendar,
    like any child
by that tall friendship and the quiet moon beguiled?)

Do you remember the Dom Rémy you knew,
   the plain, and the small mountain-range of ricks,
the poplars at their goose-step, two by two,
the brown hen-church that folded her stone-chicks,
    your father's farm,
so dear, so small it almost fitted in your arm?

HUMBERT WOLFE

Do you remember (even through the flame)
   after the long day's labour in the field
   how with the Angelus you heard your name
   mixed with the bells, and hid your face and kneeled
     when sweet and high
   a peasant heard *"ecce ancilla Domini"*?

"Behold the servant of the Lord—and France,"
   and in your hands, that never held a sword,
   the country staff was lifted like a lance
   in the hushed aisles of evening, to the Lord,
     and you were gone
   for ever, Joan, to put immortal iron on.

What was your sainthood, Joan? You did not guess
   when you restored his lilies to your king
   that you had found beyond the fleur-de-lys
   the lilies in an everlasting spring
     whose wind is blown
   across the centuries, and is fragrant, Joan.

You were not a proud saint. You went alone
   among the soldiers, and you understood
   how men are only frightened angels, Joan,
   and evil only unprotected good;
     you knew these things,
   and knew how pardonable are the hearts of kings.

And, being a woman, you lifted mankind up
   against the devil in their own despite,
   and when they feared, you drank the bitter cup

for all your cowards as by woman's right,
   and even when
you burned, you did not blame them, knowing
      they were men.

Saint Joan, it may be all things human must
   be dull with earth, and with the darkness faint,
but if it be so, then your mortal dust
   was purged with flame till you were all a saint,
     and when you prayed
fire spoke to fire, and mixed in heaven, Maid.

Snow

AUSTERE, removed, grave as the thought of
    death,
   and whiter than white hands for ever lost,
tangible shape of beauty's frozen breath,
   incredible and noiseless as a ghost,
snow, be saluted. All our magics else
   are green as Merlin woven about with leaves,
green turf, green lilies ere they break their shells,
   green buds in April's green and luminous eves.
All that the kingfisher or peacock owes
   of dyes that flame together and rejoice
   in sunsets fallen are gathered in thy white,
thou in whose pale dominion the heart knows
   the presence of the legendary voice,
   whose candid accent blossomed into light.

HUMBERT WOLFE
Iliad

FALSE dreams, all false,
mad heart, were yours.
The word, and nought else,
in time endures.
Not you long after,
perished and mute,
will last, but the defter
viol and lute.
Sweetly they'll trouble
the listeners
with the cold dropped pebble
of painless verse.
Not you will be offered,
but the poet's false pain.
Mad heart, you have suffered
and loved in vain.
What joy doth Helen
or Paris have
where these lie still in
a nameless grave?
Her beauty's a wraith,
and the boy Paris
muffles in death
his mouth's cold cherries.
Aye! these are less,
that were love's summer,
than one gold phrase
of old blind Homer.
Not Helen's wonder

nor Paris stirs,
but the bright untender
hexameters.
And thus, all passion
is nothing made,
but a star to flash in
an Iliad.
Mad heart, you were wrong!
No love of yours,
but only what is sung,
when love's over, endures.

284 *Journey's End*

WHAT will they give me, when journey's done?
    Your own room to be quiet in, Son!

Who shares it with me?   There is none
shares that cool dormitory, Son!

Who turns the sheets?   There is but one,
And no one needs to turn it, Son!

Who lights the candle?   Everyone
sleeps without candle all night, Son!

Who calls me after sleeping?   Son,
You are not called when journey's done.

HUMBERT WOLFE

285 From 'Kensington Gardens'

(a) *Lamb*

THE old bellwether
  looked at the lamb
as a gentleman looks
when he mutters 'Damn!'

'If you jump and frisk,
you little fool,
you'll only end
by losing your wool.

When I was a lamb
I always would
Behave as like a sheep
as I could.'

'Did you!' the lamb
replied with a leap,
'I always thought
you were born a sheep.'

The park-keeper said
to the boy on the fence,
'Let's have less
of your impudence!

Off with you now,
and do as you're bade,
or you'll end in prison.
When I was a lad . . .'

HUMBERT WOLFE

(b) *The Green Parrot*

'I WANT a green parrot,'
  the little boy said.
'Now what's put a parrot
into 'is 'ead,

unless 'e 'eard father
last night with the 'orrors?'
said ma. 'Now be quiet
and look at the sparrers!'

But the little boy wouldn't
be comforted:
'I want a green parrot,
green parrot,' he said.

(c) *Two Sparrows*

TWO sparrows, feeding,
  heard a thrush
sing to the dawn.
The first said, 'Tush!

In all my life
I never heard
a more affected
singing-bird.'

The second said,
'It's you and me,
who slave to keep
the likes of he.'

HUMBERT WOLFE

'And if we cared,'
both sparrows said,
'we'd do that singing
on our head.'

The thrush pecked sideways,
and was dumb.
'And now,' they screamed,
'he's pinched our crumb.'

(d) *Thrushes*

THE City Financier
 walks in the gardens
, stiffly, because of
his pride and his burdens.

The daisies, looking
up, observe
only a self-
respecting curve.

The thrushes only
see a flat
table-land
of shiny hat.

He looks importantly
about him,
while all the spring
goes on without him.

WILLIAM BUTLER YEATS
1865-1939

286 *The Song of Wandering Aengus*

I WENT out to the hazel wood,
Because a fire was in my head,
And cut and peeled a hazel wand,
And hooked a berry to a thread;
And when white moths were on the wing,
And moth-like stars were flickering out,
I dropped the berry in a stream
And caught a little silver trout.

When I had laid it on the floor
I went to blow the fire a-flame,
But something rustled on the floor,
And some one called me by my name:
It had become a glimmering girl
With apple blossom in her hair
Who called me by my name and ran
And faded through the brightening air.

Though I am old with wandering
Through hollow lands and hilly lands,
I will find out where she has gone,
And kiss her lips and take her hands;
And walk among long dappled grass,
And pluck till time and times are done
The silver apples of the moon,
The golden apples of the sun.

WILLIAM BUTLER YEATS

287 *The Wild Swans at Coole*

THE trees are in their autumn beauty,
　The woodland paths are dry,
Under the October twilight the water
Mirrors a still sky;
Upon the brimming water among the stones
Are nine-and-fifty swans.

The nineteenth autumn has come upon me
Since I first made my count;
I saw, before I had well finished,
All suddenly mount
And scatter, wheeling in great broken rings
Upon their clamorous wings.

I have looked upon those brilliant creatures,
And now my heart is sore.
All's changed since I, hearing at twilight,
The first time on this shore,
The bell-beat of their wings above my head,
Trod with a lighter tread.

Unwearied still, lover by lover,
They paddle in the cold
Companionable streams or climb the air;
Their hearts have not grown old;
Passion or conquest, wander where they will,
Attend upon them still.

But now they drift on the still water,
Mysterious, beautiful;
Among what rushes will they build,
By what lake's edge or pool
Delight men's eyes when I awake some day
To find they have flown away?

288 *The Rose of the World*

WHO dreamed that beauty passes like a dream?
For these red lips, with all their mournful pride,
Mournful that no new wonder may betide,
Troy passed away in one high funeral gleam,
And Usna's children died.

We and the labouring world are passing by:
Amid men's souls, that waver and give place
Like the pale waters in their wintry race,
Under the passing stars, foam of the sky,
Lives on this lonely face.

Bow down, archangels, in your dim abode:
Before you were, or any hearts to beat,
Weary and kind one lingered by His seat;
He made the world to be a grassy road
Before her wandering feet.

WILLIAM BUTLER YEATS

289   'Down by the Salley Gardens'

DOWN by the salley gardens my love and I did meet;
She pass'd the salley gardens with little snow-white feet.
She bid me take love easy, as the leaves grow on the tree;
But I, being young and foolish, with her would not agree.

In a field by the river my love and I did stand,
And on my leaning shoulder she laid her snow-white hand.
She bid me take life easy, as the grass grows on the weirs;
But I was young and foolish, and now am full of tears.

290   Aedh Wishes for the Cloths of Heaven

HAD I the heavens' embroidered cloths,
Enwrought with golden and silver light,
The blue and the dim and the dark cloths
Of night and light and the half-light,
I would spread the cloths under your feet:
But I, being poor, have only my dreams;
I have spread my dreams under your feet;
Tread softly because you tread on my dreams.

WILLIAM BUTLER YEATS

291 *'When You are Old'*

WHEN you are old and gray and full of sleep,
    And nodding by the fire, take down this book,
And slowly read, and dream of the soft look
Your eyes had once, and of their shadows deep;

How many loved your moments of glad grace,
    And loved your beauty with love false or true;
But one man loved the pilgrim soul in you,
And loved the sorrows of your changing face;

And bending down beside the glowing bars,
    Murmur, a little sadly, how love fled
And paced upon the mountains overhead,
And hid his face amid a crowd of stars.

292 *The Fiddler of Dooney*

WHEN I play on my fiddle in Dooney,
    Folk dance like a wave of the sea;
My cousin is priest in Kilvarnet,
My brother in Moharabuiee.

I passed my brother and cousin:
They read in their books of prayer;
I read in my book of songs
I bought at the Sligo fair.

WILLIAM BUTLER YEATS

When we come at the end of time,
To Peter sitting in state,
He will smile on the three old spirits,
But call me first through the gate;

For the good are always the merry,
Save by an evil chance,
And the merry love the fiddle,
And the merry love to dance:

And when the folk there spy me,
They will all come up to me,
With, "Here is the fiddler of Dooney!"
And dance like a wave of the sea.

BIOGRAPHICAL NOTES

A.E. (George Russell)—1867-1935. Born in Lurgan, County of Armagh. Educated in Dublin, attending Rathmines School and later Metropolitan School of Art where he met William Butler Yeats and several others who were to be prominent in the Irish Literary Movement or Renaissance as it is sometimes called. Worked as an accountant for some time but in 1897 became an organiser of the Irish Agricultural Society with which he was long associated. He edited the important Irish publication, "The Irish Homestead" (1904-'30). Associated with Yeats, Katharine Tynan and Lady Gregory in sponsoring and organising the Irish Renaissance. Made a careful study of theosophy and oriental philosophy. In his later years he lectured about both and became an acknowledged authority in Britain, the United States and Canada. He published many volumes of verse and was well known in addition as an essayist and painter.

Aiken, Conrad Potter—Born at Savannah, Georgia in 1889. Educated in Massachusetts, entering Harvard where he was a contemporary of Robert Benchley, Van Wyck Brooks, Heywood Broun, T. S. Eliot, Walter Lippman and Alan Seeger. Graduated in 1912. Then followed three years of travel abroad. Returning to the United States he began a life of devotion to literature. He settled some years ago in Cambridge, Mass., became an instructor in English at Harvard. Aiken showed talent in versification even at College. His style has undergone many influences and has developed in a variety of ways. At its best it is characterised by subtlety of rhythm, which is perhaps related to Aiken's passionate love of music, and exquisite diction. The thought is at times elusive.

BIOGRAPHICAL NOTES

ARMSTRONG, MARTIN—Born at Newcastle-on-Tyne in 1882. His maternal grandmother was Elizabeth Wordsworth, cousin of the great William. Educated at Charterhouse and Pembroke College, Cambridge. Married Jessie McDonald, formerly the wife of Conrad Aiken. Served in the World War from 1914-1919. "The Buzzards and other Poems" appeared in 1921. He has not written a great deal of poetry since. Has unusual ability as short story writer. "The Goat and Compasses" (a novel) appeared in 1925 and attracted much attention.

AUDEN, WYSTAN HUGH—Born in York in 1907. **Educated at Gresham's College, Holt, and at Christ Church, Oxford.** Schoolmaster for a short time. Became a member of group of young "leftist" poets in London (sometimes referred to as young Communist Poets). His friend Spender says Auden was never in complete agreement with communist doctrine. In 1937 drove ambulance for Loyalists in Spanish Revolution. Married Erika Mann, daughter of Thomas Mann. On return from Spain received the King's Poetry Medal. **In 1939 came to** United States to live. Has written much in collaboration with Christopher Isherwood. Much of his verse is extremely obscure. He seems at times to indulge in verbal acrobatics, a fact that may have some relation to his own admission that he is something of an exhibitionist. He says he would like above everything else to be an expert diver—it would be "such a marvellous way of showing off". Such statements are doubtless made with his tongue in his cheek. There is much beauty and dignity in his poetry and behind it one feels a great seriousness of purpose.

AYLEN, ELISE—Mrs. Duncan Campbell Scott lives in Ottawa. She has not published a great deal of verse but what she

BIOGRAPHICAL NOTES

has is distinguished by fine, sensitive poetic feeling. In 1930 a volume, "Roses of Shadow" appeared with an introduction by Dr. Scott.

Belloc, Hilaire—Born near Paris in 1870. Father was a French barrister, Mother an Englishwoman. Belloc lived as a small child in France, then went to England. Attended the Oratory School at Edgbaston where he came in contact with Cardinal Newman. Later entered Balliol College, Oxford where he had a brilliant scholarly career. In 1903 became a naturalized Englishman. 1906-1910 was Liberal member for South Salford. He lost interest in politics and devoted himself largely to literature. He has a widely varied talent—novelist, essayist, master of epigram and poet. Is almost invariably associated with his contemporary, G. K. Chesterton. He has long been known for his opposition to radicalism whether in politics or art.

Benét, Stephen Vincent—Born at Bethlehem, Pa., 1898; died 1943. Father was colonel in permanent U.S. Army. Son's education secured at various points where the father was stationed. Early interest in literature—when only 17 published volume of dramatic monologues. Entered Yale University where Archibald MacLeish, Thornton Wilder and Philip Barry were among his contemporaries. Graduated from Yale in 1919. In 1926 was awarded a Guggenheim Fellowship which he used to make an intensive study of the American Civil War. One result of his study was "John Brown's Body" which won the Pulitzer Prize for poetry in 1928. Benét was deeply stirred by the outbreak of the present war. This is shown in his poem "Nightmare at Noon" published in 1940. "Western Star", a great dramatic narrative poem based on the American pioneer, was left unfinished at his death.

BIOGRAPHICAL NOTES

BINYON, LAURENCE—Born at Lancaster in 1869; died 1943. Educated at St. Paul's School and at Trinity College, Oxford. Won the Newdigate Prize for Poetry in 1890. In 1893 entered the service of the British Museum where he was many years in charge of Oriental Prints and Drawings. Early verse was admired by Browning and Arnold. Perhaps partly because he was kept so busy at the Museum his poetic ability developed slowly but continuously. Has written a good deal about the relation of painting and poetry, notable among his volumes being "The Drawings and Engravings of William Blake" (1922). He came to be recognized as an authority on Asiatic Art. He was Norton Professor of Poetry at Harvard during the year 1933-34.

BIRNEY, EARLE—Born in Calgary, Alberta, in 1904. Educated at University of British Columbia and Toronto. He did post graduate work at the University of California and at London University. Birney has lived an extremely varied existence, working at a large number of different occupations—newsboy, delivery boy, farm hand, ditch-digger, mountain guide, logger, sailor, bank clerk, teacher. He has taught at the University of Utah and at the summer sessions of the University of British Columbia. He is Professor of English at University College, Toronto.

BRIDGES, ROBERT—Born at Walmer, Isle of Thanet, in 1844; died near Oxford in 1930. Educated at Eton and Corpus Christi, Oxford. He studied medicine receiving his degree at the age of 30. Then took post of casualty surgeon at St. Bartholomew's Hospital, London. Had long been interested in literature and writing. First volume of poetry published in 1873. In 1882 Bridges

BIOGRAPHICAL NOTES

retired from medical practice and devoted himself to literature exclusively. (He was all his life an ardent lover and student of music and had many friends among the group of contemporary British composers. A great many of his lyrics were set to music.) He devoted much time to the study of the technique of verse and was one of the founders of the Society for Pure English in 1913. In that year he became England's 16th poet laureate succeeding Alfred Austin. In 1918 he made a great contribution to English literature by the publication of the poems of his former friend, Gerard Manley Hopkins. The later years of his life were filled with honours both state and academic. He was one of the most learned of English poets. He wrote with authority and facility on art, music, science, philosophy, medicine as well as literature. He knew and spoke many European languages. Perhaps surprising in so scholarly a man, Bridges was an unusually sensitive poet. This is best seen in his brief lyrics. His long philosophical poem, "The Testament of Beauty" was published in 1929 only a few months before his death. It is considered by many critics to be the crowning achievement of his long and distinguished career as a poet.

BROOKE, RUPERT—Born at Rugby in 1887; died at Skyros on April 23rd, 1915. Educated at Rugby where his father was an assistant master, and at King's College, Cambridge. As an undergraduate he attracted much attention by virtue of his handsome physique and his prowess in athletics. Edward Thomas described him as "a golden young Apollo". Spent much time in travel on the continent. Settled in 1909 at Grantchester and devoted himself to literary studies, specialising in the Elizabethan period. First volume appeared in 1911. There was in his verse a sense of boredom with society

BIOGRAPHICAL NOTES

and occasional cynicism. Suffered a nervous breakdown and travelled on the continent. Returning to England he found his existence intolerable and in 1913 set sail for New York and, via San Francisco, for the South Sea Islands. Spent three months in Tahiti. Returned to England via Canada and the United States early in 1914. The outbreak of the World War brought a great challenge to him as to many other young men of the time for whom life had become a savourless routine. Brooke wrote:

"Now, God be thanked Who has matched us with
    His hour
And caught our youth and wakened us from sleeping."

He joined the Royal Naval Reserves in September, 1914, saw service at the Defence of Antwerp. In 1915 (February) he set sail with the ill-fated expeditionary force for the Dardanelles campaign. He never reached his destination. He died of blood-poisoning on April 23rd off the Island of Skyros. His body was buried there by his friends. He bequeathed the proceeds of his literary estate to three poet friends—Lascelles Abercrombie, Walter de la Mare and Wilfred Gibson. Brooke is perhaps the most widely known and popular of the Georgian poets. His sonnet sequence, 1914, and his untimely death made him a sort of symbol of courage and patriotic sacrifice.

BROWN, AUDREY ALEXANDRA—Born at Nanaimo, B.C., in 1904. Has been an invalid during almost her whole life. Her first volume, "A Dryad in Nanaimo" (1931) revealed her as a gifted poet. She had undoubtedly been much influenced by her reading of 19th Century Poetry, particularly by Keats and Morris. Her later war poem, "The Phoenix", shows a very remarkable advance in originality and freshness of technique. Her work has

BIOGRAPHICAL NOTES

been described by Professor L. A. Mackay,—"Allied with vivid and even luscious description is a strong and delicate poignancy of feeling, a dignified, tragic sensitiveness".

CAMPBELL, ROY—Born at Durban, Natal, in 1902. As a boy, when not at school, he was brought up in the wilds of Natal and Rhodesia. At the University of Natal he was an outstanding rugby player. Went to Oxford but failed in his examinations and left on a walking tour through southern France. He lived among the fishermen at Marseilles for a time. He has been very famous as a bull-fighter. He fought in the arena of Arles and Nimes, taking three cocardes in 1921. When he lived in Martigues he jousted for the city in the championships of the Mediterranean. At the Taurine Gala at Istres in 1931 he won the cocarde, fighting without cape and throwing the bull single-handed. He is a member of several famous bull-fighters' clubs. As a youth he was a free-thinker but joined the Roman Catholic Church in 1935. He claimed to be a Fascist and served with Franco's forces during the Spanish Revolution. Campbell has always had an interest in writing. His first volume, "The Flaming Terrapin" (1924), caused a mild sensation. There was a vigour in the work which led Edith Sitwell to refer to him as a "poetic tornado". This strong virility, sometimes an almost brutal force, is present in all his work. In many of his poems one finds a dark, brooding, rebellious spirit which is distinctly Byronic.

CARMAN, BLISS—Born in Fredericton, N.B., in 1861; died at New Canaan, Conn., in 1929. Received a thorough education at University of N.B. and Edinburgh. Returning to Canada he taught for a time, then attempted to take up engineering and law. Succeeding in neither he went to Harvard where he studied history and

BIOGRAPHICAL NOTES

philosophy. In 1890 he went to New York where he did editorial work on several magazines. He spent most of the remainder of his life in the U.S.A. He had a long and distinguished career as teacher, poet, editor and lecturer. He was one of the first Canadian poets to establish an international reputation. At his death he was recognized as Canada's leading poet.

CHESTERTON, GILBERT KEITH—Born in London in 1874; died in 1936. Educated at St. Paul's School and the Slade School of Art. He has made a great reputation for himself as a journalist and essayist. He is a master of paradox and has continued the tradition of the London city wits. He has written everything from keen criticism to an amazing series of religious detective stories ("The Innocence of Father Brown"). But it is perhaps as a poet that he will be longest remembered. "Lepanto" is one of the most stirring of modern ballads. "The Rolling English Road" captures a truly English humour. Many of his poems set aside the bantering, sometimes facetious manner for which Chesterton is famous and reveal a devout religious spirit. He became a convert to Roman Catholicism in 1922.

COFFIN, ROBERT P. TRISTRAM—Born in Brunswick, Maine, in 1892. Educated in Brunswick Schools and at Bowdoin College. A brilliant scholar, he went to Princeton for a year, then was chosen Rhodes Scholar from Maine and spent three years at Trinity College, Oxford. Was in England from 1916 to 1921, his studies at Oxford being broken by service in France during the World War. Returned to the U.S. to teach at Wells College, Aurora, N.Y. In 1934 became Professor of English at Bowdoin where he has been ever since. In 1936 "Strange Holiness" won the Pulitzer Prize for Poetry. At Bowdoin

BIOGRAPHICAL NOTES

Coffin gives reading recitals of poetry. He says, "I have a feeling that poetry can still be a *public function,* as it once was, can be *oratory* and can convince people of the possibility of design in living and supply the pattern that once was inherent in religion but that religion is losing for many people today".

COLUM, PADRAIC—Born at Longford, Ireland, in 1881. He is living now at New Canaan, Conn. He was educated at the local schools and when he was only twenty years of age he became identified with the Irish National Theatre, later known as the Abbey Theatre. Colum's first writing was in dramatic form, many of his plays being presented by the Abbey Theatre Players. By 1916 Colum had come to the United States where he has lived almost continuously ever since. His verse concerning simple Irish characters and his interest in folk lore brought him an interesting appointment—in 1923 he was invited by the Government of Hawaii to go to the Islands to study the native myths and stories and put them into form suitable for children. In this task he was highly successful thanks to his skill in story telling and his talent for simplicity.

CORNFORD, FRANCES—Born in Cambridge, England, in 1886. She is a daughter of Sir Francis Darwin, third son of the late Charles Darwin.

CUMMINGS, EDWARD ESTLIN—(prefers to be known as e e cummings). Born in Cambridge, Mass., in 1894. Educated at Harvard. On the outbreak of the World War he enlisted and went to France as an ambulance driver. When the United States entered the war he re-enlisted as a private. After the war he remained in France for several years. He then returned to New York where he has lived since. Cummings is now well known as a

BIOGRAPHICAL NOTES

painter, a novelist and a poet. His novel, "The Enormous Room", based upon an experience in a military detention camp, was published in 1922 and gained him considerable success. In painting and verse Cummings has been a confirmed experimenter. His experiments in verse have not been with the poetic form alone but even with typography and punctuation. He has invited and received violent attacks from many readers and critics who believe that a first function of art is to say something in an intelligible manner. One critic has summed up the situation thus, "It is a sort of super-verbalism that drives some readers to frenzy and others to disgust, but it conceals in its depths, if one has sufficient patience and tolerance, much brilliant irony and much poignant beauty".

DAVIES, WILLIAM HENRY—Born at Newport in Monmouthshire, Wales, in 1870. Left school at an early age and was apprenticed, by his grandfather, first to an ironmonger and later to a picture framer. He grew weary of this and came to America. Arriving in New York with $10.00 in his pocket he set about making a living. He fell in with a professional beggar who taught him the tricks of his trade. For several years he led a most precarious existence as a tramp in the United States and Canada. At 30 he set out for the Klondike but an accident interfered with that plan—in attempting to board a moving train he fell under the wheels and had his right foot cut off. He went back to England and during his convalescence returned to his early interest in writing. At first he attracted no attention and eked out a very poor living as a pedlar. In 1905 he succeeded in having printed at his own expense his first volume, "The Soul's Destroyer and other Poems". He sent copies to a number of people asking that they either send him half a crown or return the book. George Bernard Shaw to whom a copy was sent was intrigued by this "attractively simple and sensible" proposition, saw great merit in the work and sponsored Davies before the public. His position was thus at once established. It was further consolidated by the publication of the "Autobiography of a Super Tramp" (1907) with its frank descriptions of the life of the beggar and professional tramp. Since that time Davies has written prolifically—both prose and poetry.

DE LA MARE, WALTER—Born in Charlton, Kent, in 1873. Descended from an old Huguenot family. Educated at St. Paul's School in London where he revealed brilliant scholarly ability. Left school at 17 and entered employ of Anglo-American Oil Company. He worked in their London office as an accountant for 18 years. He had long been interested in writing and had become fairly well known as a reviewer, essayist and poet. He first wrote under the pseudonym Walter Ramal. His first volume of verse, "Songs of Childhood", was published in 1902. Since 1908 he has devoted himself entirely to literature. He is one of the most prolific of contemporary writers. His verse is characterised by great sensitiveness to beauty of rhythm and verbal sound, by a whimsical attitude towards people and things and by a very unusual sense of the mysterious and uncanny. He explores little understood recesses of human experience and often "takes his fascinated reader to the edge of that other world which surrounds the material and physical". J. B. Priestly says he "remains to criticism an elusive figure whose outline and gestures are not easily fixed in memory—a shadowy Pied Piper". These qualities are clearly to be seen in his amazingly discerning children's verse and in such poems as "The Listeners", "Sam's Three Wishes". They have endeared him to great numbers of readers who

BIOGRAPHICAL NOTES

were first captivated by the sheer beauty of the imagery and diction and by the subtle loveliness of the rhythmic movement of his verse.

DRINKWATER, JOHN—Born at Leytonstone, London, in 1882; died in 1937. Father was a schoolmaster and later a travelling actor. The boy lived with his grandfather in Oxford and was educated at the Oxford High School. From an early age and for many years he worked in an insurance office. He early showed interest in writing and in the theatre. He helped found the Pilgrim Players who later developed into the Birmingham Repertory Theatre. Several of Drinkwater's plays were produced successfully in London and New York. His best known and most successful drama, "Abraham Lincoln", was published in 1918.

ELIOT, THOMAS STEARNS—Born in St. Louis, Missouri, in 1888. Educated at Harvard, the Sorbonne and Merton College, Oxford. He has lived almost continuously in London since 1913. He has been a lecturer and teacher and for many years now has been a member of the editorial staff of Faber and Faber. In 1922 he established "The Criterion", a literary magazine which for the next 17 years exerted a far-reaching influence. Eliot has undoubtedly been one of the most sensitive and accomplished observers of life during the past thirty years. He has written much verse and a great deal of fine critical prose. His early verse which was objected to by many because of its difficulty, even at times obscurity, and its uncompromisingly ironical approach to life is often held by critics to be his finest. This position is challenged by his later work, for instance "The Journey of the Magi" (1927), "Ash Wednesday" (1930), "Four Quartets" (1943)—work in which there is great beauty and dignity of style, profundity and nobility of thought.

BIOGRAPHICAL NOTES

Field, Michael—Behind this pseudonym lies one of the strangest collaborations in literary history—a pooling of literary talent and effort by Katherine Harris Bradley (1846-1914) and her niece, Edith Emma Cooper (1862-1913). The secret of the disguise under which their poems were produced was penetrated by few people during the lifetime of the writers. Their work was welcomed with enthusiastic admiration by Robert Browning, Herbert Spencer, George Meredith, George Moore and Oscar Wilde. It had a great vogue during the late 80's and since has experienced alternate periods of neglect and adulation. Sturge Moore published a selection of their poems with an introduction in 1923.

Flecker, James Elroy—Born in London in 1884; died in Switzerland in 1915. Educated in Uppingham and at Trinity College, Oxford. Took special courses in Oriental languages at Cambridge. Travelled extensively and went to Constantinople in the British Consular Service in 1910. He later spent two years in Beirut (1911-13). His work shows his constant preoccupation with the craftsmanship of verse. It reveals two important influences—his sojourn in the East and his passion for the French Parnassians. He was very much opposed to the growing cult of realistic diction in poetry.

Fletcher, John Gould—Born at Little Rock, Arkansas, in 1886. Educated at Phillips Academy (Andover) and at Harvard which he entered in 1903. During his senior year he lost his father. A modest legacy made him financially independent. In 1908 he went to Europe, visiting Italy. Returned to London where he lived for several years. He was encouraged in his first attempts at verse by the Imagists—Ezra Pound, Harriet Monroe and Amy Lowell. He was deeply interested in modern French painting and music. Returned to the United States in

BIOGRAPHICAL NOTES

1914 but, after two years, went back to England where he lived until 1933. He then came back to America settling in Arkansas. He won the Pulitzer Prize for Poetry in 1939. Gould's verse has shown a remarkable and steady development. Beginning as a rather colourless writer, influenced by the Imagist Group, he has achieved a strong vigorous style which matches very well the rugged subjects which he often chooses.

FLINT, F. S.—Born in 1885, son of a commercial traveller. Early years were impoverished. Left school in early teens and worked at odd jobs. At 19 he entered the Civil Service as a typist. In that same year he was deeply stirred by the poetry of Keats and felt the urge to write himself. Attended night school, studying Latin and French. Discovered a great aptitude for languages. Later became known as an authority on French verse, was deeply impressed by modern French poets and translated the works of Verhaeren and Jean de Bosschère. In 1919, after serving in the World War, he entered the Ministry of Labour. Flint's verse often shows the influence of the Imagist Group.

FREEMAN, JOHN—Born in London in 1880; died in 1929. He was for many years chief executive officer in the Department of National Health Insurance. He was prominent as a poet, critic and novelist. Won the Hawthornden Prize for Poetry in 1920. His most successful poems are his highly sensitive and atmospheric descriptions of nature. He wrote a number of very beautiful love lyrics. One of his friends is reported as saying, "If ever a poet sang simply to please himself and because he could not help singing that poet was John Freeman".

BIOGRAPHICAL NOTES

Frost, Robert—Born in San Francisco in 1875. At the age of ten went East to New England States where his family had lived for generations. It is here that he has found the inspiration of his work. Attended High School at Lawrence, Mass., then entered Dartmouth College but stayed only a short time. Went to work in a mill. Began to write verse but attracted no attention. At 22, already married, he went to Harvard remaining only two years. His unusually original, independent cast of mind and his love of the soil have always made it difficult for him to submit to academic routine. After his time at Harvard Frost followed various occupations—shoe-making, school-teaching, farming. In 1900 he bought a farm in Derry, New Hampshire, and for 11 years tried to wrest a living from the stubborn soil. In 1912 his wife who had always been his inspiration and best critic suggested that the family move to England. This proved a fortunate decision. During the three years which he spent in England where he lived in London and later on a farm in Gloucestershire he received his first encouragement as a poet and published his first volume (1913). Returning to the United States in 1915 he found himself famous. Since that time he has taught at various colleges and universities and has lectured widely throughout the country. He has been the recipient of many honours. He has a farm in Vermont where he spends some time each year.

Frost's position is now secure. There is no more authentic voice in American poetry than his: he is often referred to as the poet laureate of New England. He has avoided all posing, whether aesthetic or philosophical. The easy simplicity of his style conceals from some readers a remarkable subtlety both of thought and poetic technique. The discerning reader will find here grace

BIOGRAPHICAL NOTES

and beauty, homely wit, humour, occasional irony and, pervading the whole, an honest, earthy, courageous philosophy of life.

GIBSON, WILFRED WILSON—Born at Hexham, Northumberland in 1878. Educated at private schools. In 1912 he went to live in London. On the outbreak of war in 1914 he volunteered for service but was not accepted. It was not until 1917 when he returned from a speaking trip in the United States that he was finally accepted in the Army Service Corps with which he served until 1919. His verse has undergone many changes. He was deeply affected by his experiences in the War. He has written much about simple characters and life in the English countryside and has made considerable use of English dialects in his verse. In this respect he has been compared with Wordsworth.

GRAVES, ROBERT—Born at Wimbledon of Irish parentage in 1895. Educated at Charterhouse and St. John's College, Oxford. Joined the British Expeditionary Force at the outbreak of War, serving in France in the same regiment as Siegfried Sassoon. Began to write verse seriously while in the trenches. Like Sassoon and Read he was deeply moved by the horror and human waste of war but his war verse lacks the bitterness of Sassoon's. Later works reveal whimsical humour and broad human sympathy. Has written several volumes of prose. "Goodbye to All That" was a provocative work and was at first suppressed in England. "I, Claudius" and "Claudius, the God", novels dealing with life in ancient Rome, brought him outstanding success.

GRENFELL, JULIAN—1888-1915. Eldest son of Lord Desborough. Educated at Eton and Balliol College, Oxford. Obtained a commission in the Royal Dragoons

BIOGRAPHICAL NOTES

in 1910. Died of wounds in 1915. His literary output was very small. His fame rests upon the one poem, "Into Battle", which was sent home in a letter from the trenches. His reaction to war was very different from that of Sassoon, Read and Owen.

GUSTAFSON, RALPH—Born near Sherbrooke, Quebec, in 1909. Educated at Bishop's College and at Oxford where he spent three years, graduating in 1933. He has done some fine experimentation in verse and is recognized as one of the most prominent members of the group of young poets in Canada. He has published several volumes of original verse and a very good "Anthology of Canadian Poetry" which was brought out in the Penguin Library in 1942. Critics note in the latest work of Gustafson a definite influence of Gerard Manley Hopkins.

(H.D.) DOOLITTLE, HILDA—Born at Bethlehem, Pennsylvania, in 1886. When she was still a small child her father was appointed director of the Flower Observatory and moved his family to Philadelphia. Hilda attended private schools there and in 1904 entered Bryn Mawr College. She went to Europe in 1911 intending to make a brief trip. After visiting France and Italy she went to London where she met a number of young and enthusiastic poets, among them Ezra Pound. She helped to found the Imagist Group. Her own work which was signed "H.D." appeared in the leading English literary magazines. In 1913 she married the talented young English critic and poet, Richard Aldington. With him she began the translation of Greek lyrical poetry, work which seems to have had a profound influence on her. She has remained one of the most consistent and faithful members of the Imagist Group. She has adhered strictly to its credo which was published in 1914. For H.D. this

BIOGRAPHICAL NOTES

creed was never a pose—it described the way in which she could best give expression to her vision of beauty. Hilda Doolittle has remained in London with the exception of one brief visit to America.

HARDY, THOMAS—Born near Dorchester in 1840; died in 1928. Educated at Dorchester Primary School and, for one year, by a French governess. At 16 entered an ecclesiastical architect's office. Later he went up to London to study architecture more intensively. In 1863 he won a prize offered by the Royal Institute of British Architects. For five years he was assistant to the celebrated British architect, Sir Arthur Blomfield. His work took him into some of the oldest and finest churches in England. Attended night classes at King's College. During this early London period Hardy was writing verse and prose but his work was not taken seriously. Finally abandoned architecture and devoted himself to literature. In 1871 his first novel, "Desperate Remedies", appeared. Then followed a succession of great novels, among them, "Far from the Madding Crowd" (1874), "The Return of the Native" (1878), "Tess of the d'Urbervilles" (1891), "Jude the Obscure" (1895). They brought him international prominence but the public reaction to his work, particularly in England, was largely unfavourable. Hardy's frank, sincere, uncompromising courage in facing the facts of life and human experience was denounced by the public as cynicism, unbounded pessimism and destructive atheism. He was attacked in pulpit and press. Partly as a result of such attacks upon "Jude the Obscure" he turned away from the novel, going back to his early love, poetry. In 1898 "Wessex Poems" appeared. The next few years saw many volumes of verse, among them his great epic drama of the Napoleonic era, "The Dynasts". He achieved a very

BIOGRAPHICAL NOTES

great fame as a poet and for many years before his death was recognized as England's most distinguished literary figure. After his death his heart was removed and buried in the grave of his first wife in the little cemetery at Woking, Surrey; his body was cremated and the ashes were buried in the Poets' Corner in Westminster Abbey.

Hardy's verse was at first considered angular, awkward in expression and difficult to understand. We now see that it possesses great beauty and dignity, directness and incisiveness of style, at times remarkable grace of expression. There is always a lofty objectivity in his treatment of life situations. His poetry is perhaps Hardy's surest guarantee of permanent literary fame.

HODGSON, RALPH—Born in Yorkshire in 1871. He has always been something of a recluse avoiding publicity. Little is known definitely about his biography—even the date and place of his birth are not known with certainty. This is perhaps not the least of Hodgson's achievements in an age so publicity-conscious as ours. He lived in America and in 1924 went to Japan as a lecturer at Sendai University. He has a great admiration and love for animals and birds. He has often championed them in his writing revealing their dignity and deploring man's stupid, cruel treatment of them. He is the leading authority in the British Isles on English bull-terriers. Poetry is for Hodgson an avocation, a hobby. He has achieved moments of intense lyric inspiration and great beauty of expression.

HOPKINS, GERARD MANLEY—Born at Stratford, Essex, in 1844; died in 1889. Educated at Highgate Grammar School and Balliol College, Oxford. While at Oxford he came under the influence of Jowett and Newman. When, at the age of 22, he was received into the Society

BIOGRAPHICAL NOTES

of Jesus he burned all his early poems and resolved to write no more, a resolution to which fortunately he did not adhere strictly. He spent some time with Newman doing mission work in Birmingham, later obtained a Church in Oxford and, in 1884, was appointed to a teaching fellowship in the Catholic University at Dublin where he remained until his death five years later. At his death Hopkins' manuscripts, including those of his poems, went to Robert Bridges, a close friend from his Oxford days. In 1918 Bridges published Hopkins' poems. The poems reveal profundity and exalted beauty of thought. The style was at once recognized as strikingly original. It presents very real obstacles to the reader but he who will face these and proceed to an understanding of these lyrics will be richly rewarded. It is pertinent to say that the peculiarities of style are never superficial, self-conscious tricks of the poet. They are closely related to the thought and arise out of the process of the thought itself.

HOUSMAN, ALFRED EDWARD—Born in Shropshire in 1859; died in 1936. Educated at Bromsgrove School and St. John's College, Oxford. In 1882 he was appointed Higher Division Clerk in the British Patent Office. During his ten years there he spent his leisure hours in most diligent classical studies. In 1892 he was appointed Professor of Latin at University College, London. In 1911 he became Professor of Latin and Fellow of Trinity College at Cambridge, posts which he held until his death. He published many scholarly essays and articles on classical subjects and edited the works of Manilius, Juvenal and Lucan. Poetic inspiration with Housman was deep and disturbing. (*Cf.* introductory note to "Last Poems".) During his lifetime he published only two volumes of verse—"A Shropshire Lad" in 1896 and

BIOGRAPHICAL NOTES

"Last Poems" in 1922. After his death Lawrence Housman, acting upon the permission but not upon the request of his brother, published a slim volume, "More Poems". It is doubtful whether any poet in English has written with more intense concentration than Housman. The themes which recur most frequently in his lyrics are the ironic spectacle of lads and lasses regarding wistfully the inconstant, fleeting quality of time, the brevity of beauty, a passionate determination to live the moment to the full and a stoicism which is at times bitterly resentful. These lyrics (only 124 of them published during his lifetime) have established themselves in the hearts of hosts of readers by virtue of the sheer beauty of their concise statement and the sensitive loveliness of their thought.

HUXLEY, ALDOUS—Born in Godalming in 1894; a grandson of the great Thomas Huxley. Educated at Eton and Balliol College. Has become well known as a journalist, critic, lecturer, a short story writer of distinction and a brilliant novelist. His poetry, as indeed all his literary work, shows great variety both of style and subject matter. It is at times almost academic and conventional—at others it is highly individual and original, elusive and ironical. At times Huxley reveals a deep, disillusioned bitterness. For some years now he has been living in the United States.

JEFFERS, ROBINSON—Born in Pittsburg, Penn., in 1887. Educated in local schools and in Switzerland. A small legacy from an uncle in 1914 made it possible for him to pursue his own life. He settled at Carmel in California, built himself a house with stones gathered from the beach and has lived there, with his wife and two sons, a curiously lonely, almost isolated existence. Civiliza-

BIOGRAPHICAL NOTES

tion, according to his view of things, is doomed; humanity is unnecessary; animals and birds make a more dignified showing in the world than men. He has published several long poems, tragic and sometimes violent in their thought and expression, and many brief lyrics. For the most part he has adhered to conventional form in his writing but there is always a strong originality, even at times daring in the thought.

JOYCE, JAMES—Born in Dublin in 1882; died in 1940. Educated at the famous Jesuit School, Clongowes Wood College, and the Royal University, Dublin. Joyce lived for many years in Paris; studied medicine and music there. Had a great desire to be a singer. Joyce is best known as a writer of highly experimental prose. His "Ulysses" and "Finnegan's Wake" have attracted much attention largely because of their great, most readers would say completely impenetrable, obscurity. "Ulysses" was for many years banned in England and the United States. In contrast his verse is almost always clear-cut and beautifully suggestive. Whatever may be the individual reader's reaction to Joyce's work all agree that he was a master of diction, highly sensitive to the allusive, connotative power of words.

KIPLING, RUDYARD—Born in Bombay, India, in 1865; died in England in 1936. After a childhood spent in India he went to England where he was educated at the United Services College, Westward Ho. Returned to India and began his literary career as an editor and journalist. He early achieved popularity for his rousing tales and ballads about Anglo-Indian life. He was a most prolific writer. He endeared himself to the British reading public by his short stories of which he published several volumes, his novels and his children's stories. But he will

BIOGRAPHICAL NOTES

undoubtedly be longest and most fondly remembered for his poems. His verse, which occasionally lapses into what his critics have called jingoistic imperialism, has a fine virile quality. Under its distinct romanticism of form there is always a preoccupation with the realities of life and human character. It is on occasion sharply ironical. Kipling received many honours. In 1907 he was awarded the Nobel Prize for Literature and in 1926 he received the highest literary distinction in Great Britain, the Royal Society of Literature's Gold Medal.

LAMPMAN, ARCHIBALD—Born at Morpeth, Ont., in 1861; died in Ottawa in 1899. Educated at Trinity College, Toronto. Attempted school teaching and then entered the Civil Service in Ottawa, in the Post Office Department. His duties in this post permitted him some leisure for study and writing. He had a very sensitive nature and was devoted to the out-of-doors. His lyrics show these qualities very clearly. There is ample evidence too, in the beauty of his poetic style, of Lampman's thorough classical education and deep culture. After his death a comprehensive collection of his poems was published by his devoted friend Duncan Campbell Scott.

LAWRENCE, DAVID HENRY—Born in Nottinghamshire in 1885; died in 1930. He was the son of a coal miner. Educated at Nottingham High School and Day Training College. Taught school for a time, then travelled extensively, particularly on the continent. He was successful in various types of writing—the novel, essay, short story and verse. Several of his novels were the cause of deep controversy because of their frank descriptions of life situations. Lawrence was a very intense individual, a quality which is reflected clearly in his literary work—for instance in his fine lyric, "The Ship of Death" and the successful novel, "The Rainbow".

BIOGRAPHICAL NOTES

LEWIS, CECIL DAY—Born in 1904 at Ballintubber, Ireland. Educated at Sherborne School, Dorset and Wadham College, Oxford, where he was a contemporary and friend of Auden, Spender and Isherwood. He has taught at various schools and colleges. In 1927 he and Auden collaborated in editing *Oxford Poetry*. Since 1935 he has devoted himself entirely to writing and political activities. He is a member of the young group of English poets, so-called communists. He is consciously revolutionary both in politics and literature. He has remained a close friend of Auden and Spender. He owes his financial independence to his successful detective stories written under the pseudonym *Nicholas Blake*.

LINDSAY, VACHEL—Born in Springfield, Illinois, in 1879; died in 1931. Educated at Springfield High School and Hiram College, Ohio, later at the Art Institute of Chicago and the New York School of Art. Lectured and did settlement work for two years. He then set out on his long trips on foot through America, preaching his gospel of beauty, reading his own verse and seeking to influence the lives and taste of the people who heard him. He felt himself definitely called to be the people's poet. He insisted that verse must be partly read and partly sung, invoking in support of his theory the example of Greek poetry. Lindsay attempted in his verse to give expression to the intensity, the violence, the rugged virility, the speed and noise of American life. Beneath these qualities there is often a very fine lyric feeling. This can be seen in "General Booth Enters Heaven" and especially in one of the finest of his lyrics, "The Chinese Nightingale".

LIVESAY, DOROTHY—Born in Winnipeg in 1909. Both her parents had definite literary interests. Educated at the University of Toronto and the Sorbonne in Paris. She

BIOGRAPHICAL NOTES

now lives in New Westminster, B.C. She has been a careful student of the technique of verse. She has always been deeply interested in social and economic problems. These enthusiasms are clearly evident in her highly sensitive lyrics.

LOWELL, AMY—Born in Brookline, Mass., in 1878; died in 1925. Sister of Dr. Lawrence Abbot Lowell, a former President of Harvard, and niece of James Russell Lowell. Her family was for generations distinguished for its literary and scholarly achievements. From earliest childhood she had all the advantages of wealth and culture. Her early education was supervised by her mother. She travelled widely in Europe and Asia. Not until her late twenties did she decide to become a poet. She prepared herself by intensive study, reading widely in the literature of many countries. Her first volume, "A Dome of Many-coloured Glass" (1912) gave little indication of what her later work was to be. She visited England in 1913 and became identified with the young group of poets who described themselves as Imagists. After Ezra Pound left this group it was Amy Lowell who held the members together and made possible the publication of their three important anthologies (1915, 1916 and 1917). In these collections appeared the work of D. H. Lawrence, Richard Aldington, F. S. Flint, H.D., John Gould Fletcher and Amy Lowell herself. She wrote some criticism the most notable being her two-volume work, "John Keats". Her last volume of poetry, "What's O'clock", was published posthumously in 1926 and was awarded the Pulitzer Prize for Poetry.

MACDONALD, WILSON—Born at Cheapside, Ont., in 1880. Was educated at Port Dover Public School, Woodstock College and McMaster University. His work has appeared

BIOGRAPHICAL NOTES

in many periodicals and several published volumes of verse. His public, though not large, is discriminating and enthusiastic.

MacKay, Louis A.—Born in 1901. Educated in Toronto and at Oxford. He taught for a time at the University of Toronto and is now Professor of Classics at the University of British Columbia. Mackay has published only a small amount of verse, some of it in a Ryerson Press Chapbook, "Viper's Bugloss", under the pseudonym, John Smalacombe. Many of his poems have appeared in Saturday Night, the Canadian Forum, Contemporary Poetry and other Canadian periodicals. He has been referred to by E. K. Brown as "our most angry and clever satirist". He is assuredly an accomplished and gifted craftsman in verse and a most intelligent student of Canadian literature.

MacLeish, Archibald—Born in Illinois in 1892. After graduating from Yale he studied law at Harvard. In 1917 he went to France as a captain in the American Expeditionary Force. Returned to America after the war, taught at Harvard for a time and practised law for three years in Boston. He then went to live in France. Travelled extensively in Europe, particularly in the Mediterranean. Has published several volumes of verse. "Conquistador" won the Pulitzer Prize for poetry in 1932. Among other outstanding longer works are— "Panic" (1935), and "The Fall of the City", a radio play (1937). MacLeish was appointed Librarian of Congress in 1939.

Magee, Pilot Officer John Gillespie—Born in Shanghai, China, where his parents, the Rev. and Mrs. John G. Magee were American missionaries; educated at Rugby and later at Yale University. He enlisted in the R.C.A.F.

BIOGRAPHICAL NOTES

in Montreal in October, 1940. In December of the following year, at the age of 19, he was killed on active service in Britain. His sonnet, "High Flight", will take its place as one of the noblest lyrics inspired by the present war. It was found scribbled on the back of an envelope and sent to his parents.

Hearing of his son's death Mr. Magee wrote to the R.C.A.F.:

"When my wife and I saw how deeply he felt about the situation in September, 1940, we gave our consent and blessing to him as he left us to enter the R.C.A.F. We felt as deeply as he did and we were proud of his determination and spirit. We knew that such news as did come might come. When his sonnet reached us we felt then that it had a message for American youth but did not know how to get it before them. Now his death has emblazoned it across the entire country. We are thinking that this may have been a greater contribution than anything he may have done in the way of fighting, for surely our American youth must enter this conflict in the high spirit of idealism and faith. . . .

"May we thank the R.C.A.F. for all the training and help you have given to our boy. We saw a tremendous change in him when he returned to us from his training, a change that was all for the good. We do not regret that we gave our consent to his going and will be forever proud of him."

MARQUIS, DONALD—Born in Illinois in 1878; died in 1937. A journalist, actively associated with various newspapers. Became famous for his satiric wit. Attracted much attention through his column, The Sun Dial, in the New York Evening Sun. Wrote short stories, plays and serious verse ("Dreams and Dust", 1915). Best known creations are Archie, the cockroach who had literary ambitions and

BIOGRAPHICAL NOTES

his friend, Mehitabel, the cat. His humorous sketches, supposedly written by Archie, are justly popular.

MARRIOTT, ANNE—Born in Victoria, B.C., in 1913. Educated at private schools there. She has published several small volumes of verse. Her longest work, "The Wind our Enemy" (1939) is a searching statement of the tragic frustration due to drought, dust and consequent crop failure on the Canadian prairies. It is a brief, poetic condensation of a Canadian theme which is the counterpart of Steinbeck's "The Grapes of Wrath". The poem is justly described as an experiment—but it is an extremely able one. Miss Marriott's work shows the incisive, clear-cut style which we have come to associate with the Imagists.

MASEFIELD, JOHN—Born at Ledbury, Herefordshire, in 1878. Brought up by an aunt. Indentured at 14 to the Captain of a merchant ship, the Conway; he served three years before the mast. At 17 he left the sea and went to live in the United States where he worked at a variety of jobs in and around New York. While working in a carpet factory there Masefield was able to indulge his passion for reading. He spent all his spare money buying books and his spare time reading them. He tells the story of this period of his life in a prose volume, "In the Mill". It was then he read Chaucer "with passion and system" and Shakespeare, Milton and Keats. In 1897 he returned to England and began his literary career. His first volume of verse, "Salt Water Ballads" appeared in 1902. It brought him considerable attention, notably from Synge and Yeats. The latter encouraged him to go on with his writing. He wrote a great deal— tales of adventure in prose and verse and several dramas. His first great success came in 1911, "The Everlasting

BIOGRAPHICAL NOTES

Mercy". This was his first serious venture in the genre that he was to make peculiarly his own—the long narrative poem. During the first World War he served in France and at Gallipoli with the Red Cross. He has been a prolific writer. Popularity has come to him in generous measure and many honours have been showered upon him. In 1930 he was chosen Poet Laureate to succeed Robert Bridges.

MEREDITH, GEORGE—Born at Portsmouth, Hampshire, in 1828. Early education undertaken privately. After his mother's death he was raised by relations. At 14 he was sent to the Moravian School at Neuwied, Germany. In 1844 he went into a London lawyer's office but law had no real attraction for him and after a short period he decided upon a literary career. He had a very hard struggle with poverty and gained recognition slowly. As a journalist he was able to give encouragement to several young writers, notably to Gissing and Thomas Hardy. His first important novel "The Ordeal of Richard Feverel" was published in 1859. In 1862 he published "Modern Love", a sequence of fifty sonnet-like poems inspired by his unhappy first marriage. In spite of the fact that he was the intimate friend of most of the great Victorians and assisted many of them, popularity came to him very slowly. In 1905 he received the Order of Merit. At his death a memorial service was held for him in Westminster Abbey. During his life Meredith was best known as a novelist but now his poetry is held by many to be his most notable literary achievement. In many respects Meredith is typically Victorian but in the technique and style of some of his poems he prepares for the work of the moderns. This is notably the case in some of his short lyrics and in the long poem "The Woods of Westermain". Like many of the later

BIOGRAPHICAL NOTES

Victorian writers Meredith was preoccupied by a worship of Nature, of Earth, "our stern, genial Mother".

MEW, CHARLOTTE—1870-1928. Born in Bloomsbury; educated privately. Daughter of an architect, she had a life-long struggle with poverty. Published very little during her lifetime—only one slim volume—and yet she was one of the most gifted of modern English poets. She had to an extraordinary degree the gift of expressing herself with intensity of feeling in highly condensed, concentrated poetic form. There is grave, poignant beauty in everything she wrote. In 1922, at the instigation of Thomas Hardy, Masefield and de la Mare she was given a Civil List Pension of £75 a year. In 1928 she fell desperately ill and was confined to a nursing home. Having lost her mother, two sisters and a brother there seemed nothing left to live for and, in a fit of despondency, she took her own life.

MILLAY, EDNA ST. VINCENT—Born in 1892 at Rockland, Maine; educated at Vassar College. Following her graduation she has lived mostly in New York. She has travelled extensively and spent a few months in Europe in 1922. During her early years in New York she encountered many difficulties. She was an active member of the Provincetown Players both as writer and actress. Her stage name was Nancy Boyd. In 1922 she won the Pulitzer Prize for poetry. In the following year she married Eugen Jan Boissevain, a New York importer. She has had many honours. She has achieved perhaps her greatest distinction through her mastery of the sonnet, especially in its Shakespearian or Elizabethan form. Her best known volumes are "Buck in Snow" (1928), "Fatal Interview", a sonnet sequence (1931) and "Conversation at Midnight" (1937).

BIOGRAPHICAL NOTES

MONRO, HAROLD—1879-1932. Born in Brussels, Belgium, of English parents. Educated abroad and in England at Radley and Caius College, Cambridge. Was an accomplished linguist. He travelled extensively in Europe. He early revealed serious literary interest and ambition but his first published work did not appear until 1906. In 1912 he established the Poetry Bookshop in London. This for years was a unique establishment, a true literary centre seeking to bridge the gap between poets and the public. In the same year he began the publication of a quarterly, "Poetry and Drama" which, after the War, was resumed as "The Chap Book". This publication gave genuine encouragement and practical assistance to many young writers. Monro served during the World War. At its conclusion he returned to the Poetry Bookshop which he carried on until his death in 1932. As a writer he is perhaps most successful in dealing with the small, often unnoticed, things of life.

NEWBOLT, SIR HENRY—1862-1938. Educated at Clifton and Corpus Christi College, Oxford. Practised law until 1899. His interest in the sea and British naval history led to his appointment as official historian of the Admiralty in 1923. His verse is traditional in form and is marked by the imperialistic enthusiasm common in the late Victorian and Edwardian periods.

NICHOLS, ROBERT—Born at Shanklin in the Isle of Wight in 1893. Educated at Winchester and Trinity College, Oxford. Served in the World War and was invalided home suffering from shell-shock in 1916. From 1922 to 1925 he was Professor of English Literature at the University of Tokyo, a post formerly held by Lafcadio Hearn.

BIOGRAPHICAL NOTES

NOYES, ALFRED—Born in Staffordshire in 1886. Educated at Exeter College (Oxford). Began to write verse as a boy; published his first volume in 1902. Came to the United States in 1913 as lecturer at the Lowell Institute; his subject was "The Sea in English Poetry". Was Professor of English Literature at Princeton from 1914 to 1923 when he returned to England. During the World War he was attached for some time to the Foreign Office of the British Government and in 1918 he was created a Commander of the Order of the British Empire. He has written a great deal of verse which is traditional in form. As a critic he has been consistently opposed to the experimentation in form and subject matter which has been so characteristic of many of the best of his contemporaries and has defended with great zeal the traditional work of older poets.

OWEN, WILFRED—1893-1918. Born at Oswestry; educated at the Birkenhead Institute and at London University. Went to France where he taught as a private tutor. In spite of very delicate health he joined the Artists' Rifles in 1915 and served in France until invalided home in 1917. In 1918 he returned to France. He was awarded the M.C. for conspicuous gallantry in October of that year and was killed on November 4, seven days before the Armistice. His early death removed a young poet of very unusual ability and promise. He was sensitive to the pity and tragedy of war, speaking of it in his verse with a restrained intensity that places his work high among the poets of that period. His poems were collected and published in 1920 by Siegfried Sassoon. In his introduction to the little volume Sassoon quoted an illuminating passage from one of Owen's letters to his mother, written only a month before his death: "My nerves are in perfect order. I came out again to help these boys; directly, by

BIOGRAPHICAL NOTES

leading them as well as an officer can; indirectly, by watching their sufferings that I may speak of them as well as a pleader can".

PICKTHALL, MARJORIE—Born in London, England, in 1883. Lived in Canada as a child but returned to England at the outbreak of the Great War. After the war she returned to Canada. She lived in British Columbia, largely in Victoria and Vancouver until her death in the latter city in 1922. A. J. M. Smith says of her verse, "Her poetry is romantic and literary" and that is a very just summing up. She has a light poetic fancy at times (*cf.* "A Modern Endymion"), a genuine sympathy with people and a deep and sincere piety.

POUND, EZRA LOOMIS—Born in 1885 in Hailey, Idaho. Educated at Hamilton College and later at the University of Pennsylvania where he took the degree of A.M. in Romance Languages. He went abroad in 1908 and has lived in Europe ever since—in England, in France and in Italy. His early verse was well received in England— "A Lume Spento" (1908), "Personnae" (1909). He was for a time an enthusiastic member of the Imagist Group of poets. He has produced several volumes of verse, some of it exquisitely beautiful, some of it excessively obscure and baffling (*cf.* Cantos). Much that seemed twenty years ago exciting and significant because of its originality and defiant strangeness has ceased to interest readers and its permanent value is questionable.

PRATT, EDWIN J.—Born at Western Bay, Newfoundland, in 1883, the son of a Methodist minister. Educated at Methodist College, St. John's and at Victoria College, Toronto. He was first trained for the ministry. He was ordained and did some "student preaching". After graduation from Toronto he was appointed a lecturer in

BIOGRAPHICAL NOTES

Psychology at the University. He was at this time writing verse which showed the influence of his boyhood, the life of the sea and the rugged existence of the poor fisherman with whom his early years were associated. He has written and published a good deal of verse and is now recognized as a central figure in Canadian poetry. His writing is strong and virile like "Ned" Pratt himself. His narratives of the sea have a fine racy quality; his long poem, "Brébeuf and his Brethren" has a deep seriousness and a sensitive appreciation of character; his shorter lyrics show wit, fantasy and a capacity for irony. Dr. Pratt has been for many years a Professor of English at Victoria College, Toronto.

READ, HERBERT—Born in Yorkshire in 1893. Educated at boarding school and later at the University of Leeds. He served in the Great War winning the M.C. He has done some important criticism both in literature and in the field of general art. He edited the literary remains of T. E. Hulme who was killed in the war. He has held some important posts—Assistant at the Victoria and Albert Museum, South Kensington and Professor of Fine Arts at Edinburgh. He has published several works on Art, notably "The Meaning of Art" and "Art Now!" As a poet he is perhaps best known for his bitter verse of the World War but actually some of his finest work has been done during the last few years. He is now in London doing war work. He is recognized as a distinguished and able critic.

ROBERTS, SIR CHARLES G. D.—1860-1943. Born near Fredericton, N.B., a cousin of Bliss Carman. He was educated at Fredericton and the University of New Brunswick. There he received a thorough classical education. He taught school, practised journalism and wrote

BIOGRAPHICAL NOTES

verse. He went to the United States and lived in New York from 1896-1907. He was in the active forces during the World War, in the final year working with Lord Beaverbrook on the writing of the official story of Canada's part in the War. He devoted himself thereafter to a literary career and became one of the best known of Canadian poets. In his verse, which is sometimes Wordsworthian in flavour, he has revealed a true and sensitive feeling for the Canadian landscape. He achieved a considerable reputation for his animal and general nature stories.

SACKVILLE-WEST, THE HONOURABLE VICTORIA (VITA)—Born in 1892, daughter of Baron Sackville. As a member of one of the very old, aristocratic families of England she has been familiar from childhood with the finest in English culture. She has a profound love of the English countryside. This is clearly evident in her work, particularly in her long poem, "The Land", and her novel, "All Passion Spent".

SANDBURG, CARL—Born at Galesburg, Ill., in 1878, the son of Swedish immigrants. His education was a very haphazard affair. At 13 he left school and went to work. At 17 he "rode the freights" to the Western States where he worked at every conceivable kind of job. Returning after a short time to the East he went back first to his old job of delivering milk and, later, house painting. In 1898 he joined the Illinois Infantry in the Spanish American War. Following this he attended Lombard College for four years. Since that time he has worked as a journalist, a salesman, a representative of the Social-Democratic Party and has written verse. From the first ("In Restless Ecstasy", 1904) his poetry has been free in form and particularly vigorous in style and diction. He

BIOGRAPHICAL NOTES

has been accused of vulgarity and many deny him the name of poet. As a matter of fact he has continued the Whitman tradition, speaking frankly of the whole man and the whole of life.

SASSOON, SIEGFRIED—Born in 1886, son of a wealthy country gentleman of Anglo-Jewish stock. His mother was an Englishwoman. Sassoon was educated at Marlborough and Clare College, Cambridge. He was always fond of poetry, music and out-door sports, particularly fox hunting. His early verse which is colourless and almost negligible was published privately for circulation among friends. On the outbreak of war he enlisted at once and went to France. He rose to the rank of captain in the Welsh Fusiliers. He served in Palestine for a brief period and three times in France. He won the Military Cross for gallantry in bringing in severely wounded men under enemy fire. His first important verse arose out of his war experience. "The Old Huntsman and other Poems" (1917) and "Counter-Attack" (1918) contain lyrics which for angry, ironical protest against the waste and tragedy of war are unsurpassed. In his Introduction to "Counter-Attack" Robert Nichols quotes Sassoon as saying, "Let no one ever from henceforth say one word in any way countenancing war. It is dangerous even to speak of how here and there the individual may gain some hardship of soul by it. For war is hell and those who institute it are criminals." That was the theme in one way or another of Sassoon's war poetry. In recent years he has turned to more general themes (*cf.* "The Heart's Journey", 1928).

SCOTT, DUNCAN CAMPBELL—Born in Ottawa in 1862, son of a Methodist preacher. Educated in the public schools and at Stanstead College, Quebec. At 17 he entered the

BIOGRAPHICAL NOTES

Civil Service in the Department of Indian Affairs. He later became head of this department, a post which he held with distinction until his retirement. As a young man he was an intimate friend of Archibald Lampman and after the latter's death he edited a collection of his poems with an introductory Memoir. Throughout his life he has had a passion for music and still delights in playing the music of Bach. In his quiet, unobtrusive way he has taken an interest in all intellectual and artistic activities in Canada.

His poetry has won him recognition as the most distinguished living Canadian poet. It has great variety of style and subject matter. There is much fine nature poetry, distinctly romantic in feeling; there are poems of character and situation, such as "The Forsaken" and "At the Cedars"; there are love lyrics of an exquisite loveliness and poems of pure fantasy like "The Piper of Arll" which was singled out for the highest praise by the poet laureate. In all his work the reader will find great precision of diction, a subtle sense of the music of words and a quiet pervasive beauty which gives to the whole a peculiar dignity and serenity.

SCOTT, GEOFFREY—1885-1929. English critic and essayist. He edited the private papers of Boswell. His poetic output was small but his lyrics have a fine individual quality.

SHOVE, FREDEGOND—Born in Cambridge, England, in 1889. Her poetry was little known until the appearance of four poems in the Poetry Bookshop's publication, "Georgian Poetry" for 1919. In the same year appeared her own volume "Dreams and Journeys". Her verse is distinguished by great beauty of imagery and by simple and effective diction. A critic writing in The Chapbook said,

BIOGRAPHICAL NOTES

"Her poetry is like sunlight on a green hill. It is always the same sun and the same hill, but the imagination of the beholder sees it each time in a new and beautiful light".

SMITH, A. J. M.—Born in Montreal in 1902. Educated at McGill and the University of Edinburgh. Now Professor of English at Michigan State College, East Lansing. His poetry has been published in periodicals in the United States and England and in anthologies. His volume, "News of the Phoenix" (1943), contains some of the finest of his verse. Smith is an important member of what has come to be known as the Montreal Group of Poets. He has a fine critical sense. Speaking of poetry in an article recently he said, "And remember lastly that poetry does not permit the rejection of every aspect of the personality except intuition and sensibility. It must be written by the whole man. It is an intelligent activity and it ought to compel the respect of the generality of intelligent men. If it is a good it is a good in itself". That is surely a striking and useful thing to say to the poets of this period. E. K. Brown says of Smith's work, "Whatever the theme the execution is beautifully deliberate and the feeling or thought fully mature and intense". Professor Smith was awarded the Harriet Monroe Memorial Prize in 1941. In 1943 he published "The Book of Canadian Poetry", a most comprehensive and carefully chosen collection of Canadian verse with an admirable critical intrtoduction.

SPENDER, STEPHEN—Born in London in 1909, of German-Jewish descent on his mother's side. His father was a journalist and lecturer. Spender was educated at University College, Oxford, where he was a close friend of Auden, Day Lewis, Isherwood and MacNeice. He has taken part in left-wing activities, associating himself with the

BIOGRAPHICAL NOTES

work of the other "young communist" poets. His approach has been to a large extent individualistic and his interest intellectual rather than downright political. His verse has been more lyrical, less obscure and perhaps more romantic than has Auden's or MacNeice's. He has a strong sense of humanity and a fine sensitiveness to man's rich inheritance from the truly great of past ages. Spender has remained in England during the war: he is a member of the London Auxiliary Fire Service.

STEPHENS, JAMES—Born in Dublin in 1882. Had little formal education. George Russell (Æ) saw some of his early writings and found him a position as clerk in a solicitor's office. He encouraged him to devote himself to writing. He has written a great deal and is one of the most successful of the group of Irish poets. He has spent much time in the United States as a lecturer.

SYNGE, JOHN MILLINGTON—Born at Rathfarnham, near Dublin, in 1871; died in Dublin in 1909. Spent his childhood in Wicklow where he heard the rich and colourful Irish speech which became so distinguished and characteristic an element in his writing. Like many of his contemporary Irish poets he was interested in other arts than poetry. He spent some time studying music in Germany, then went to live in Paris. There Yeats found him in great poverty, persuaded him to return to his native land and identify himself with the Irish Literary Renaissance. In preparation Synge lived for some time in the remote Aran Islands. There he shared the existence of the fisher folk. As a result he wrote his dramas which remain one of the most successful achievements of the Irish Movement. They are written in a poetic prose which is beautifully cadenced. They deal with simple Irish characters caught in the toils of tragic circumstance. They were performed in this

BIOGRAPHICAL NOTES

country by the Abbey Players with great artistic success. After Synge's death a volume of translations of Petrarch and Villon was published. These are remarkable for their fidelity to the originals and for a fine racy individual style which they possess and which marks them as being Irish.

TEASDALE, SARA—Born at St. Louis, Missouri, in 1884. Educated there, then travelled for two years (1905-07) in Europe and the Near East. In 1916 she moved to New York. Her verse reveals her a master of lyric brevity and condensation—she is perhaps a little too conscious of this gift at times. Her lyrics are highly effective, particularly those published in "Flame and Shadow" (1920) and "Dark of the Moon" (1926). Always in frail health she contracted pneumonia while in London in 1932. She returned to America and suffered a nervous breakdown. In January, 1933 she was found dead in her New York apartment. She was one of the most consistently subjective of contemporary American poets.

THOMAS, EDWARD—Born in Lambeth, London, in 1878 of Welsh parentage. Educated at Lincoln College, Oxford. His father opposed his wish to follow a literary career. Consequently Thomas left home and had a long struggle with poverty. Though he hated hack work he had much of it to do. Two volumes of prose essays reveal great literary talent. His association with Robert Frost, during the latter's sojourn in England, gave him his first encouragement to follow his desire to write verse. His first volume of poems, dedicated to Frost and using the pseudonym, Edward Westaway, was on the press at the time of his death. He was killed in an observation post

BIOGRAPHICAL NOTES

at Arras in 1917. His verse is usually marked by a sadly contemplative note.

TURNER, W. J.—Born in Melbourne, Australia, son of an organist, in 1889. Educated at Scotch College, Melbourne. Went to Europe, studied in Germany, then settled in England where he has lived almost continuously ever since. He has achieved much note as a critic. He has been musical critic of The New Statesman since 1916. His verse has a delicate beauty both of style and thought. Its most frequently recurring theme is the contrast of the material world and the "ideal world of the imagination".

WICKHAM, ANNA—Born at Wimbledon, Surrey, in 1884. Went to Australia at 6; at 21 she returned to Europe. She studied opera with de Reske in Paris. She suddenly abandoned music as a career and turned to poetry. Her sensitive, imaginative verse makes a limited appeal—a fact that has led to her being described as a "poet's poet".

WOLFE, HUMBERT—Born of Jewish parentage in Milan in 1885; died in London in 1940. Educated at Bradford Grammar School and Wadham College, Oxford. Early began writing verse. Entered the British Civil Service in 1908. During the great war he was an ardent militarist and held an official post in the Ministry of Munitions. He was created a Companion of the Order of the British Empire in 1918 and a C.B. in 1925. He wrote a great deal, both verse and criticism, devoting his leisure time to this avocation.

YEATS, WILLIAM BUTLER—1865-1939. Born in Dublin, son of an attorney who later became well known as a painter. His family was Protestant. Yeats' childhood was divided between London where he went to school

BIOGRAPHICAL NOTES

and County Sligo. For years he studied painting and achieved some success in that art though he was not as well known as a painter as were his father and his brother Jack. From boyhood he was well acquainted with Irish folk lore and legend. It is not surprising that at 21 he turned definitely to Literature as a career. He was intensely interested in the Irish Movement both politically and artistically. He was a moving spirit with Lady Gregory and others in the Celtic Renaissance, as it is sometimes called, and helped found the Irish Literary Theatre (later known as The Abbey Players) in 1899. From 1922-28 he was a senator in the Irish Free State government. He received the Nobel Prize for Literature in 1923. He wrote a great deal. His early work was almost entirely Irish in subject matter and markedly Celtic in style. Later he turned to more general, philosophic themes. Although his early poems are the best known, many critics contend that his finest verse was written during the last years of his life.

INDEX OF TITLES AND FIRST LINES

About me the night, moonless, wimples the mountains,	55
Above my head the shields are stained with rust,	335
Abraham Lincoln (Choruses)	134
A cold coming we had of it,	141
Across the years he could recall	109
Adlestrop	407
Admonition for Spring	265
A Dream in Early Spring	385
Aedh Wishes for the Cloths of Heaven	424
A Fire at Night	110
A Flower given to my Daughter	228
A flower has opened in my heart . . .	369
After Battle	372
After they have tired of the brilliance of cities	392
Afterwards	199
Ah, bird	187
A January Morning	235
All lovely things will have an ending	6
All our Joy is enough	382
All that's Past	125
All we make is enough	382
A man should kindle once a year	110
Ambassador Puser the ambassador	268
A Modern Endymion	336
An Ancient to Ancients	203
And I have learned how diving's done	256
And he cast it down, down, on the green grass,	386
And since to live men labour, only knowing	361
An old thorn tree in a stony place	389
An image of Lethe and the fields	341
An Old Woman of the Roads	111
An Old Woman's Lamentations	402
A Northern Vigil	94

469

INDEX OF TITLES AND FIRST LINES

Anselmo Speaks	298
A Passer-by	60
Apologia pro Poemate Meo	331
Are you awake, Gemelli,	178
As I came to the edge of the woods,	174
As I gird on for fighting	217
As I walked down the waterside	124
A snake came to my water-trough	238
A Song	377
A Song for Simeon	143
A Summer Evening	235
At dawn they launched the ships; and all went well.	78
A Time to Dance	248
Austere, removed, grave as the thought of death,	415
A wind sways the pines,	293
✳ Babylon ('Æ')	1
✳ Babylon (Graves)	180
Base Details	368
Bavarian Gentians	244
Beautiful must be the mountains whence ye come,	62
Because of body's hunger are we born,	411
Before Action	177
Be not so desolate	4
Bent double, like old beggars under sacks,	330
Beyond the Last Lamp	196
Binsey Poplars	213
Birches	171
Birds	227
Blue Squills	404
Booth led boldly with his big bass drum—	250
Bredon Hill	215
Burial at Sea	349
Call not thy wanderer home as yet	3

470

INDEX OF TITLES AND FIRST LINES

Canto XIII	338
Cedar and jagged fir	387
Chamber Music	229
Chicago	364
Children of Love	301
Choosing a Mast	83
Christmas Eve, and twelve of the clock.	200
Cities and Thrones and Powers	230
Clifton Chapel	310
Come In	174
Consider this and in our time	16
Conversation at Midnight (Anselmo Speaks)	298
Cool Tombs	366
Cuckoo Song	187
David	44
David and I that summer cut trails on the Survey,	44
David's Reconciliation with Absalom	151
Death is another milestone on their way.	393
Dedication	183
Deirdre	396
Dirge in Woods	293
Do not let any woman read this verse!	396
Doom is dark and deeper than any sea-dingle	19
Down by the salley gardens my love and I did meet;	424
Do you remember, Joan (O vain to wonder if you remember),	413
Drake he's in his hammock an' a thousand mile away,	307
Drake's Drum	307
Dulce et Decorum Est	330
Duncton Hill	21
Dust	69
Easily to the old	263
Eau-Forte	161

471

INDEX OF TITLES AND FIRST LINES

Ecstasy	410
Emerging at midnight	353
Empty are the ways,	341
Eternal Father by Whose Might	378
Evening (H.D.)	186
Evening (Lampman)	236
Exit	263
False dreams, all false,	416
Fancy's Knell	221
Fantasia	256
Farewell	131
Faster	381
Fear is a wave	352
Felix Randal the farrier, O he is dead then? my duty all ended	209
Fifty Quatrains	151
Fish (fly-replete, in depth of June,	71
For the Fallen (1914)	40
For those who had the power	248
For when the winds have ceased their ghostly speech	89
Fountain, fountain, what do you say	403
Fragment Thirty-six	191
Frail lilies that beneath the dust so long	355
Frail the white rose and frail are	228
Frolic	1
From upland slopes I see the cows file by,	236
From where I sit, I see the stars,	236
Full Moon	364
Gather for festival,	189
General William Booth enters into Heaven	250
Germinal	3
God flings in air His box of things;	381
God of our fathers, known of old,	231

INDEX OF TITLES AND FIRST LINES

God's Grandeur	208
Good Friday	390
Grandeur of Ghosts	367
Had I the heavens' embroidered cloths,	424
Hands	57
Harp Song of the Dane Women	232
Hate	398
Hath Hope Kept Vigil	355
Hats	161
Haulms burn in distant fields:	354
Haunted	133
Heaven	71
Heaven, you say, will be a field in April,	9
He closed the Bible carefully, putting it down	25
He does not die that can bequeath	21
'He Fell among Thieves'	308
He is Jealous of the Heavens and Earth	399
He lay, and those who watched him were amazed	311
Here by the gray north sea,	94
Here is the soundless cypress on the lawn:	303
Here on the valley's slope is the olive grove,	379
Here was gold,	383
He understands the Great Cruelty of Death	401
He went, and he was gay to go;	177
He wishes he might die and follow Laura	400
High Flight	278
His heart, to me, was a place of palaces and pinnacles and shining towers;	296
His wild heart beats with painful sobs,	353
Hog Butcher for the World,	364
Honey Harvest	10
How many million Aprils came	404
How splendid in the morning glows the lily: with what grace he throws	155

473

INDEX OF TITLES AND FIRST LINES

How to keep—is there any any, is there none,	210
Humming-Bird	238
Hunger	39
Hymn for Those in the Air	378
I can imagine, in some other world	238
I come among the peoples like a shadow;	39
If I could come again to that dear place	291
If I should die, think only this of me:	73
If I should ever by chance grow rich	407
If I were fierce and bald and short of breath,	368
I have been so great a lover: filled my days	67
I Have been through the Gates	296
I have seen old ships sail like swans asleep	152
I have seen that which is mysterious,	156
I heard a linnet courting	59
I heard it all, each, every note	207
Iliad	416
I love all beauteous things	60
I know I am but summer to your heart,	297
I know not what to do,	191
I laid me down upon the shore	117
I leant upon a coppice gate	195
I lift the Lord on high,	333
I'm glad to lie on a sack of leaves	112
I'm going out to clean the pasture spring;	173
Immortal Autumn	267
Impression—IV	120
I must go down to the seas again, to the lonely sea and the sky,	287
Inbetweentimes	353
In Spring-Time	125
In summertime on Bredon	215
In the air there are no coral-reefs or ambergris,	377
In the amber morning by the inlet's high shore	57

INDEX OF TITLES AND FIRST LINES

In the Fields	294
In the loam we sleep,	366
In the years of her age the most beautiful and the most flowery—	400
In this buff-gray cliff	286
In this meadow starred with spring	370
In Time of 'The Breaking Of Nations'	200
Into Battle (1915)	181
'Ione, Dead the Long Year'	341
I saw a frieze on whitest marble drawn	410
I saw God! Do you doubt it?	398
I saw with open eyes	207
I see a farmer walking by himself	384
I shall not care	404
I sit beside the brazier's glow,	177
Isled in the midnight air,	133
I speak this poem now with grave and level voice	267
'Is there anybody there?' said the Traveller,	130
It is I, Odysseus—Elpenor:	270
It seemed that out of battle I escaped	328
It's no use raising a shout.	14
I think continually of those who were truly great,	391
I, too, saw God through mud,—	331
It was the lovely moon—she lifted	167
It was the Rainbow gave thee birth,	121
I've heard them lilting at loom and belting,	246
I went out to the hazel wood,	421
I who am dead a thousand years,	153
I will pluck from my tree a cherry-blossom wand,	412
I wonder about the trees.	170
John Brown's body lies a-mouldering in the grave.	34
John Brown's Body (Prelude and Finale)	25
Journey of the Magi	141
Journey's End	417

INDEX OF TITLES AND FIRST LINES

Kensington Gardens	418
Kinsmen, you shall behold	134
Kung walked by the dynastic temple	338
Labour	361
Lament	178
Laodamia	78
Late in March, when the days are growing longer	10
Late November	237
Laura waits for him in Heaven	401
Lean out of the window,	229
Lepanto	98
Life Laughs Onward	202
Loam	366
London, my beautiful,	165
Look away now from the high lonesome hills	265
Lord, the Roman hyacinths are blooming in bowls and	143
Lord, when I look at lovely things which pass,	294
Love is not all; it is not meat nor drink	297
Loveliest of trees, the cherry now	219
Love to Love calleth,	63
Low Tide on Grand Pré	92
Lucifer in Starlight	292
Martha	126
Memorial Rain	268
Midnight	236
Milk for the Cat	303
Moon Spell	20
Moorland Night	295
Morning Glory	370
Music comes	166
Music I heard with you was more than music,	9
My aspens dear, whose airy cages quelled,	213
My enemy came nigh;	398

INDEX OF TITLES AND FIRST LINES

My face is against the grass—the moorland grass is wet—	295
My flowery and green age was passing away,	401
My young love said to me, 'My brothers won't mind,	116
'next to of course god america i	119
Nightingales	62
Night Litany	343
1933	270
Nod	132
Non Nobis	265
Not every man has gentians in his house	244
Not for our sake your life was ended thus,	265
Nothing is so beautiful as spring—	214
Now first, as I shut the door,	406
Now when I sleep the thrush breaks through my dreams	385
Ode: On the Death of W. B. Yeats	389
Ode to Music	63
O Dieu, purifiez nos coeurs!	343
Oh, I have slipped the surly bonds of earth	278
Oh see how thick the goldcup flowers	219
Old Olives at Bordighera	379
Old Susan	128
On a starred night Prince Lucifer uprose.	292
On black bare trees a stale cream moon	161
Once in my garret—you being far away	176
Once in the winter	372
'Once . . . once upon a time . . .'	126
Only a man harrowing clods	200
On Reading the War Diary of a Defunct Ambassador	370
On the Beach at Fontana	228
O, to have a little house!	111
Out in the dark over the snow	408
Out of the complicated house come I	119
Out of the earth to rest or range	288

477

INDEX OF TITLES AND FIRST LINES

Over the hills of April	90
O why do you walk through the fields in gloves,	118
Peace is the heir of dead desire,	226
Perched on my city office-stool	175
Père Lalement	333
Pity the innocent. There are none innocent, none.	266
Portion of this yew	201
Pre-Existence	117
Prelude for Spring	252
Prelude XIV	6
Promise	4
Pure blood domestic, guaranteed,	345
Purple Grackles	258
Rambling I looked for an old abode	202
Recessional	231
Rend your Heart and not your Garments	266
Reveille	218
Rich Days	122
Romance	409
Rose-bosom'd and rose-limb'd	168
Rupert Brooke	176
Sam	128
Sandstone	286
Sea-Fever	287
See, they return; ah, see the tentative	342
Sehnsucht	411
September Fires	354
She Moved through the Fair	116
Shepherd, to yon tall poplars tune your flute:	225
She was wearing the coral taffeta trousers	364
Sightless, I breathe and touch; this night of pines	222
Silences	346

478

INDEX OF TITLES AND FIRST LINES

Snake	238
Snore in the foam: the night is vast and blind,	85
Snow	415
So Abram rose, and clave the wood, and went,	331
Softly along the road of evening,	132
Song	74
Song of Poplars	225
Songs from Cyprus	189
Sonnet XXIX	291
So that's your Diary—that's your private mind	370
Spring	214
Spring goeth all in white,	60
Spring has caught up the eager earth	376
Spring in the Valley	376
Spring's Saraband	90
Star-Talk	178
Stopping by Woods on a Snowy Evening	173
Strange Holiness	107
Strange Meeting	328
Strict I walk my ordered way	412
Stride the hill, sower,	114
Stupidity Street	207
Suicide's Stone	226
Summers and Summers have come, and gone with the flight of the swallow;	357
Sunset and silence! A man: around him earth savage, earth broken;	115
Suppose that we, to-morrow or the next day,	247
Sweet as Eden is the air,	293
Sweet Stay-at-Home, sweet Well-content,	123
Tantramar Revisited	357
Tell me not here, it needs not saying,	216
The Barrel-Organ	314
	479

INDEX OF TITLES AND FIRST LINES

The Bells of Heaven	206
The blue dusk ran between the streets; my love was winged within my mind,	1
The Bridge	383
The Buzzards	13
The Cherry-Blossom Wand	412
The child alone a poet is:	180
The children were shouting together	1
The Cicadas	222
The clouds grow clear, the pine-wood glooms and stills	235
The Coming of War: Actaeon	341
The crooked paths go every way	395
The Darkling Thrush	195
The Dead	72
The Decision	346
The Donkey	106
The Eagle soars in the summit of Heaven	148
The Evening Sky	168
The Farmer, 1917	384
The Fiddler of Dooney	425
The fierce musical cries of a couple of sparrow-hawks hunting on the headland,	227
The first day she passed up and down through the Heavens,	401
The Flaming Terrapin	89
The Forsaken	372
The Fountain	403
The Funeral	393
The Furrow and the Hearth (I)	114
The fury of a creature when it drips	151
The glittering roofs are still with frost; each worn	235
The Glory of Women	368
The Goat Paths	395
The Golden Journey to Samarkand	154
The grackles have come.	258

480

INDEX OF TITLES AND FIRST LINES

The Grand Canyon of the Colorado	156
The Great Lover	67
The Heart's Journey (V)	369
The Heart's Journey (XXXIV)	369
The hen and the oriole	279
The Highwayman	322
The Hills	119
The hills and leafless forests slowly yield	237
The Hollow Men	144
The hollow sound of your hard felt hat	161
The holy boy	301
the hours rise up putting off stars and it is	120
The House of Christmas	105
The Ice Cart	175
The Kingfisher	121
The Lamp of Poor Souls	335
The Land (Labour, Vintage)	361
The Last Chrysanthemum	194
The Leaden Echo and the Golden Echo	210
The light passes	186
The Listeners	130
The Lonely Land	387
The man I had a love for—a great rascal	402
The moon has set fire	20
The Moth	133
The Mummer	412
The naked earth is warm with Spring,	181
The New Ghost	386
The New House	406
The Nightingale near the House	303
The old bellwether looked at the lamb	418
The Old Ships	152
The Oxen	200
The Parable of the Old Men and the Young	331
heart	298

481

INDEX OF TITLES AND FIRST LINES

The Passing Strange	288
The Pasture	173
The Phoenix said to me	75
The Plougher	115
The Prize Cat	345
The rabbit in his burrow keeps	133
There are some men, of course, some men, I know,	305
There fared a mother driven forth,	105
There is no peace on earth today save the peace in the	
There is no point in work	242
There is no silence upon the earth or under the earth	
like the silence under the sea;	346
There is strange holiness around	107
There's a barrel-organ carolling across a golden street	314
There's many a pool that holds a cloud	125
The Return (Gibson)	177
The Return (Pound)	342
There will be stars over the place for ever;	403
The Rock (Two Choruses)	148
The Roosevelt and the Antinoe (Burial at Sea)	349
The Rose of the World	423
The Saint (She)	413
The Scene of War: Fear	352
The Scene of War: The Happy Warrior	353
The Secret Heart	109
These dreams abound:	252
These hearts were woven of human joys and cares,	72
The Sirens	41
※ The Slaver	25
The Sleepers	124
The smell of woodyards in the rain is strong	286
The Soldier	73
The Solitary Woodsman	355
The Song of Honour	207
The Song of Wandering Aengus	421

482

INDEX OF TITLES AND FIRST LINES

The Sound of the Trees	170
The South Country	22
The Sprig of Lime	311
The sun goes down, and over all	92
The Swan	160
The trees are in their autumn beauty,	422
The Way through the Woods	233
The Wild Swans at Coole	422
The Wind our Enemy	280
The wind was a torrent of darkness among the gusty trees,	322
The world is charged with the grandeur of God.	208
'They shall not die in vain,' we said.	183
They shut the road through the woods	233
This day upon the bitter tree	390
This is the Chapel: here, my son,	310
This mast, new-shaved, through whom I rive the ropes,	83
This speaking were enough	182
Time, you old gypsy man,	205
To a Fat Lady seen from the Train	118
To a Poet a Thousand Years Hence	153
Transformations	201
Trees	**305**
Tristan da Cunha	85
'Twas fifty quatrains: and from unknown strands	151
'Twould ring the bells of Heaven	206
Uncertain still, new-mated birds	20
Under a wall of bronze	160
Vancouver Lights	55
Very old are the woods;	125
Vintage	362
Wake: the silver dusk returning	218
Watch any day his nonchalant pauses, see	16

INDEX OF TITLES AND FIRST LINES

We are the hollow men	144
Welcome to you, rich Autumn days,	122
well boss did it	279
We who are left, how shall we look again	178
We who with songs beguile your pilgrimage	154
What a grudge I am bearing the earth that has	399
What is a woman that you forsake her,	232
What the Shuiler Said as she Lay by the Fire in the Farmer's House	112
What Tomas Said in a Pub	398
What will be left when my life is over?	74
What will they give me, when journey's done?	417
When Abraham Lincoln was shoveled into the tombs,	366
When evening came and the warm glow grew deeper	13
When fishes flew and forests walked	106
When I am dead and over me bright April	404
When I am living in the Midlands	22
When I have heard small talk about great men	367
When I lie where shades of darkness	131
When I play on my fiddle in Dooney,	425
When I see birches bend to left and right	171
When I set out for Lyonnesse,	198
When I was but thirteen or so	409
When lads were home from labour	221
Where once we danced, where once we sang,	203
When Sam goes back in memory,	128
When Susan's work was done she'd sit,	128
When the first larks began to soar,	372
When the grey lake-water rushes	355
When the Present has latched its postern behind my tremulous stay,	199
When the tea is brought at five o'clock,	303
When the white flame in us is gone	69
When you are old and gray and full of sleep,	425
While rain, with eve in partnership,	196

INDEX OF TITLES AND FIRST LINES

White founts falling in the courts of the sun,	98
Whither is she gone, wing'd by the evening airs,	41
Whither, O splendid ship, thy white sails crowding,	60
Who dreamed that beauty passes like a dream?	423
Who live under the shadow of a war,	394
Whose woods these are I think I know.	173
Why should this flower delay so long	194
Wild Apple	20
Will you come as of old with singing,	405
Wind flattening its gaunt furious self against	280
Wind whines and whines the shingle,	228
Winter Night Song	405
With proud thanksgiving, a mother for her children,	40
With separated phrase and smothered word	349
Woodland Peace	293
Woodyards in Rain	286
Work	242
Yasmin	155
'Ye have robb'd,' said he, 'ye have slaughter'd and made an end,	308
Yes. I remember Adlestrop—	407
Yet I recall	362
You left the field and no one heard	346
You love us when we're heroes, home on leave,	368
You that love England, who have an ear for her music,	245
You went to the verge, you say, and came back safely?	6
You were glad tonight: and now you've gone away.	369
You!—You stealing violets where the snail-tracks glisten	336